Men's Health

Life Improvement Guides®

Good Loving

Keys to a Lifetime of
Passion, Pleasure, and Sex

by Donna Raskin, Larry Keller,
and the Editors of **Men'sHealth** Books

Reviewed by Jonathan M. Kramer, Ph.D., clinical psychologist and marriage
and family therapist in La Jolla, California, and author of *Losing the Weight of the World*
and *Why Men Don't Get Enough Sex and Women Don't Get Enough Love*

Rodale Press, Inc.
Emmaus, Pennsylvania

Sex and Values at Rodale Press

We believe that an active and healthy sex life, based on mutual consent and respect between partners, is an important component of physical and mental well-being. We also respect that sex is a private matter and that each person has a different opinion of what sexual practices or levels of discourse are appropriate. Rodale Press is committed to offering responsible, practical advice about sexual matters, supported by accredited professionals and legitimate scientific research. Our goal—for sex and all other topics—is to publish information that empowers people's lives.

Notice

This book is intended as a reference volume only. It is not intended as a substitute for any treatment that may have been prescribed by your doctor or counselor.

Other titles in the *Men's Health Life Improvement Guides* series:

Command Respect	*Maximum Style*	*Stress Blasters*	*Vitamin Vitality*
Fight Fat	*Powerfully Fit*	*Stronger Faster*	
Food Smart	*Sex Secrets*	*Symptom Solver*	

Library of Congress Cataloging-in-Publication Data

Raskin, Donna.
  Good loving : keys to a lifetime of passion, pleasure, and sex /
by Donna Raskin, Larry Keller, and the editors of Men's Health Books.
    p. cm. — (Men's health life improvement guides)
  Includes index.
  ISBN 0–87596–441–9 paperback
  1. Marriage. 2. Sex in marriage. 3. Communication in marriage.
4. Men—Health and hygiene. I. Keller, Larry. II. Men's Health
Books. III. Title. IV. Series.
HQ734.R245 1998
646.7'8—DC21   97–44353

Distributed in the book trade by St. Martin's Press

2 4 6 8 10 9 7 5 3 1   paperback

OUR PURPOSE

*"We inspire and enable people to improve
their lives and the world around them."*

Good Loving Editorial Staff
Managing Editor: **Jack Croft**
Senior Editor: **Stephen C. George**
Contributing Editor: **Jeff Bredenberg**
Writers: **Donna Raskin, Larry Keller, Alisa Bauman, Perry Garfinkel, Kelly Garrett**
Contributing Writers: **Dave Caruso, Jennifer L. Kaas, Nanci Kulig, Deanna Moyer, Lorna S. Sapp**
Assistant Research Manager: **Jane Unger Hahn**
Lead Researcher: **Deborah Pedron**
Editorial Researchers: **Leah B. Flickinger, Deanna Moyer, Kathryn Piff, Lorna S. Sapp**
Senior Copy Editor: **Amy K. Kovalski**
Copy Editors: **Kathryn A. Cressman, David R. Umla**
Associate Art Director: **Charles Beasley**
Series Art Director: **Tanja L. Lipinski**
Series Designer: **John Herr**
Cover Designer: **Tanja L. Lipinski**
Cover Photographer: **Robert Whitman**
Part Opener Illustrator: **J. Andrew Brubaker**
Spot Illustrator: **Mark Matcho**
Layout Designer: **Donna G. Rossi**
Manufacturing Coordinator: **Melinda B. Rizzo**
Office Manager: **Roberta Mulliner**
Office Staff: **Julie Kehs, Mary Lou Stephen**

Rodale Health and Fitness Books

Vice-President and Editorial Director: **Debora T. Yost**
Executive Editor: **Neil Wertheimer**
Design and Production Director: **Michael Ward**
Research Manager: **Ann Gossy Yermish**
Copy Manager: **Lisa D. Andruscavage**
Production Manager: **Robert V. Anderson Jr.**
Studio Manager: **Leslie M. Keefe**
Associate Studio Manager: **Thomas P. Aczel**
Book Manufacturing Director: **Helen Clogston**

Photo Credits

Page 148: **Alison Miksch**
Page 150: **Harry Langdon**
Page 152: **Hilary Schwab**
Page 154: **Courtesy of Sam Keen**
Back flap: **Photofest**

Contents

Part Four
Sharing Your Lives

Part Five
Real-Life Scenarios

Quest for the Best

You Can Do It!

Introduction

Bringing It Down to Earth

Casanova. Valentino. James Bond. The Fonz.

Mythic lady-killers, one and all. The poster boys, in the eyes of many, for good loving. But if these are the icons we're expected to emulate, it's no wonder that men have gotten such a bad rap in the romance and relationship department. Look at that list again: An oyster-gobbling, inveterate gambler. A silent actor (a guy who never had to open his mouth, for Pete's sake). A government killer. A motorcycle hoodlum. These are good lovers?

Not in our book.

We wrote *Good Loving* because we wanted to make an acknowledgment. We wanted to give men the credit that most women won't, which is simply this: We know that your relationship with your partner is important to you. You want to know her—yes, in the biblical sense—but also to understand her, to do the little things that make her happy. That way, you'll both enjoy more peace and quiet at home, more action and noise in the bedroom, and best of all, mutual respect and the certain knowledge that there is at least one person who truly understands you and is there for you. No matter what.

Of course, wanting these things and actually attaining them are very different. It's not like she makes things any easier, sitting there all coy, expecting you to pick up her signals, to read her mind like some telepathic alien. Who knows? Maybe there is something to all this talk about men and women being from different planets. But given the choice, you'd rather have your sex life be X-rated than an X file. Well, stop worrying. *Good Loving* brings it all back down to earth.

Make no mistake: We gratefully, cheerfully acknowledge the fact that men and women *are* different. In fact, they are so different that sometimes the idea of pairing two of these creatures up and expecting them to live together for an extended or indefinite period of time, and love each other while doing it, seems crazy—except for one simple fact: It happens all the time.

And if it's happening to you right now, here's the really good news. It can get even better, if you follow the expert advice you'll find in this book. As you'll see, good loving isn't just about having great sex, although there's much to be said for great sex—and we found plenty of experts to say it. No, good loving is about opening your mouth and your mind, not to mention your ears and your heart. It's about understanding your partner and helping her to understand you.

Finally, ultimately, good loving is about sharing your life, your dreams, your self with another person. Not that you'd learn any of that from our male icons. But what would you expect? They're either dead or fictional. Either way, they're not much help.

But it's not like you're on your own. *Good Loving* is your personal guide to a more passionate and satisfying relationship. The kind you've dreamed about.

Be good. Hell, be great.

Jack Croft

Jack Croft
Managing Editor

Part One

Building a Lasting Relationship

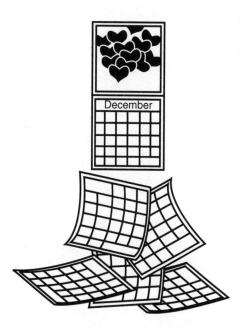

Where We Are

The State of the Union

Companionship, great sex, a best friend, a nicer home, great sex, more exotic vacations, romance, great sex—these are just some of the things we hope to find when we begin a promising romantic relationship. And, for the most part, relationships deliver these things—and more. Consider the facts.

- Men are 2.7 times more likely to be influenced by a member of the opposite sex to see a doctor, and thus stay healthier, than women. Also, married men are more likely to be influenced to seek health care than unmarrieds.
- Guys with wives say that they are happier than guys without them. Could it be because they...
- Have more sex? Yes, it's the husbands who score in this category. Depending on age, sexual activity is 25 to 300 percent more frequent in married couples than among divorced and never-married people. It's obvious, but bears repeating, that having a steady partner around makes it a whole lot more convenient to have sex more often.
- Despite the rise of divorce (5 out of 10 couples will get one), almost 75 percent of all men will be married at some time in their lives.

Taking the Good with the Bad

Committed relationships and marriage are also a good way to make life less complicated. "You wash, I'll dry" and "two can live as cheaply as one" are just two of the clichés that committed relationships can fulfill for individuals. It's just easier and simpler—and a lot less stressful—to share your life with someone.

"Although men and women bring different things to a relationship, it's clear that marriage has enormous quality-of-life benefits for both people," says Linda Waite, Ph.D., professor of sociology at the University of Chicago.

That's not to say that relationships themselves aren't complicated, or occasionally problematic. The external pressures of children, financial worries, and extended-family issues can infiltrate even the happiest couple's plans. Likewise, internal stresses, such as having grown up in a divorced home or struggling with the changing roles of men and women, can leave people feeling confused.

"We've had massive changes of historical importance in the last 20 years," says John Mirowsky, Ph.D., professor of sociology at Ohio State University in Columbus and editor of the *Journal of Health and Social Behavior.* "But there has been a lag in how we're adapting to these changes. There's still an abundance of traditional roles being played out on both sides of the marriage bed." For example, even though the majority of women today work outside of the home, they still do most of the housework. Men, on the other hand, still make more money and work longer hours outside of the home.

Simple Solutions

Relationships, as you'll learn in the pages of this book, are made, not found. Happiness isn't so much a matter of choosing the right person with whom you could have a conflict-free relationship (as you may have realized on your own, such a beast does not exist). Instead, it's really more about learning how to deal effectively with the issues that arise in virtually every relationship. "Sometimes the strains in life are fairly simple and obvious," says Dr. Mirowsky. "It's possible that all of this talk about being from different planets and having conflicting goals is actually turning innocent issues into complicated problems."

So, for example, it's easy to experience the feelings of love (as well as those of frustration and vulnerability), but it takes grown-up intelligence to communicate them effectively.

It takes even more energy to put your feelings aside in order to compromise and solve problems. It's easy to have sex, but it takes commitment to continue having it for years and years—and make it good. It's easy just to live in a house together, but it takes respect and patience to cohabit comfortably and without major disagreements—especially if children are involved.

Staying Focused

The good news, however, is that it only takes some practice at skill-building to become a guy who knows how to handle what comes up between you and the woman you love.

For example, "one of the best ways to improve a marriage is to shift the focus from what you're getting to what you're giving," says Dr. Mirowsky.

In other words, if you earn more money than she does, and therefore work overtime three days a week, don't focus on how small her paycheck is. Instead, try to help her out around the house. It may seem paradoxical, but taking responsibility will actually make you happier in the long run.

Marriage Waits, Sex Doesn't

It's a hot summer night, 1963. A guy and a girl are under the boardwalk (from the park you can hear the happy sounds of the carousel). They want to have sex. What do they do? That's right, they get married first.

Today, there's another young man under the boardwalk with another young lady. They want to have sex. What do they do? Well, hopefully, he'll wear a condom, but marriage? Not necessarily. At least, not yet. Times have changed, especially the amount of time we wait to get married. Consider these facts.

- Since 1970, the rate of living together has increased fivefold. More than one-third of adults roughly 25 to 35 years of age cohabit before getting married the first time. And for second-timers, 61 percent of people ages 25 to 44 live with their spouses before getting remarried.

- On average, couples now live together for 1.3 years before either getting married or breaking up. Approximately 40 percent of them get married within two years.

- Thirty-some years ago, the median age at which guys entered their first marriages was 22 to 23. Today, it's 26 to 27.

In fact, lending a hand around the house, learning to communicate more effectively, and taking more responsibility for the health of the relationship might bring you all of the substantial benefits—including better health and more sex—we talked about earlier.

And the payoff won't just happen tonight in the bedroom, or tomorrow in the doctor's office. Studies have shown that the longer they stay together, the more likely it is that couples will begin to experience a resurgence of love and passion. In fact, with the kids gone and work issues.out of the way, you and she could be just like newlyweds.

Attraction

Finding the Perfect Chemistry

It turns out that sex really can light up the sky. Researchers working in Roaring River State Park in Missouri found that when male fireflies want to "turn on" the ladies, they simply flash their fire as fast as possible. The fastest flasher draws the most females, possibly because you have to be fit to flash fast. Meanwhile, to signal her interest, when a female firefly is feeling a little flirty, she'll flash fast, too, just to let the fit flasher know that he's the light of her life.

Among humans, flashing—regardless of how fast it's done—gets you arrested, not a date. But men and women have their own unique mating rituals, some of which are as rooted in biology as the flashing of fireflies.

A Whiff of Love

It all starts with a sense of smell. Hers, to be exact. "Women have a stronger sense of smell than men, and their bodies respond to the odors of the men in their lives," says Winnifred Cutler, Ph.D., founder and president of the Athena Institute for Women's Wellness in Chester Springs, Pennsylvania. It has long been theorized, and is only now being supported by research, that men and women give off chemical signals—called pheromones— that attract us to particular kinds of people.

"Through pheromones, a man's body odor can actually send unconscious genetic information to a woman, telling her if the two of you will produce

genetically superior children," Dr. Cutler says. In other words, a woman attracted to your natural odor could unconsciously be more receptive to having sex with you—with good biological reason.

In fact, because we have numerous scent glands on our upper lips, kissing seems to have begun as a courting ritual that allowed men and women to get a good whiff of each other. (Eskimos, of course, simply skipped the mouth part and went right to the rubbing of noses.) Kissing, then, is the biological equivalent of studying someone's genetic résumé.

Pheromones are most obviously seen in the animal kingdom, where they are used to mark territories or help find fertile mates. Dogs sniff the ground to pick up pheromone information and find out what other dogs or animals (who sprayed the ground) live in the neighborhood, and whether they are male or female.

Scents and Sensibility

In human beings, smell is only a small part of the equation of attraction. We have come to rely on our full range of senses to impart necessary sexual information. "Once humans became standing animals, they depended less on smell for sexual arousal and more on sight," says sex therapist Theresa Crenshaw, M.D., author of *The Alchemy of Love and Lust.*

Giving someone the once-over imparts not just biological information but also a psychological background. "You can tell a lot about someone by how she stands and dresses," says Al Cooper, Ph.D., clinical director of the San Jose Marital and Sexuality Centre in California. "Of course, you have to talk to someone to really get a full picture, but I think first impressions are quite trustworthy."

That's because your brain responds to a woman's looks on both a rational level (She looks intelligent) and an instinctive level (Pant, pant, pant!). "At this stage in evolution, we've found that just looking at a certain person can cause some of the chemicals in our brains to change levels," says Dr. Crenshaw.

Indeed, all of your senses contribute to falling in love. Hearing your lover's voice, smelling her clothes, seeing her face across a crowded room, touching her arm, and, of course, tasting her with a kiss, create a chemical surge in your head, filling you up with love and emotion.

"Infatuation is a result of the rush of hormones into your brain," says Dr. Crenshaw. Indeed, the chemical effects of love are similar to what happens if you take amphetamines or smoke pot—you have a spike of increased energy, along with feelings of happiness and a lowering of inhibitions. The levels of these druglike hormones, phenylethylamine (PEA), dopamine, and dehydroepiandrosterone (DHEA), rise and fall within your body, depending on whom you're with and what you're doing.

"These naturally occurring love drugs in your brain are a lot like illegal drugs," Dr. Crenshaw says. "Basically, you're stoned on PEA, dopamine, and DHEA, among others."

For example, in your brain, PEA—a naturally occurring hormone that is also found in marijuana and chocolate—functions as an antidepressant. You have more of it in your brain when you're feeling "in love," which explains why some people feel "high" at the beginning of a

Love...or Infatuation?

Being drawn to someone doesn't mean that you should commit to someone. There is a big distinction between infatuation and love.

When you are infatuated with someone, you idealize her—which means you tend to ignore her negative qualities. But when you truly love someone, you see her honestly. It's a bit of a paradox. "You can't truly love someone until the glow of being 'in love' has worn off and you're aware of the other person's faults," says Dr. Al Cooper of the San Jose Marital and Sexuality Centre.

Studies have shown that togetherness will kill infatuation, and that's a good thing. In fact, an on-again, off-again relationship will actually keep you from finding out if you want to love someone since yo-yoing will continually rekindle the flame of infatuation.

Unfortunately, when a relationship like this drags on for years, it rarely changes into a truly satisfying or loving experience.

"Only time can allow an infatuation to develop into love," Dr. Cooper points out. "No amount of hormonal surges can replace what happens as you get to know someone."

On the other hand, beware the marriage that holds two people together who have never experienced the joint hormonal rush of being in love. "That's a problem," says Dr. Cooper. "Everyone wants to feel that feeling. If you miss out on it, you're going to want to act on it when you feel it later down the road—with someone other than your partner."

new romance. With hormones like these working on the side of love, maybe it's not so surprising that women have inspired men to do things like build the Taj Mahal or fight the Trojan War.

Committed to Biology

Hormones play a role not just in your feelings of love but also in your sense of commitment. Chemicals such as oxytocin, pro-lactin, and vasopressin all have a bonding effect on the human mind, explains Dr. Crenshaw. Women have greater amounts of these hormones washing through their bodies at all times, although the levels rise and fall with various activities.

For example, the primary bonding hormone, oxytocin, reaches its highest levels in a woman just after she has had an orgasm, when she is giving birth, and when she is breastfeeding. Oxytocin is the reason women bond with their newborns when breastfeeding and why they love to be held after sex.

Although men don't have as much oxytocin as women, their levels will increase steadily as they experience more touch and affection. So, for example, if you move in with a woman but feel unsure about making a deeper commitment, chances are that regular touching will start an addiction to her in your mind.

"Touch, which releases the oxytocin, can make or break your hormonal surges," Dr. Crenshaw explains. "If, for any reason, you end up spending more time rather than less time with the woman in question, there's a good chance that you'll remain together and not roam into another relationship."

Your brain, however, doesn't surrender easily to those attachment hormones. "Before these love-making hormones can work their magic on your heart, the big T, testosterone, pulls you away from your new interest and gets you looking at all the other women walking by," Dr. Crenshaw says.

Produced in the hypothalamus and pituitary glands, testosterone is the hormone that creates a sex drive in both men and women.

However, testosterone is anything but picky. Its rather single-minded goal is to make sure that your seed travels far and wide, rather than staying home to star in the home video version of *Father Knows Best.* "Love and attachment hormones fight testosterone's best interests, which drive you to be alone and seek out novelty in sex," says Dr. Crenshaw.

This can make for quite a battle raging inside our brains and bodies. "Men are very much in tune with their lust, especially when they are being visually stimulated," Dr. Crenshaw says. "But just when they find themselves becoming more emotionally hooked, men often make an effort to walk away." Men naturally struggle with two biological urges—loving one person and looking at lots of others.

"Men have a biological imperative to preserve our species by finding healthy, fertile women, so we look at women a lot," Dr. Cooper says. We also have lots of indecision. Indeed, if you're in a volatile relationship that yo-yos between attachment and separation, your hormones will also ride that pendulum.

"That's why they call it madly in love," says Dr. Crenshaw. "You feel out of control and not quite sane because the levels of these emotional hormones change so dramatically from one minute to the next." But if you do break up, the chemicals of attraction exact a high price. Love hormones drop off, which can be traumatic to the body. "When your PEA and other hormonal levels fall off, you suffer from lovesickness," Dr. Crenshaw says. "That's how a love addiction can start, because you'll be forever trying to get a new fix to feed your chemical addiction."

This explains why it's so difficult to withdraw from long-term relationships and why some people end up in codependent relationships. On the positive side, the science of attraction also refutes the old notion that men don't readily attach and commit to one person. The fact is that once your body is hooked on someone else's narcotic presence, your brain won't ever want to say goodbye.

Compatibility

Finding Common Ground

A perfect match? No such thing.

You hear a lot of talk from people—and maybe these words have come out of your mouth, too—about finding the ideal mate, the one you're perfectly compatible with. Everyone wants to be compatible, as if men and women were software packages made by different computer companies. Well, forget about it.

First of all, compatibility isn't about finding a perfect match—never has been. The definition of *compatibility* is, simply, being "capable of existing together in harmony." So being compatible doesn't mean that the two of you agree on everything. It means that you can still love each other and get along, even when you disagree.

That being the case, there are some factors that can determine how likely you are to be compatible with one another, and the more you see eye-to-eye on these core issues, the better your chances of staying together. For example, if you come from the same cultural, racial, or religious background, your odds of being compatible throughout your relationship are much higher than if you come from vastly divergent backgrounds. If you don't share these traits, however, you're hardly doomed to a bad relationship.

"Compatibility, we believe, is pretty overrated," says Scott Stanley, Ph.D., co-director of the Center for Marital and Family Studies at the University of Denver and co-author of *Fighting for Your Marriage.* People worry far too much about how alike or how different they are from their partners, says Dr. Stanley. The bigger

issue—and the one that is the measure of *true* compatibility—is how well you complement one another.

Learning to Take a Complement

By "complement," we mean finding a person whose views and opinions you can respect but who also brings some fresh ideas and excitement into your life.

"It's great to be in a relationship with someone who is strong in a way that you aren't," says Dr. Al Cooper of the San Jose Marital and Sexuality Centre. For instance, let's say you've just fallen in love with Amy, a woman who sits down once a month and balances her checkbook—while you take 20 bucks out of the automated teller machine every other day but never write it down. Also, Amy can tell a great joke, even to strangers, whereas you always get stuck somewhere in between "A horse walks into a bar..." and "Why the long face?"

Now perhaps after reading the above, you're thinking, "I'm doomed. These experts say that you need to find someone who complements your personality, but I'm already committed to someone who's just like me." Or maybe you're with someone who's your complete opposite. Does this mean you're incompatible? Of course not; it only means that you may have to work a little harder in some areas to achieve a certain level of compatibility. But first, let's take a quick look at each couple type—likes and opposites—to see what obstacles you have to overcome and what benefits you have to look forward to.

On the face of it, being with someone who is just like you seems about as close to that mythical perfect match as you can get. It makes a certain kind of intuitive sense: The more two people agree about the world around them, the easier it is to get along day to day.

"If you fall in love with someone who has the same interests as you as well as the same education level, you'll very likely have a great environment to raise children in," says Rebecca Cutter, a retired marriage and family therapist and author of *When Opposites Attract.*

Still, if there's a danger in this kind of relationship, it's in finding someone who is so like you that she doesn't challenge you. Or she does challenge you, and you both fight about the same things over and over. You're each just as stubbornly attached to your viewpoint as the other, so nothing ever gets resolved. Or you both have the same viewpoint about everything, all the time. After 20 or 30 years of this sort of thing, it's bound to get pretty boring.

Counting on Your Opposite Number

Your whole life, you've heard women referred to as the opposite sex. But that's not at all what we're talking about when we say that opposites attract. (As most of us have found out, it's nowhere near that easy.)

"I don't think being opposites has anything to do with gender," Cutter says. "It has much more to do with the way a person thinks and how he looks at the world." In fact, Cutter has found that opposites are divided not by sex but by thought process. In looking at 20 years of research, she concluded, for example, that right-brain people (intuitive, subjective, spatially oriented folks) are balanced by left-brain people (linear, objective, logical thinkers).

Such small differences can make a big difference in the long run of a relationship. They can provide enough spark and mystery to hold two very different people together. "Without conflict, there is often no challenge, and that can lead to boredom in a relationship," Cutter says.

The problem, however, arises when your lover is so different from you that you never find anything to agree on, or you do things that constantly offend one another. "There's a big difference between being challenged by someone and being overwhelmed by chronic conflict," Cutter says. "Being opposites should have less to do with personality traits and more to do with hobbies, political parties, career choices, and other opinion-type differences."

Building Bridges

Whatever type of relationship you have, you're going to hit speed bumps, and when you do, the best way to smooth them over is to work together to resolve—for want of a better term—the incompatibility. This is true even of couples who truly do complement each other. As is often the case, the very quality you once appreciated about your partner—the thing that complemented your abilities and traits—often becomes the thing that ends up annoying you the most. That checkbook balancing? Anal-retentive money issues. Her ability to tell a joke? She always has to be the center of attention. "First they attract us, then they repel us," says Dr. Cooper.

Couples who could be twins, ideological opposites, and infuriatingly well-balanced complementary couples—Dr. Stanley has seen them all, and they've all had their problems. What makes the difference, and what will help them keep their relationships enjoyable and satisfying, is how well they negotiate and handle the conflicts that arise in any union. When it happens to you, here are three simple guidelines to help you find some common ground.

Be open to change. In other words, don't insist on remaining exactly as you are, while expecting your partner to do all the changing, Dr. Cooper says. Most new relationships, especially committed ones, require some change within both people's lives. By both being open to change, you'll find that you move that much closer to complementing one another, no matter how similar or different you are.

Be honest about change.
Try to step back from the love and passion you feel for your partner to objectively examine how you feel about what this person brings into your life. You and your partner should be honest with each other about which changes are okay and which aren't. If either of you decide to compromise on something that you're uncomfortable with, sooner or later you're going to regret it or resent it, Cutter says. Take the time to figure out which differences each of you can live with and which you can't.

"If you feel uncomfortable with what someone asks of you, then it's not a healthy relationship," Cutter says. "Healthy love just doesn't hurt that much."

Celebrate your differences.
No matter what type of couple you are, it helps to look for the differences you have and to celebrate them. When you fall in love with someone who has skills that you don't, you're getting the benefit of her wisdom for the price of love, which makes it a bargain in any book. And even if your partner is very much like you, remember that she's amazingly, wonderfully different in at least one important respect—she's a woman.

"Try to realize the value of the other person's traits and see if you can incorporate some of those things into your own life," Dr. Cooper says. Then you'll find yourselves becoming much more complementary to one another. And that, you'll see, is the path to true compatibility.

Hole-Filling Fallacies

Before looking for someone who perfectly complements you and fills in all the holes of your empty spaces, take a look in the mirror. If you don't like what you see, you're not likely to find the right mate.

That's because you have to like yourself before you can feel worthy of being loved by and being close with another. And the more intact and self-sufficient you are, the more likely you are to be able to do just that. "Invest your time in getting your own act together, and don't look for someone to fill your holes," says retired marriage and family therapist Rebecca Cutter. "You're more at risk to fall for the wrong person if you don't feel complete on your own."

While a good relationship is healing and growthful, the healthier and happier we are on our own, the greater the odds of our having a healthy and happy relationship, says Jonathan M. Kramer, Ph.D., a clinical psychologist and marriage and family therapist in La Jolla, California, and author of *Losing the Weight of the World* and *Why Men Don't Get Enough Sex and Women Don't Get Enough Love.*

Here are some of the things we can do to help ourselves have a fulfilling relationship in the future, according to Dr. Kramer.

- Sustain one or more satisfying, nourishing friendships.
- Develop new skills that empower you and help you cope with real-life situations (such as a computer class, dance lessons, or a public speaking class).
- Create a home for yourself where you can relax and rejuvenate.
- Learn to enjoy your own company and develop hobbies and activities that you truly enjoy.

Commitment

Sharing Your Life

Marriage? It sends chills down most single men's spines—even when they're in a relationship where everything is going great. Are we really so skittish about commitment as most women would have us believe? Well, yeah. But we do have darn good reasons (no, we really do!).

Many men avoid commitment because they worry that they can't be in an exclusive relationship with one woman for the rest of their lives. And in some cases, they don't just worry—they know it for a fact, says clinical psychologist and marriage and family therapist Dr. Jonathan M. Kramer.

Naturally, we'd like to think things through—thoroughly—before we make a long-term promise, and that's exactly what the experts advise us to do.

"Commitment is the cognitive, willful part of love. It isn't ruled by your emotions or hormones. It's the part of love that is a decision," says Leslie Parrott, Ph.D., a marriage and family therapist, co-director of the Center for Relationship Development at Seattle Pacific University, and co-author of *Becoming Soul Mates*.

But what goes on in your head—and in your relationship—to inform that decision? Women and the experts have been telling us for years when and why we should make a commitment, but no one bothers to say how we should go about doing it. It turns out that commitment requires a bit more than a conscious effort.

In fact, there are three

essential components that your relationship needs before you can—or should—even think about committing to another person. The first two, says Dr. Scott Stanley of the University of Denver, are "constraints, which keep you together, and dedication, which allows the relationship to thrive."

The glue that holds it all together, says Harriet Lerner, Ph.D., clinical psychologist at the Menninger Clinic in Topeka, Kansas, and author of *Life Preservers*, is intimacy.

Fostering Security

Constraints are outside factors that discourage you from leaving a relationship. These can start out as an emotional investment, but over the course of a relationship, constraints will get stronger, arriving in the form of children and financial pressures. Right now, you're probably thinking that those things sound more like *re*straints. That's because it's easy to imagine that constraints are going to shackle you—and maybe that's why it's not such a good idea to commit. But in fact, most constraints in a relationship aren't enslavements but investments. With constraints, it's more likely that you will stay put because you don't want to lose something in which you've already invested a lot of yourself, not to mention time.

Dedication, meanwhile, is a much more internal force. It is reflected in that sense of "we-ness" two people have when their relationship is going great, says Dr. Stanley. It makes the relationship a priority in each person's life, so much so that we cease to look for other partners.

More important, we start to feel safe. Gradually, the fear of getting burned—always a danger where emotions are in-volved—is itself burned away. And that sense of safety feeds on itself. If you trust that the other person is dedicated to sticking around and treating you well, then you're that much more likely to feel safe and stay put yourself.

Choosing Intimacy

To make a committed relation-ship a happily committed relationship, you need one more thing: intimacy.

"People sometimes mistake in-tensity for intimacy, but the two aren't the same," Dr. Lerner says. While pas-sion, excitement, anger, and other strong emotions can be seen within intimate relationships, they aren't the norm. Instead, an intimate relationship has other qualities. In such a relationship, Dr. Lerner says, both people can:

- Talk openly and honestly about things that are important to them
- Define their values, beliefs, con-victions, and principles and keep their own behavior in the relationship in line with these beliefs and values
- Take a clear position on where they stand on important emotional issues
- Clarify the limits of what is acceptable and tolerable in a re-lationship
- Define the limits of what they can comfortably do or give
- Openly share their competence as well as their problems and vulnerabilities with each other.

Commitment Quiz

To determine how committed your relationship is, ask yourself these questions.

1. Does this relationship energize you? Does it give you strength to face other situations in your life?
2. Do you have an accurate picture of yourself and of the other person?
3. Does the relationship allow your sense of self-worth to remain intact, or to be even stronger?
4. Are you not only making a deeper connection to the other person but also creating rich relation-ships with other people, such as friends and family?
5. Do you feel sufficiently grown-up? Do you have a strong sense of your own identity?
6. Are you more than happy to give up other romantic and sexual relationships?

If you answered "yes" to all of the above, you're a committed man—stand tall, walk proud. If you answered "no" to one or two questions, you have some work to do to truly solidify your commitment. And if you answered "no" to question number six, you might have a problem.

Where commitment is concerned, this last question may be the most important one of all. "People think differently when they're committed to a relationship," says Dr. Scott Stanley of the University of Denver. "When people are dedicated and committed to one person, they don't spend as much time thinking about what it would be like to be with other people. In fact, they begin to perceive being attracted to another available person as a threat to the already-existing rela-tionship." If you're not ready to make this kind of choice, the odds are that you're not ready to make a commitment.

Monogamy

Is It Natural?

Back in the good old days, when men wore bearskins and women wore fur bikinis just like the one Raquel Welch sported in *1,000,000 B.C.*, it was a man's job to have sex with as many females as possible. In fact, the whole human race depended on each man doing his duty, casting his seed as far and wide in the gene pool as possible.

Man, how times have changed. Now we're overcrowding the planet. Our emotions have evolved enough to create jealousy and attachment. And somewhere in the intervening eons, morality and ethics cropped up, making things a lot more complicated than they used to be. Yet while society's rules have changed, some aspects of a man's being have gone unaltered since the dawn of the species. For example, the urge to sleep around is still very much a part of your genetic makeup.

Born to Stray?

In a major twist of biological irony, our emotional and physical systems have evolved to encompass both sexual infidelity and emotional attachment, "while our primitive relatives were totally promiscuous," says Helen Fisher, Ph.D., research associate in the department of anthropology at Rutgers University in New Brunswick, New Jersey. This is why, throughout history and in almost all societies, we have patterns of adultery.

For millennia there was a Darwinian payoff to having sex with lots of women over one

lifetime, says Dr. Fisher. In the interest of ensuring the survival of the species, it made more sense for men to "spread their seed," as Dr. Fisher puts it. The line of the promiscuous breed lived on, while a man who didn't stray had fewer children—and thus less of his genetic code survived.

That's clearly not the end of the story. Despite the sexual revolution and the prevalence of no-fault divorce, marriage has become overwhelmingly popular. "There's a very deep need in the human psyche to build an intimate, sexy, happy relationship," Dr. Fisher says. "And, to my amazement, many of us succeed."

In fact, even in cultures where multiple partners are allowed or even encouraged, human beings still tend to pair off. "A whopping 84 percent of all human societies permit a man to take more than one wife at once," writes Dr. Fisher in her book, *Anatomy of Love*.

But despite the permission given to them, only about 20 percent of the men in those cultures actually have several wives at once, Dr. Fisher says. Instead, individuals choose to form nuclear families. "Human beings almost never have to be cajoled into pairing," writes Dr. Fisher. Something must drive this urge to bond.

The Right Chemistry

There are two main forces that make us bond with a particular person: body chemistry and a deeply instinctual sense of attachment and possessiveness.

First, the chemistry. There are hormones that work in the brain to counteract the stimulation your roving eye provides. For example, vasopressin (nicknamed the monogamy molecule) and oxytocin are two "bonding" chemicals that promote attachment to another person.

One of the other basic reasons that we may tend to stay together has to do with a more mysterious but equally powerful primitive directive—a sense of territoriality. Once we bond with someone, a certain sense of possessiveness kicks in, says Dr. Fisher. We don't want any other male interacting with our partner; we want her all to ourselves. "The human animal," concludes Dr. Fisher, "is not built to share."

Choosing Faithfulness

As if biological and territorial urges weren't enough, nowadays the urge to stay with one person is bolstered by a more evolved sense of morality. "People work hard at being monogamous because of their values," says Richard L. Meth, clinical director of the Humphrey Center for Marital and Family Therapy at the school of family studies at the University of Connecticut in Storrs. "But some men will struggle more than others with the question of monogamy."

Your own ideas about monogamy will be shaped by numerous family, cultural, and ethnic factors, Meth says. Ultimately, the decision to be monogamous becomes not a genetic predestination, nor a territorial imperative, nor even a moral choice, but a personal one. Let's say, for example, a man wants to have sex four times a week, but his wife wants to be intimate twice a week. "One guy will watch erotic videos and masturbate twice a week and that will satisfy him," says Meth. "Another man, however, might be out having sex with other women."

The difference between Guy #1 and Guy #2? "It's just more important to Guy #1 to be monogamous than to have sex four times a week with a partner," Meth says. "He has made a choice based on his value system. For him, monogamy is necessary and important."

Her Cheatin' Heart

Just because men have the drive and the equipment necessary to cast their seed broadly, don't believe for a second that they're the only ones inclined to sleep around.

"Men are fooling themselves if they think that women are naturally faithful," says Dr. Helen Fisher of Rutgers University. "They are no more naturally faithful than men are." The only real difference is that while men will often go out of a marriage simply for sex and adventure, women have affairs because they have strong emotional feelings for someone else.

This emotional component gives rise to a long-existing myth that says that if a man cheats, the marriage stays together, but if a woman cheats, that same marriage will break up. Not true, says the University of Connecticut's Richard L. Meth.

"There are numerous factors that will predict whether couples will survive an affair," Meth says. "The most compelling one, though, is the quality of their relationship before the affair." For example, how long was the couple together prior to the affair? How strong is their bond?

Making the choice to be monogamous, for both a man and a woman, usually means that you're ready to make a commitment to the person you're with, Meth says. "And that person doesn't have to be the one you have the best sex with, because sex changes as your relationship changes, and the quality of the sex you have doesn't guarantee that you won't cheat. Cheating isn't always about sex, for men or women."

Communication

The Key to a Lasting Relationship

"We just grew apart." That's one of the main reasons couples cite for divorce—over and above infidelity, physical abuse, substance-abuse problems, money, and a myriad of other infractions, both major and minor. In fact, the majority of relationships die because the two individuals involved feel that they simply drifted away from each other.

Even though two people may meet by chance, that doesn't mean that they can stay together that way. While people are quick to say that relationships "take work" and that the most important thing in a relationship is "good communication," no one ever explains what these two things mean. Here goes.

"Relationships take work" means that even when you don't feel like talking or going to the store or staying faithful, you sometimes have to bite the bullet and do it anyway. You have to get over yourself and accept that your partner isn't there to take care of you or the relationship. That's your job, too. And like any job, it requires work.

"Good communication" means that you send clear, accurate messages; are empathetic and responsive; and are generous with supportive and positive statements. Like the relationship itself, all of this takes work, too.

Communication isn't just about speaking and listening, though. For example, if your partner is worried and you put your arm around her, you've communicated support. Likewise, if you're angry and you walk through the house

slamming doors, then you're communicating something, too.

But—and these are the tricky bits—good communication must be consistent. If you tell your partner you care about her career but don't listen when she tells you about what's going on at work, you aren't communicating effectively. Good communication also has to address problems in a relationship. This, of course, may lead to conflict and arguments. And while you might think that an argument is a form of bad communication, it's not. In fact, it's one of the most vital forms of communication a relationship can have.

Practicing good communication—in all its forms—is a skill that two people learn, separately or together. While you can't create a spark of attraction where one doesn't exist, and you can't fake respect or compatibility with someone you don't like, you can learn to communicate well.

The Languages of Love

Okay, mid-chapter quiz: Which of the following is a form of language?

- Preparing dinner three nights a week so that she can go to the gym
- Sending a dozen roses to your partner for no reason
- Spending three hours in five stores while she tries on dresses
- Scratching her back and smoothing her hair
- Saying, "I love you"

It's a no-brainer, but yes, all of the above are forms of language. Acts of service (doing things your spouse likes you to do), gifts (not the cost, but the thoughtfulness), quality time (it doesn't matter what you do, as long as it's together), physical touch (not just sex, but affection), and words of affirmation ("I know you can land that account") are all known as love languages, says Gary Chapman,

Ph.D., senior associate pastor at Calvary Baptist Church in Winston-Salem, North Carolina, and author of *The Five Love Languages: How to Express Heartfelt Commitment to Your Mate.*

"It's not enough to simply feel love for someone," Dr. Chapman says. "You have to express your feelings in such a way that they can hear you." However, learning how to show your partner love is sometimes a lot like learning a second language.

"And learning a second language as an adult can be a real task," Dr. Chapman says. "There's a good chance, however, that part of the reason you admire this person is because of the way she expresses love. That second language simply increases your own vocabulary."

So, let's say your partner always calls friends and relatives to talk about important events in their lives—not just birthdays and anniversaries but day-to-day things, too—how the job interview went, what the doctor said, how their vacation was. In learning this, you've discovered three things. First, you've gleaned a clue about your partner's primary love language—likely the "words of affirmation" language, given that she makes a point of talking with friends and family at times when they need recognition or support. If that's the case, then you've also learned a way you can show your love to her (by remembering to ask her about day-to-day happenings in her life, even if they seem ordinary to you). Finally, by discovering this fact, you've learned a new way you can show love to other people in your life (by asking them about events in their lives, too).

Another way to discover her primary love language is to listen to her complaints. "Believe it or not, that's her way of telling you what she needs from you to feel loved," Dr.

Communicating Distress

How married couples handle conflict is one of the best predictors of divorce, says Howard Markman, Ph.D., co-director of the Center for Marital and Family Studies at the University of Denver and co-author of *Fighting for Your Marriage*. Happier couples seem to have more effective communication skills, especially during times of conflict.

"Conflicts and disagreements are inevitable in all relationships," says Dr. Markman. "You can't wait around for someone to come along with whom you'll have no problems. Instead, you have to develop ways to handle what comes up between you and another person."

In other words, it doesn't really matter what issues the two of you disagree on. It's how you each approach the problem—and choose to solve it together—that makes the difference, says clinical psychologist and marriage and family therapist Dr. Jonathan M. Kramer.

Keep the big picture in mind. You're supposed to be a team that pulls together for the long haul. Besides, conflict is not just inevitable, it's actually good in a weird sort of way.

Not only is conflict necessary for growth but it's also a sign that two people are intimate, allowing their partners to see other aspects of their personality. So don't shy away from conflicts as they arise—engage them, recommends Dr. Kramer. In the long run, you'll be a stronger, more loving couple for it. And the words "we just grew apart" need never pass your lips.

Chapman says. For instance, if you buy flowers for your sweetheart every Friday, but she complains because you forgot to ask about her presentation on Tuesday, you're not speaking her language. Quit spending money on rosebuds and start asking about her job.

Culture

How Hollywood Shapes Our Attitudes

Volcanic sex. Stirring romance. Inspiring bravery. Unwavering friendship. True love. When it comes to life and love on the grand scale, you can almost get it all at the movies. Oh, except for one little thing: reality.

It's rare to find a movie—or a TV show, for that matter—that accurately reflects the day-to-day issues that people confront in relationships. It's just not the stuff of high ratings and boffo box-office hits. Instead, Hollywood believes that audiences want on-screen relationships to be about:

- Sexually driven affairs that have no hope of becoming happy marriages
- Strong, silent men who must choose between fighting off enemies and settling down
- Marriages threatened by affairs because of an evil, yet irresistible, third party

And despite the dysfunction of these different scenarios, the couples almost always walk off into the sunset—together. "If it doesn't end with a chase scene, chances are that it will end with a wedding," says David Schwartz, chief curator of film and video for the American Museum of the Moving Image in Astoria, New York.

The problem is that, in real life, relationships don't end at the wedding. In many ways, that's when it is only beginning. And the information we get from our popular media doesn't do much to help us figure out what should happen next.

Celluloid Women

Television shows and movies don't give us very accurate knowledge about women in general. "The movies teach us that if she's beautiful on the outside, she's beautiful inside," Schwartz says. "Rarely is a beautiful woman worthless in a movie."

Oddly enough, though, despite the power a woman's beauty has over a leading man, she's often portrayed as a victim, too. "Suffering makes women seem virginal and virtuous," Schwartz adds. "These characterizations create a false ideal of desirable qualities in a woman."

At the same time that these characterizations create sympathy for the suffering female lead, not one of these women—despite the harrowing experiences they've undergone—has so much as a pimple or a bad hair day. "In fact, the camera lingers on their smiles, hair, and breasts, forcing the viewer to objectify women's body parts," says Gary Brooks, Ph.D., chief of psychology at the Central Texas Veteran's Health Care System in Temple and author of the book *The Centerfold Syndrome.*

"There's something wrong with the way we teach men to be sexual," Dr. Brooks says. "Men are taught to be sexual voyeurs, sexual predators, and to compete with other men to use women's bodies as trophies. The problem is that men can't be intimate with women if they are looking for a centerfold or a movie star."

In real life, most couples meet at work or through friends and family, not in bars or on the street. Then they "settle down," which means living together or getting married. While this might seem natural and satisfying in the real world, the scenario would look quite a bit different through the eyes of a screenwriter.

"Movies usually present marriage as something that ends the adventure of life," says Schwartz. "If a man is seen as independent, then he rarely settles down, and if he does, we're often shown the temptations he's faced with after marriage."

Of course, the biggest threat to a happy marriage isn't education, travel, or world peace, even according to Hollywood. It's usually The Other Woman.

Violent Femmes

"The Femme Fatale can always lure a nice guy into doom," says Schwartz. "In fact, a woman is almost always blamed for the bad things that happen, so much so that the audience often wants to see her killed at the end of the movie."

Fatal Attraction, for example, is just one in a long list of movies that shows men being enticed into and then condemned for committing adultery. *The Postman Always Rings Twice* and *Body Heat* are just a couple of more memorable examples of films that feature women who not only manage to look irresistible but also manipulate some of the most iconoclastic men of the silver screen.

If there's one saving grace to this repeated formula it's that, on screen, the men who stray rarely get away with it. "Despite Hollywood's love of passion and drama, a character always pays for his or her sins," Schwartz says. "Audiences want to see people behaving badly, but then they want to see the characters pay for their crimes." And maybe that's not such a bad message to send.

In Your Living Room

Although more and more movie stars are choosing to come into your homes every week through television, and the plots of TV and film are similar, the way we react to the different media are very different.

"A movie is something you visit, whereas a television show is something you invite into your home every week," Schwartz says. "In some ways, TV is more like married life, while a movie is more like an affair." Because producers know the public makes plans to see a television family on a regular basis, TV shows tend to have more of an emphasis on character development. Movies, on the other hand, have to keep the characters in action.

Despite this, even TV shows are given to extremes in their characterizations of most families or groups of characters. Shows depict idealistic families, such as *The Cosby Show* or *Mad about You,* or, conversely, paint melodramatic portraits of evil siblings and untrustworthy friends, as in *Melrose Place* or *Dallas.*

Like other aspects of our popular culture, for the most part TV simply gives us beautiful people with easily resolved problems—and scant few glimpses into how to resolve real-life problems.

It's Only Reel Life

It's hard to look at TV programs or movies without some sense of irony. Everyone knows that behind-the-scenes Hollywood is a world filled with broken marriages. How is it, then, that this same world can place such emphasis on showing audiences an idealized image of relationships?

"I think that basically our society values marriage and raising a family," Schwartz says. "So it's a goal that everyone identifies with."

In welcoming viewers into a world of "perfect" relationships as well as unlikely scenarios, audiences have begun to hold up the image as a standard. Despite their tendency to ultimately punish people with questionable morals, movies and TV are not the place to learn life's little lessons.

"In the end, movies let you live vicariously through their characters," says Schwartz. "They encourage you to experience things that you can't do in real life, and so the experience has to be fun."

Spiritual Values

Keeping the Faith

Contrary to popular belief, sex isn't the most private thing you can share with a woman. Spirituality is.

And there happens to be a direct link between the two, says marriage and family therapist Dr. Leslie Parrott. In fact, according to Dr. Parrott, couples who consider themselves religious have more active sex lives than those who don't.

In their book *Becoming Soul Mates*, Dr. Parrott and her husband, Les Parrott III, Ph.D., wrote about spiritual connection. "For most of us, our greatest goal in life is to really be known and loved by someone," Dr. Leslie Parrott says. In order to be known, however, we have to make ourselves vulnerable, which can only happen if we know that the person we reveal ourselves to is trustworthy.

Being a soul mate doesn't just happen. Organized religions may provide a road map, but the journey is still unique for each couple. For some people, it involves understanding beliefs and traditions from a heritage that is different from their own.

"Marrying someone who is the same religion as you is only important if that's important to you," says Dorothy Becvar, Ph.D., a family therapist who practices in St. Louis. "What matters the most is that you respect her opinion and she respects yours."

A Matter of Spirit

All couples, even those of the same faith, have numerous issues to discuss regarding their spiritual beliefs. Just because two people were brought up in

the same religion doesn't mean that they will agree on all aspects of it.

When you do sit down to talk about differences of faith, follow these commandments.

Be respectful. When she talks about her beliefs, understand their importance in her life. Don't demean her, and don't engage her in a theological debate. You wouldn't want her to pick apart your beliefs, would you?

Explore your differences. Couples of different faiths should make an effort to examine each other's religions. If she attends church and you don't, go along with her. What harm can it do? If you hold different beliefs, try to learn how your religions differ. In the process you might even find that you hold certain beliefs and practices in common—and you never even knew it.

Seek counsel. Couples who marry within a church or temple will receive spiritual counseling from the pastor or rabbi who plans to marry them. If the two of you are from different spiritual communities, it's a good idea to speak to both leaders as well as an outside counselor, who won't take sides, recommends Dr. Becvar.

Holidays and Holy Days

On a more practical note, differing spiritual beliefs can upset your social calendar. Big events—often revolving around religious occasions—come up all the time, which can create problems if you don't plan for them. Here are some of the situations you'll likely encounter.

Wedding ceremonies. In this case, your own. This is usually the first series of major decisions a couple makes together. They will have to find answers to questions such as, "Who will marry us?" "Where will we have the ceremony?"

and "What vows do we want to say?" The answers to these questions, however, will depend very much on the input you receive from any house of worship you turn to.

No conflict has to be seen as an either/or situation, says Dr. Becvar. In the case of weddings, two heads can dream up a more ideal wedding than one head committed to his or her own idea but unwilling to listen to the input of a partner.

Holidays. For a textbook example, let's say that one of you is Jewish and the other is Christian. The Jewish person is uncomfortable having a Christmas tree in the house. What should you do?

There are numerous ways to compromise on this issue.

- Move to neutral ground. Instead of turning your living room into a war zone, you could split the holiday by visiting family members of each faith.
- Honor both holidays. Who says it has to be either/or? Have symbolic decorations from both faiths on display.
- Start a new tradition. Volunteering together at a homeless shelter is a prime example of ways you can both still celebrate a holiday, while serving your fellow man.

However, if compromises on religious beliefs are made by either partner, you both should question the motives behind any significant changes. "Are you doing this because you want to or because you want to please your partner?" asks Dr. Becvar.

Kids. Ah, children—religious events in and of themselves. In-laws, pastors, and rabbis alike will have plenty of ideas and may even try to assert a divine right in telling you how to raise your children in a spiritual manner. But this is also one of the most significant times a couple can assert their independence. Your first

---

Act of Faith

In their book *Saving Your Marriage before It Starts*, Dr. Les Parrott III and Dr. Leslie Parrott suggest that couples take some time to consider certain issues about their faith and spiritual beliefs before they marry.

- Is it important to either of you that you belong to the same church or synagogue?
- How often do you expect to attend a religious service?
- How much money does one of you give to your place of worship every week or throughout the year? Is that okay with the other one?

"In the best of all possible worlds, questions of spirituality shouldn't be posed as either/or scenarios," says family therapist Dr. Dorothy Becvar. "While everyone is entitled to their opinion, you need to determine what level of differences you're comfortable living with. And you should do these things before you make a commitment."

---

step should be to find out the rules and regulations of your particular faith.

Jewish law, for example, says that children are Jews if the mother is Jewish. Meanwhile, in most Catholic churches, if two individuals want to be married within the church and only one person is Catholic, that person is informed that they are obligated to baptize and rear the children in the Catholic faith. The non-Catholic party is notified of the Catholic party's obligation to do so. There's no signing of a legally binding document involved, but it sure carries a spiritual heft.

Church rules aside, it's a good idea to expose the child to each of your beliefs. Ultimately, when your kids are old enough, it's really their decision about what kind of faith they want to pursue, Dr. Becvar says. As parents, the best you can do is give them as much information as you can to help them make their own choices.

Family Values

A Role-Playing Game

If there were classified ads for husbands and fathers, what do you think the job qualifications would be? Breadwinner? Disciplinarian? Protector of the home? Certainly these requirements would have topped the list a few generations ago, but they aren't necessarily the most important, or the only, responsibilities for most men these days. Nor is it assumed that these roles automatically fall to the man of the house. Today's husband and father has an opportunity his own dad didn't have—to loosen the restrictive bonds of traditional masculinity, which dictated that he had to be responsible for all the major decisions in the family, says Dr. Gary Brooks of the Central Texas Veteran's Health Care System. "Men can now move from a position of authoritarian leadership to a relationship of cooperation, participation, and supportive nurturing," Dr. Brooks says.

So forget all the self-serving political blathering and posturing over family values. What it comes down to is demonstrating in concrete, specific ways that you value your family.

Your New Jobs

The easiest way to redefine a man's role in contemporary relationships is to look at the responsibilities that used to automatically fall to women, says Donna M. Hastings, Psy.D., clinical psychologist at Naticook Counseling Resources in Merrimack, New Hampshire. For example, it wasn't too long ago that most wives did all of the cooking, the shopping, the decorating, and the caretaking of chil-

dren, plus the nurturing of most other relationships (such as with parents, in-laws, and friends). Today's woman is more likely to work outside of the home (often at least part-time) and can hardly manage to do all of those things by herself.

This means that men are expected to add new job descriptions to their household résumé, just as their wives or girlfriends have done. Here are some examples. If you already fulfill these roles, you're on the fast track to a long and satisfying career as husband, father, and lover. If you don't, you could find yourself on probation or even downsized to:

Part-Time Cook and Bottle Washer. In a house where you're both working, who has time to make dinner? Answer: You both do. If you don't, Dr. Hastings suggests that maybe you should. Julia Child wasn't one of your childhood heroes? Pick up some Chinese food on your way home from work. Puttering around the kitchen can be great fun. She's not expecting duck à l'orange every night, just a meal that she doesn't have to be responsible for.

Contact Keeper. Ironically, most guys have no problem maintaining professional contacts, but historically they've let personal contacts go untended. Again, with both of you likely to be so busy, maintaining your network of family and friends ought to be a team effort. And we don't mean just keeping in touch with your pals and family members, but hers, too. "This is a great way for a man to score some major points," says Dr. Harriet Lerner of the Menninger Clinic. "And if you really want to show your wife how much you value her family, give her mother or sister a call once in a while on your own to find out how they are."

If you (or she) have children, take more responsibility for them. Try getting down on the floor and playing with youngsters. Or talk honestly with the resident teenager. The point is to look for opportunities to be closer and warmer with family and friends, rather than leaving all the socializing up to her.

Men give women a hard time for spending so much time worrying about the state of their relationship, but she might not fret so much about it if she sensed you were thinking about it, too. You demonstrate that by talking about the relationship and by making an effort to remedy things when you feel you and your sweetie haven't been spending enough time together lately. Show her that she's not the only one thinking about the two of you.

Mr. Mom. Even the most liberated of couples are thrown for a loop when their first baby enters the family, says Jay Belsky, Ph.D., distinguished professor of human development at Pennsylvania State University in University Park and author of *Transition to Parenthood*. In fact, one of the biggest problems new parents face is the sudden and unexpected return to traditional expectations once a baby comes along, Dr. Belsky says.

Studies show that the division of labor between two people tends to divide along gender lines more after the birth of a child. Mom ends up doing lots of housework, while Dad ends up staying out in the bad old world, earning the money. This can be a difficult adjustment for any modern couple.

It's also tempting to expect that because she stays at home more, she's responsible for all domestic and child-rearing responsibilities. But you know better than that. Unlike your own dad, you've probably changed a few diapers in your day (or plan to). But you have to be ready to do more than that, says Dr. Hastings. That may mean taking children to school or to soccer practice. Or cleaning up after them. Or getting them out of Mom's hair when she needs a break.

How We Become Our Parents

Even as we work to create a fair and equal partnership with our mate, we end up doing things the way our parents did without even thinking about it. For better and for worse, we study our parents' relationship closer than any other in our lives, so it becomes both a conscious and an unconscious model of how we will behave in our own partnership. It can be a helpful template, but also a liability to our own relationships.

"A lot of people go through their relationships on autopilot, but it's important to once in a while switch to manual," says Dr. Donna M. Hastings of Naticook Counseling Resources. "That means that you should take the time to slow down and study your past for clues about two things: the kind of husband and father you want to be as well as the kind of husband and father you *don't* want to be."

Likewise, you need to learn how to deal with your partner's parents as people, not as in-laws. "These people have a much longer history with your wife, and they love her in a very deep way," says Dr. Harriet Lerner of the Menninger Clinic. "She may be critical of her family, but it would be helpful if you don't jump on the bandwagon immediately."

Unfortunately, it's easy for one spouse to blame the other spouse's family of origin for problems in the relationship, says Dr. Lerner. Instead of looking for blame, talk to your spouse about how you would like your own relationship to function.

If she continues to worry about her parents' reactions, opinions, and judgments of the things she and you do as a couple, then she needs to re-commit herself to making her marriage—not her status as a daughter—her first priority.

Respect

It's Strictly Mutual

A man says he wants respect from his family and friends. A woman says she wants love. Two different things? We don't think so. Consider the following definitions.

Respect: high regard for; giving special attention to.

Love: affection based on admiration; unselfish loyalty and concern for the good of another.

Do you see a whole lot of difference between the two? Neither do we.

"Ultimately, the meat of these two matters is the same," says Verdi Lethermon, Ph.D., a staff psychologist for the Houston Police Department. "If a woman is being loved, then she is also being respected. And if a man is being respected, then he usually feels loved."

As in most things in life, the key to getting what you want is to give her what she wants. In other words, if you give her lots of love, odds are that she's going to give you lots of respect.

Giving Freely

Even though we've all been told that respect is something that you earn in life, in fact, that's not really the case.

"We give love and respect to people out of our commitment to them. We don't wait for them to do something to earn it," Dr. Lethermon says. In fact, it's impossible to offer love if all you're thinking about is whether you're getting respect in return. Instead, you must give love freely.

Of course, you can't just talk the talk. Offering love is not simply saying "I love you." You have to learn to walk the walk.

"Love is a feeling that must be turned into an action," says Dee L. Shepherd-Look, Ph.D., professor of psychology at California State University, Northridge. "There are four behaviors that move love from an adjective to a verb. I call them the four A's: acceptance, affection, acknowledgment, and appreciation." Naturally, these are also the building blocks of respect.

Here are some practical and necessary ways to show love and earn the respect you deserve.

Let her in. Show her that she's part of your life by sharing that life with her. Talk with her, share your good days and your bad days with her. By letting her into your life, you're showing that you accept her. She'll respect you for that.

Do the things you say you'll do. "Consistency is very important to people," Dr. Shepherd-Look says. "Your partner needs to know that you're a man of your word. If she learns that she can trust you, then she'll respect you." That's part of acknowledging her need for consistency and to know that you're someone she can count on.

Give her what she needs. "I encourage men to get into the habit of asking their women how they want to be loved," Dr. Lethermon says. Some women want physical attention, others want verbal praise, while others might need someone to wash the dishes after they cook dinner. If your partner tells you what's important to her, what kind of affection she craves, do your best to give her that act of love.

Show appreciation. "Of the four A's, appreciation is the one most linked to respect," Dr. Shepherd-Look says. "If she does something around the house, for example, don't take it for granted. Instead, let her know that you appreciate the choice she makes every day to continue the relationship and the things she does for it."

Getting Respect

In an ideal world, every child would be raised to love and respect others as they would want to be loved and respected. Unfortunately, not everyone is so well-versed in the Golden Rule. "If you're being nice to someone and they're not returning the favor, then something's wrong," says Dr. Shepherd-Look. Here are some warning signs that respect isn't coming your way.

- When she shows contempt for things you say or do, that's as sure a sign as any that you're not getting the respect you deserve. Key signs of contempt—she rolls her eyes when you talk or laughs or demeans you when she disagrees with you.
- She asks you what you want for dinner, and you tell her Chinese. She nods and then proceeds to make lasagna. If this sort of thing happens to you all the time, it's a problem because if she doesn't respect your wishes, 9 times out of 10, she doesn't respect you.

Your best bet in this case—indeed in all cases—is to point out the disrespectful behavior to her and let her know how it felt. If her response is "Don't be ridiculous," then, buddy, you've been dissed. Let her know, in words, that your needs are as important as her own.

Of course, maybe you're getting rolling

Respect through Her Eyes

When Otis Redding first heard Aretha Franklin sing "Respect," a song he wrote, he said, "I just lost my song. That girl took it away from me."

He was right, of course. The song did become a kind of anthem for women. Still, experts know that the kind of respect a man desires and the kind a woman desires are different. While he wants respect for his wisdom and capability, she's thinking about gaining more respect as a woman with brains in a man's world (hey, James Brown said it, not us).

"It's important to see the person you love in a big context," says Dr. Harriet Lerner of the Menninger Clinic. "She doesn't just exist inside the marriage, but outside in the world."

And that world of hers is greatly affected by her gender. "Gender still shapes what men and women feel responsible for and entitled to in this world," Dr. Lerner says. For example, let's say your wife earns less than a similarly experienced male co-worker. You know how hard she works. How does that make you feel? "Wives sometimes try to tell their husbands about the pressures they feel as a woman, but it isn't always easy to listen to a story that's so different from your own," Dr. Lerner says.

Respect her for her contributions to your life and family. If she works and earns money, is a good partner or mom to the kids, or simply lights up your life with her smile, respect what she brings into your world.

eyeballs and ignored wishes because that's exactly the sort of crap you pull on her. If you want to avoid being treated contemptuously, you have to curb your contempt, too. No eye-rolling or name-calling.

Expectations

Making Them Realistic

Men and women both enter a relationship with a certain idea of how things should be. You expect her to continue giving you daily back rubs. She expects that you'll always bring her flowers on her birthday, anniversary, and Valentine's Day. Even though she doesn't like to cook now, you expect that she eventually will. Even though you don't want to have kids now, she knows that you'll change your mind later.

In short, we each have a pretty clear picture in our head of how our life with this other person is going to turn out. And when things don't turn out the way we imagined, it can lead to disappointment, disillusionment, and even dissolution.

True, sometimes a man meets a woman who fulfills all of his expectations and vice versa—just like in the movies. But such couplings are rare indeed. In most relationships, it's more the norm for couples to feel a gap between what they want from one another and what they actually get. The wider the gap, the larger the disappointment, says Lynn Lott, a marriage and family therapist and co-author of *Together and Liking It.*

have, says Emery J. Cummins, Ph.D., professor of counseling at San Diego State University.

Unfortunately, we often don't notice how far a woman falls short of our ideal until we're well into the relationship, Dr. Cummins says. "Somehow the chemistry of falling in love clouds a lot of cognitive judgment. People come together but don't talk about vital, obvious things."

And we're talking vital—like whether she wants to have children, believes in fidelity, enjoys sex, or goes to church on Sunday. Why do we overlook such traits as her complete lack of cooking skills, her nasty habit of eating crumb-producing foods in bed, her low level of sexual desire until much, much too late? We miss them because there's nothing rational about falling in love, says Beverly S. Talan, Ph.D., clinical psychologist and marriage and family therapist in private practice in Birmingham, Michigan.

"When a couple meets, they fall into romantic love, and that's not real love," Dr. Talan says. "Romantic love is based on the desire to have the perfect love you may not have received as a child. It is supported by chemical changes in your body. It feels really great. But eventually, reality sets in and you realize you are not getting the love you want."

Also, early in a relationship most of us feel uncomfortable talking about touchy topics such as babies, sex, and chores. Who wants to get in a fight and suddenly lose the greatest person in the universe? So we date on and assume she's our everything—until we find out, too late, she's not. Instead, you and she will have a much easier time of it if you spend time finding out how you're able to fulfill each other's dreams—and how you're not. Here's how you can do exactly that.

Don't sweat the small stuff. Mick Jagger and Keith Richards probably aren't the first guys you'd turn to for advice on how to build a strong, lasting relationship (although *Under My*

Sizing Her Up

Instead of waiting for the perfect partner—someone who most likely will never materialize—we'd do better spending time early in the relationship examining our expectations more closely, tossing aside our unrealistic, unimportant needs and instead focusing our efforts on what we must and can

Thumb does have a certain appeal, at times). But in this case, the Glimmer Twins hit the nail on the head: "You can't always get what you want, but you can get what you need."

That, friends, is what it comes down to: identifying what you'd like to have and what you *need* to have in your relationship. Think about the qualities in a mate that are important to you. Are you looking for someone who will have dinner on the table or someone who brings home the bacon? Someone who holds her own with the boys or someone who leaves the room when your buddies come over? Now talk about your major expectations with her and find out where she stands, says Dr. Cummins.

See the future in your past. Regardless of whether you admit it, you'll expect your relationship to work out much the same as your parents'. If your mother always picked up your father's dirty socks and lined up his shoes, guess what? You'll be expecting your wife to do the same. If her parents never fought about issues, she'll expect to sweep problems under the rug.

You can identify such expectations by talking about your families. Tell her how men acted in your family. Hear her talk about how women acted in hers. This is how you root out conflicting expectations—like discovering that her mom and dad took turns cooking dinner, while your mom did all the cooking. Going over family history helps you temper future expectations, Dr. Cummins says.

Finish the sentence. Here's a little gimmick that can help you uncover your expectations. To find out what preconceived notions you and your partner have regarding marriage, complete the following sentence: "Marriage is..." You can also do the same with other

Working on the Relationship

If you expect to stroll down Easy Street once you tie the knot, you have another think coming. Women expect to work at a good marriage.

"For men, the most important thing is having the relationship," says Linda Acitelli, Ph.D., associate professor of psychology at the University of Houston. "Once you have the relationship, you don't have to worry about it. For women, the most important thing is what's going on in the relationship: the dynamics, the emotional tone, the processes."

Most men probably want the relationship to go well, but not nearly as much as most women want, adds clinical psychologist and marriage and family therapist Dr. Jonathan M. Kramer. "She usually has much higher expectations of the relationship than he." This is a problem. A clash of expectations, you might say.

The solution? Why, compromise, of course. First, determine how closely your partner's affinity for relationship-fixing mirrors your own, suggests Dr. Acitelli. Most likely, it doesn't, especially if she's incessantly asking you, "How are we doing?" Make it clear to her that the relationship is important but that you can't talk about it every day of the week. Then, make a point to set aside time once in a while—say, every month—to talk about goals and plans and hopes.

topics, such as parenthood, fidelity, and commitment, Lott says.

Fantasize together. Obviously, some of the things you dream up you never truly expect to act on—having a beautiful stranger perform oral sex on you in the middle of a crowded train station, let's say. Some sexual fantasies, however, really count as secret wishes. Talking about your sexual fantasies lets you and your partner know where boundaries exist—and where they don't. Doing this before making a serious commitment together can help you make sure that you are playing on the same field, suggests Dr. Cummins. Of course, it can also destroy a relationship if too much is revealed too soon. Use common sense. As you build a bond, you can 'afford' to be more and more honest about your real selves without threatening your relationship.

Making Her Real

So maybe you realize she's for keeps even though she falls short of an expectation or two. Can you change her? To some extent, yes. Here are some ways to turn your expectations into reality.

Tell her. To express your expectations, you first must create a safe communication environment, Dr. Talan says. "That means no finger-pointing, hinting, and teasing. Instead, you want to talk about your expectations with compassion. Genuinely listen to her response and honor her right to a different opinion."

Date your mate. If you expected more married sex than you ended up getting, take a trip down memory lane. You probably prepared for your initial dates by shaving, splashing on cologne, and wearing your best outfit. In turn, she slipped into her sexiest black lingerie, a short skirt, and heels. During the evening together, you focused attention on each other, held hands, stared into each other's eyes, and maybe even whispered provocative remarks to each other like, "I can't wait to undress you." You mentally had hours of foreplay. By the time you got to the bedroom, you ripped each other's clothes off.

Then you got married or moved in together. You stopped your pre-sex rituals. "Somehow couples think that being naked in the same room is all they need," Dr. Cummins says. "Often that leaves one or the other feeling cold. The joy goes out of their sex life." To rev

up your sex life, ask her out on a date. Plan evenings together where you both know ahead of time what you are building up to. Remember to splash on the cologne. Make sure that she leaves those white circus tent panties at home. Give each other a lot of attention. Compliment her. Talk dirty. And make love.

Please her in bed. Good lovers ask their partners to teach them how to please. You can broach this touchy subject by at first talking around it. Talk about messages you both got about sex when growing up, suggests Lott. Then move on to sexual beliefs you had as a child. Eventually, when you feel comfortable, talk about what you like and don't like sexually now.

Ask. We often assume she wants or doesn't want something without taking the time to find out for sure. For instance, men who refer to their partners as "the ball and chain" often bow out of various activities because they expect the ball and chain will get mad, says Randall B. Davis, a marriage and family counselor in Corona, California. Yet we never take the time to find out whether she'd actually care if we, say, stayed out late on a Friday night to play poker. You'll never know how she feels about something unless you ask. So ask her.

Measuring Up to Her

Now, you knew that this expectation thing wasn't a one-way street. If you want her to live up to your expectations, you have to live up to hers. Here are some of the more common expectations women have and ways you can satisfy them.

Ask her opinion. She needs to feel that she's a part of your life, and not just your home or sex life either. On a certain level, she expects you not just to include her in what you're doing but also to solicit and rely on her opinions about the things you're doing. So solicit, already. Whenever you're thinking about a career move, whenever you're planning a vacation, find out what she thinks, says

Jacqualine Cosper Truitt, a marriage counselor at NewLife Counseling Center and Family Institute in Pasadena, Texas. It sounds like you're letting yourself in for unnecessary grief, but really all you're doing is showing how you value her—and she has a right to expect that.

Study her dad. Just as you will expect your partner to fulfill many of your mother's roles, so many of her expectations about how a man should behave will come directly from her father, Dr. Cummins says. To find out what she expects from you, ask her what she admires about her father, or any other male figures who played a paternal role in her life. In all likelihood, this is a man she respects, admires, and depends on, as much for the tasks he performed as for the way he treated her. If her father did it, and she loves her father, then you want the job.

Call ahead. If you told her you were going to be home by 5:00 P.M. and you're running late, call and let her know, suggests clinical psychologist and marriage and family therapist Dr. Jonathan M. Kramer. If you're on the road for business, call every night. If you're at work and thinking about her, call her. This is not about being a kept man. This is about letting your woman know you care about her.

Carry a calendar. And write her important dates in it, suggests Dr. Kramer. Her birthday is a given. So is your anniversary. And Mother's Day (if you have children). And Valentine's Day. She's going to expect to get pampered on such occasions. You can help yourself remember by highlighting the dates on your calendar as soon as you get a new one—or make it a New Year's Day tradition.

Great False Hopes

Some expectations are simply unreasonable. Here are some of the most common ones.

- *Waiting for June Cleaver.* **Often we expect that our home life will mirror the home life that we enjoyed as children—except that Mom stayed home, while your partner most likely works. So your home won't ever look as *Good Housekeeping*–perfect as the home that you grew up in, says marriage and family counselor Randall B. Davis. Neither of you has all day to clean. And don't expect a gourmet three-course meal waiting when you walk in the door. Most likely, she's walking in the door at the same time. Also, she won't always be in the mood to bring you a beer on the couch—no matter how domestic she is.**

- *Banking on frequent sex.* **You can't expect to have sex—or for her to *want* to have sex—five times a week in your fifties like you did in your twenties. Age does affect desire to some extent, says San Diego State University's Dr. Emery J. Cummins.**

- *Assuming you speak the same language.* **Your definition of *soon* probably isn't the same as your partner's. To avoid conflict, verify what your partner means with vague words such as *later*, *clean*, and *not too expensive*, suggests marriage and family therapist Lynn Lott.**

- *Expecting the same expectations.* **Give up on this idea fast. You have only a minuscule chance that she will expect the same things from you that you expect from her, Dr. Cummins says.**

- *Trying to guess correctly.* **You can't assume that you know how to romance her, how to please her sexually, how to tell when she's upset. If you really want to know, you'll have to ask her for the answers, Dr. Cummins advises. And you'll get to know each other more and more fully and accurately as time goes by.**

Money Matters

The High Price of Love

When love stinks, money usually has something to do with it.

Plenty of issues force couples to mix it up now and again—her taking too long to get ready, your not picking up your dirty socks, her belittling you in front of your friends, your watching football on your anniversary. But all these and a mother-in-law can't compare to the resentment, angst, and outright teeth-gnashing generated by disagreements over money. That filthy lucre makes even the most reasonable, laid-back, low-conflict couples lose their tempers. Indeed, money ranks as the biggest source of arguments—especially the kind that don't get resolved, says Samuel L. Pauker, M.D., assistant clinical professor of psychiatry at Cornell University Medical College at New York Hospital–Payne Whitney Clinic in New York City and co-author of *The First Year of Marriage: What to Expect, What to Accept, and What You Can Change for a Lasting Marriage.*

"It tends to be a lightning rod," says Dr. Pauker. In fact, conflicts over money generally tend to follow couples all the way to divorce court, where they continue to fight over who gets what.

Under Pressure

Most of the time, when we fight about money, we're also fighting about something else, says Daniel L. Kegan, Ph.D., a Chicago attorney and organizational psychologist with Elan Associates, which is a network of organizational consultants.

"Relationships are tough to manage. They are like a pressure cooker, with stuff getting pushed around and around. Eventually, something will push at a weak seam. Money is that weak seam," says Dr. Kegan. "Mostly, conflict over money is a symptom of other problems."

For instance, money problems can stem from poor communication. Two people with a communication problem might be able to get by for a long time without getting into a no-holds-barred fight only because they had no need to communicate—they hadn't pushed up against that weak seam. Once money enters the picture, however, communication becomes a necessity. That's because money is a powerful reflector of our deeply held feelings of security and insecurity, dependence or independence, Dr. Pauker says.

Let's say you make more money than your partner. She already feels insecure because she doesn't have as much money. She doesn't tell you about it. Instead, she shops to make herself feel better, which threatens your security. So each time she buys something, you complain about how *your money* gets spent, which makes her feel even more insecure, says clinical psychologist and marriage and family therapist Dr. Beverly S. Talan.

The Money Traps

Why does money bring all of our problems to the surface and not, say, chores, cooking, or recreation? There are numerous reasons.

Secrecy. Next time you're stuck in an airport with nothing better to do, try this experiment. Sit down next to a random guy and make small talk. After chatting about the crowded airport, the weather, your health, and your love life, ask the guy, "So, Jim, what's your net worth?" Watch him clam up. The point? People are uncomfortable talking about money.

Anxiety. We worry about money. We worry whether our health insurance will cover catastrophic illness. We worry whether we'll be able to send our kids to college, whether we're saving enough for retirement, whether we're keeping up with the Joneses, and whether we'll lose our jobs. Yet, because we link money with our manliness, we rarely ever talk about such fears with our partners. So we fight around them.

Power. Whoever keeps the checkbook, whoever determines the big expenditures, whoever has or makes more money has power. An imbalance of power can sour every aspect of your relationship, including your sex life. For instance, if you force her to send back the sofa, she may exercise whatever power she has in the bedroom by withholding sex, says San Diego State University's Dr. Emery J. Cummins.

Fear of failure. Financial decisions can be so complex that they make us feel stupid. For instance, you may know the stock market is doing better now than ever. But do you know how to play it? What if you make the wrong investment? Such fear can heighten conflict and erode communication, Dr. Kegan says.

Values. What you spend money on says a lot about what you consider important. Often, we're not so mad that money gets spent. Instead, we're mad about how money gets spent, Dr. Kegan says.

Money Doesn't Talk

You can solve many of your money problems with one easy remedy: Talk to

---

Diamonds Are a Girl's Best Friend

So you've met a beautiful lady. Things are going great. But you have just this one nagging thought: Is she a spender or a saver?

Time for some detective work. Check out her fingers, her neck, and her clothes. Is she wearing flashy clothes and jewelry? Probably a spender, says Dr. Robert O. Weagley of the University of Missouri. Now check out her car. Flashy? Another sure sign. Ready for the final test? What kind of stones does she have connected to her jewelry? "If she has fake diamonds hanging off her ears or her fingers, she's going to want real ones pretty quick," Dr. Weagley says.

The thing is that most of the women who turn our heads are the spenders, he says. They are the ones with the flashy outfits. So, if you're looking for a woman who'll sock money away until you both become filthy rich, you better start gravitating to the plain Janes— they're the real diamonds in the rough.

---

your partner about them. So simple, yet couples rarely do it, Dr. Cummins says. The following suggestions will help you and your partner better communicate about money matters.

Check out each other's checkbook. If you haven't already tied the knot, sit down and take a look at each other's checkbooks and credit card spending for up to a year's time. The exercise will give you both a sneak peak at each other's values, while easing you into a touchy area. For instance, you may learn that she turns 10 percent of her income over to her hair stylist. She may learn that you spend 10 percent of your income on beer. "Someone will be appalled at something," Dr. Cummins says. Get those differences out on the table to talk about them. Better now than later.

Learn together. The world of finance won't seem so scary if you do your homework—together. Sit down with financial magazines such as *Money, Kiplinger's Personal Finance Magazine, SmartMoney,* or a finance textbook and figure out an investment you can make as a couple. If you disagree, resist the urge to belittle. Instead, see your differences as information that can help form the best decision, Dr. Kegan says.

Share the power. Even if you alone bring home the bacon, everyone in the household should get some scraps to fry up in the pan—including children, says Robert O. Weagley, Ph.D., associate professor of consumer and family economics at the University of Missouri at Columbia. Allowing everyone to have a personal bank account—or piggy bank—reduces the number of turf wars.

Air resentment. No matter how fairly you distribute income, someone will probably feel resentful. For instance, if your wife's parents are loaded, you may feel uncomfortable every time she talks about their possessions. Tell her. It's important to make it clear that this is potentially a sore point, Dr. Cummins says.

Tell her what's really bugging you. You come home from work to find a brand-new sofa in the living room. You assume your wife is squandering your money, and you tell her so. She counters that you needed the sofa. You fight. What if, instead, you stopped to think about why buying the sofa upset you in the first place? Maybe you're worried that the company won't have a Christmas bonus this year or

Money in the Bank

Should you get joint accounts, separate accounts, or a combination of both? It really depends on your communication style. To help you decide, here's a rundown of the most common ways to manage money, according to Dr. Samuel L. Pauker of the Cornell University Medical School at New York Hospital–Payne Whitney Clinic.

Pooled money. This is the most traditional financial arrangement among couples. Spouses combine their earnings and have equal access to a joint account.

Pros: Method works well when couples agree on how much money to spend and to save, and it saves having to pay fees on several accounts.

Cons: Pooling money requires couples to communicate and cooperate about finances since both are depositing and withdrawing money from the same account. The method also can pose problems when partners harbor resentments over spending differences.

Separate accounts, joint payments. You have separate accounts but split common expenses, such as rent, utilities, and vacations. Or, rather than splitting everything 50-50, you may agree that each of you will be wholly responsible for paying certain agreed-upon shared expenses. Each partner spends the money left over in their accounts as they wish.

Pros: You maintain a degree of financial independence, which can be especially important if you

about potential layoffs at work. If you say, "I'm worried about buying a sofa now when my job might be in jeopardy," she probably won't get as defensive, says Dr. Kegan. Before you react to the expense, take a moment to identify the real issue.

have been accustomed to living on your own for many years.

Cons: The plan doesn't require either of you to talk about how you are spending your money or to develop a joint financial plan. Also, if one partner earns considerably less than the other, the lower wage earner will pay a higher portion of income on joint expenses unless adjustments are made.

Joint and separate accounts. Each spouse keeps money in both joint and separate accounts. You use the joint account for shared expenses such as rent, and the individual accounts for personal expenditures.

Pros: The system allows you to operate independently and interdependently.

Cons: Your bookkeeping becomes more difficult and time-consuming the more accounts you have.

Separate but not equal finances. Each of you keeps your finances separate, but you don't pay for expenses equally. You might live off one salary and save the other, which only works if you have one salary large enough to support both of you.

Pros: Works well for couples who can live off one partner's salary—usually the man's—with the wife free to use her income for personal expenditures.

Cons: The woman in this plan ends up with little knowledge of her husband's income and expenses, which could be important if his health falters or they divorce.

Fiscal Fitness

Though most of our money problems stem from some other issue, sometimes when we fight about money, we're really fighting about money. For instance, let's say you're flat broke, or in debt. You don't know how you got yourself into this situation. So you blame your partner. And she blames you. You're fighting about money. You can avoid such a pitfall by following this three-step process once a year.

Follow your money trail. You'll never solve anything until you know where the money is really going, Dr. Weagley says. He suggests keeping track of your expenditures for three months. Computer programs such as Quicken can help you do so. So can two other high-tech pieces of equipment—a notebook ledger and a calculator, courtesy of your local office supply store.

Plan together. Once you know where the money is going, you need a budget. Figure out generally how much money you need to spend on daily living (electricity, rent, food) and how much you want to save or pay down debt. The key to making a budget work is working it out together, Dr. Weagley says.

Make some goals. Budgets are easy to write, harder to follow. You can motivate yourself by writing down all the takes-more-than-one-paycheck-to-buy material possessions you think you want in this lifetime. Have her do the same. Just do it separately. Then trade lists and look for similar desires. Talk and compromise to come up with some common goals. Now prioritize them. Once you've whittled your list down to some reasonable dream purchases, do your homework. Figure out how much money you need. Now look at how much money is coming in versus what's going out. Then figure out what sacrifices you'll have to make to turn your dreams into reality. Putting money in the bank instead of running the air conditioner seems more reasonable when you know you'll eventually use the savings to buy something you've always dreamed of.

Support

That's What Friends Are For

Imagine how different the story would have been if Tom Sawyer had rafted down the great Mississippi with Becky Thatcher and not Huck Finn. Or what if, God forbid, Paul had only teamed up with Linda instead of John, George, and Ringo? Nothing, not even your sweetest sweetheart, is the same as a good friendship.

But ask most married men how long it has been since they've hung out with an old friend from high school or college, and they'll shrug sheepishly. The answer is often "years," and we're here to tell you that's way too long.

"Not nurturing their friendships is one of the biggest problems men in committed relationships have," says Dr. Harriet Lerner of the Menninger Clinic. "Friendships renew us. They evoke new aspects of our personalities."

Friends and Lovers

Friends make life easier for you—and especially your partner. It's true: Men without friends place a big emotional burden on their wives.

"Guys look forward to sharing their feelings with one woman, but then she becomes responsible for helping you handle all of your emotional situations," Dr. Lerner says. "It's a lot of pressure to put on one person."

Furthermore, this same guy also tends to rely on his partner to make his other emotional connections for him. For example, she'll run all communication interference between him and his parents, and him

and his children. If she were out of the picture, he likely wouldn't have an emotional or intimate connection with people who do, in fact, mean the world to him, Dr. Lerner says.

But if a guy realizes that he has been out of touch with his friends, then works to nurture those relationships, his marriage will be a bit more easygoing. "Romantic relationships only improve when we work first on our relationship with ourselves, rather than expecting everything to come out of our marriage," Dr. Lerner says. "Becoming a better friend, son, or father is, in a profound way, becoming a better friend to yourself because you're protecting relationships that mean a lot to you."

If you've placed all of your emotional eggs in the marriage basket, they're going to crack when a marital crisis such as illness, death, or divorce hits, Dr. Lerner says. And it's often because men haven't built a support system around them that includes anyone but their wives. The healthiest man—both in body and mind—has numerous relationships.

You and your partner should both have some outside interests that allow you to be involved outside the home. Mentors, clergy, co-workers, friends from the gym, and other folks should all be part of your lives.

Friends to the End

True friendship rests on our ability to reveal the more vulnerable aspects of

ourselves. "Look for a relationship where you can really be yourself and know the other person in a real way," Dr. Lerner says. "That means sharing both your confidences and your vulnerabilities, and being able to speak freely about anything that's on your mind."

Also, if you can learn to open up to a longtime friend, there's a good chance that you'll be able to speak more freely to the woman in your life. "Friendship is a wonderful place for men to practice intimacy," Dr. Lerner says.

Here are some ways for you to nurture relationships outside of your relationship.

Turn to someone, anyone. You can't wait to get home and tell your wife what a %$#&*!@ your boss is. But if you're always venting to her about work issues, why not give her ears a rest and call a trustworthy co-worker you knew at your last company? Tell him the situation and see if he can give you some helpful advice.

It's not hard—if you want to call a friend to ask for advice, simply ring them up and say, "I have a problem, and I want to hear your perspective," Dr. Lerner says. You're not exposing a vulnerability. You don't look weak. Instead, you score points. People feel flattered when someone turns to them for help. And you get some peace of mind in the process.

Be friends with women. If you've had a friendship with a woman before your wife, then there's probably no reason to change that connection now unless, says Dan Jones, Ph.D., director of the Counseling and Psychological Center at Appalachian State University in Boone, North Carolina, you see these warning signs: You don't tell your partner when you're going to see your female friend; you don't want to include your spouse when you're with your friend; or you're spending more and more time fantasizing about the friend, rather than actually being with your partner. Then there may more to this "friendship" than meets the eye.

Keep in touch. Don't rely on your partner to send birthday cards and condolence notes, or just to keep in touch with other

Your Pal, Her Enemy

He drinks too much and cheats on his wife. He drags you (twisting your arm, of course) to strip joints. If you were in a commercial with the guy, you'd be the one holding up your beer and blubbering, "I love you, man."

He's your friend, and your woman hates him.

"Too bad," says Appalachian State University's Dr. Dan Jones. "Chances are that you've known him longer than you've known her. She doesn't have to spend time with him. She just has to recognize that you might want to."

But ask yourself, "Is my buddy a bad influence on me?" If you end up drunk and in singles' bars trying to pick up other women, maybe your wife is right and you need a friend who won't bring danger and damage to your marriage, suggests clinical psychologist and marriage and family therapist Dr. Jonathan M. Kramer.

Maybe he's a loser who's really loyal. Maybe you met him in second grade and you also know what his father used to do to him if he broke any rules, and so you feel for the guy. "There's no right answer in these situations," Dr. Jones says. "It's just a matter of taste and preference. You and your wife are each entitled to your own opinion."

Still, you have to let her know that you understand and respect her feelings, but that you should be able to have this relationship on your own. It may be that she just needs reassurance that you won't drive drunk or chase women when you're with your old fraternity buddy.

people in your life. You may be a couple, but that doesn't mean the rest of the world sees you as an inseparable unit. You're still an individual with individual relationships, so be sure the people in your life know that it's you who cares about them, not just your wife, Dr. Lerner says.

Taking Inventory

What You Should Know about Each Other

Getting to know your partner before you marry her—seems like a matter of course in any relationship. In at least one state, it has become a matter of law.

In order to stem the rising tide of no-fault divorce, in 1997 Louisiana allowed a new clause in the standard marriage license: Couples could now legally declare that they were entering a "covenant marriage"—a more binding commitment than the standard marriage contract. To qualify for covenant-marriage status, couples must complete a premarital counseling course and commit to attend marriage counseling before the state will consider any request for divorce.

Regardless of whether the law requires it, experts in the field recommend that couples complete premarital preparation before they tie the knot. The idea of premarital counseling is an old one for many churches and synagogues, which typically require engaged couples to take instructional classes before clergy will perform the ceremony. Some men might balk at anything that sounds like counseling or—God forbid—therapy, but premarital counseling can be a fantastic preparatory tool to marriage, not unlike driver's ed was before you got your license. And research has demonstrated that thorough pre-marital preparation programs can help couples identify problems and issues that could snowball into divorce proceedings later, if left unchecked.

"We have increasing evidence that these programs are extremely effective when couples take part in them voluntarily," says Dr. Scott Stanley of the University of Denver. "There are fewer breakups and lower incidences of physical aggression in the marriages of graduates who learn better communication and conflict-management strategies. Other kinds of programs may also be very helpful, especially those that focus on helping couples assess strengths and weaknesses." The main gist of these programs is to alert couples to their potential "hot spots" and then help them learn to work through their conflicts effectively.

Be Prepared

The most effective premarital education focuses on communicating effectively with your partner. "The goal of most premarital programs is to get a couple talking to each other," says David Olson, Ph.D., professor of family social science at the University of Minnesota in St. Paul and developer of the PREPARE/ENRICH program, a well-known counseling program that includes a detailed questionnaire designed to help couples get at issues they may not have even considered. "For example, PREPARE asks each individual 165 questions and 30 background questions. We find in many cases that premarital couples may have talked about only 50 of those questions, so there are at least 100 things they haven't talked about."

In the PREPARE program, as in most counseling programs, questions and study

issues include both down-to-earth topics and more romantic issues. Here are some examples of topics and questions that Dr. Olson recommends you and your partner should be discussing as a way to help you take inventory of your relationship. Keep in mind that over time, you'll get to know each other a lot better, but it's valuable to talk through these issues as best you can as early

Confirm Your Compatibility

Over 30,000 counselors across the country administer PREPARE/ENRICH, a program to help couples prepare for their marriage. One of the most effective parts of the program is a questionnaire that helps couples get at tough issues that may crop up in the relationship. Wondering how your relationship stacks up? Then grab a pen and take this quick quiz, developed by Dr. David Olson of the University of Minnesota. You can do this individually or with a partner. If you both take it, answer the questions separately and then compare and discuss your answers.

Answer "yes" or "no" to each of the questions.

Realistic Expectations
1. I expect some of our romantic love will fade after marriage.

Personality Issues
2. My partner has some habits I dislike.

Communication
3. I can easily share my positive and negative feelings with my partner.

Conflict Resolution
4. We have some important disagreements that never seem to get resolved.

Financial Management
5. We have decided how to handle our finances.

Leisure Activities
6. At times, I feel pressure to participate in activities my partner enjoys.

Sexual Relationship
7. I am very satisfied with the amount of affection I receive from my partner.

Children and Marriage
8. I have some concerns about how my partner will be as a parent.

Role Relationship
9. We have clearly decided how we will share household responsibilities.

Religion and Values
10. We sometimes disagree on how to practice our religious beliefs.

If you took this by yourself:
On the odd numbers (1, 3, 5, 7, 9), count the number of "yes" responses.
On the even numbers (2, 4, 6, 8, 10), count the number of "no" responses.
Add the two categories together.

If you took this with your partner:
On the odd numbers, count the number of questions where you *both* answered "yes."
On the even numbers, count the questions where you *both* answered "no."

Total Score
8–10: Your relationship has a lot of strengths.
6–7: Many relationship strengths, but you have a few growth areas that need to be worked on.
4–5: A few relationship strengths, with several growth areas to work on.
1–3: Mostly growth areas. Keep working.

And the questions where you and your partner didn't agree? Congratulations—you found an area of your relationship that you and your partner need to discuss at greater length.

For more information about the PREPARE/ENRICH program, write to P. O. Box 190, Minneapolis, MN 55440-0190. Or ask your therapist or clergyperson to advise you on premarital counseling options.

in the relationship as you can.

Finances. There's more to decide than just who balances the checkbook, like: Do you want to buy a house or rent forever? Do you believe in saving for the future, or do you prefer to spend your money now? How does this make your intended feel about your spending habits, and how do you feel about hers? Even with a day-to-day issue such as money, a counseling program's focus isn't on outlining the correct way to live, but rather on establishing an honest dialogue about a sensitive topic.

Religion. Like money, this is a topic many couples avoid because it is such a private issue. But it's an important one to discuss. A few years down the line—when kids are involved—one partner might be shocked to discover that the other partner doesn't necessarily want to go along with certain religious rituals or conventions—baptism or circumcision, for example. Premarital counseling asks these intimate questions to avoid surprises later.

Children. Speaking of kids, how many—if any—do you want? How soon? How would you discipline them? Do you believe in hitting them? Do you want to pay for private education? Would you put them in day care, or will one of you care for them at home?

Sex. He may be scared that she's going to give up those Monday morning quickies once they're married. She may be nervous that he's going to forget all about the romance and conversation that usually begins their most intimate evenings. Any subject that a couple is afraid to talk about before marriage is a subject that must be talked about before marriage.

Acing the Test

Once you've discussed some important questions, the feedback process focuses on some concrete goals. In the PREPARE/ENRICH program, for example, couples first take a 195-question questionnaire to get an assessment of their relationship's strengths and weaknesses.

That process itself can help a couple pick up on potential problems that being "in love" may have blinded them to. "You end up thinking that you can change someone or that a particular habit or trait will go away, but it won't," Dr. Olson says. Instead, you have to work through it. That's why it's important, after a personal evaluation, to set and accomplish several goals, each of which can put the relationship on much stronger footing. Here are just a few of the important goals that Dr. Olson says you should work on.

Know your strengths and weaknesses. Once you've figured out the weak links in your relationship, don't just fret about them or push them away. Now that they're out in the open, discuss them. The more you talk through the possible conflicts highlighted by a premarital inventory, the better you'll be able to squelch them before they become insurmountable problems.

Sharpen your communication skills. Aw, you knew this one was coming, didn't you? Communication is the grease that makes relationships work smoothly. Work with your partner on being more assertive about expressing your feelings. Work together, too, on active listening skills, making sure that you truly hear one another when you're expressing yourselves.

Draw up a budget. After you've opened the discussion on money and how each of you handles finances, one of the more practical goals you can set is to sit down together and work up a budget. Think about long-term financial goals, too—factoring in kids, when or if to buy a house, and how to plan for retirement.

Set goals. In addition to finances, take time to discuss long-term goals—for each of you individually, together as a couple, and later as a family. Where do you want to be? Where do you want to go? This is the time to lay out your great hopes and dreams for the future and start laying the foundation for making these dreams come true.

Part Two

Communicating Clearly

How Men Communicate

Conversation = Competition

You know the phrase "the gentle art of conversation"? It was *not* devised by a man.

Men tend to perceive conversation with a mate as a form of competition or challenge—like playing office politics or jockeying for position in the passing lane. When we're asked a question, we don't just answer—we want to give the right answer (or the right excuse). If talking turns into a debate or argument, naturally we want to win it. If the conversation revolves around our partner's problems, 9 times out of 10, we'll move into advice-giving mode, trying to come up with solutions to the puzzle laid out before us.

Our adversarial attitude toward conversation is not just mental; it's physical, too. Conversation can be as stressful as any physical challenge men face in life. It actually quickens our heart rates and causes our temperatures to rise. Left unchecked, our impulse to wrestle with conversation can also cause tempers to rise and very quickly lead a conversation into the not-so-gentle realm of a full-blown argument. But it doesn't have to be this way.

Guy Talk

It's the basic nature of men to equate the rigors of conversation with more physical challenges. We don't talk about stuff; we do stuff. We're hands-on, proactive. "Men get their identities from their

achievements, not their relationships," says Dan Jones, Ph.D., director of the Counseling and Psychological Center at Appalachian State University in Boone, North Carolina. Thus, we have a hard time simply having a talk, empathizing with a partner, commiserating with her. We need the talk to have a point or a goal, or to address a concrete issue that can be solved with advice and specific actions.

This is just the opposite of what women want. Usually, all they want is to feel that you've heard them, regardless of whether your conversation comes to a specific resolution.

That's not the only way we differ in conversational style. Just for your own edification, here are some other examples that reveal our competitive leanings when it comes to conversation, says Dr. Jones.

- Men issue commands; women make requests. For example, a man will say, "Close the door," while a woman will ask, "Will you please close the door?" This gives men power and makes women seem subservient.
- Believe it or not, men talk more than women. While women initiate conversations, men interrupt a lot more and thus gain control of the discussion.
- In conversation, men like to give information, not get it. This, by the way, is why we don't like to ask for directions.

Speaking Her Language

Unless you want every conversation to descend into a fight or heated debate, temper your world-conquering approach to conversation, says Dr. Jones. Not only will doing this ease stress in mind and body but it can also make you closer to your partner. To become a conversational man, steal a few pages from your partner's rule book. Follow these precepts and you should find yourself well on the way to becoming a guy who speaks her language. Here's how.

Listen up. The most obvious advice is the hardest to follow, isn't it? But it's a fact that women usually just want you to listen more than they want your advice. How can you tell when she really wants your advice? She'll ask for it, says Dr. Jones. Wait to hear if she says, "What do you think?" Until then, keep your mouth shut and your ears open.

Open up. "It takes real bravery to make yourself vulnerable," says Dr. Jones. "Men should look at attempts to be intimate as maverick acts of courage." So don't be afraid to make revealing statements about yourself. To a woman, that's what conversation is all about.

Calm down. Men get very agitated in the face of disagreement. That agitation often propels us to higher levels of anxiety—which explains the rising heart rate and body temperature. So if you feel yourself getting hot under the collar, take five. Explain to your partner that you're having trouble relaxing and that you need a few minutes to calm down so that you can communicate more effectively.

Don't get angry if you're sad. In conversation, as in life, men have been trained to think the best defense is a good offense. So when we're feeling hurt or sad, rather than express those feelings in a conversation, we'll often repress them and show anger instead, says Dr. Jones. You don't necessarily have to show your hurt feelings if you don't want to, but if you're going to mask those feelings, mask them in a neutral way instead of covering them up with an angry outburst.

Practice patience. We guys are often impatient with women's conversational style.

Top 10 Things Men Should Never Say to Women

She doesn't just talk differently; she listens differently. And some of your passing remarks just aren't as funny to her as they are to you, smart guy. To keep you out of the doghouse, here are 10 lines you shouldn't utter within earshot of your woman.

10. "It's different for guys."
9. "You're just like your mother."
8. "So this is PMS."
7. "What's gotten into you?" (Asked when she initiates sex.)
6. "You're not *that* fat."
5. "Why are you so angry? She didn't mean anything to me."
4. "What's that on your chin?"
3. "I forgot my wallet."
2. "I'll call you."

And the number one thing you should never say:

1. "Why do we need a piece of paper when we already know how we feel?"

"When will she get to the point?" we wonder, as our conversational radar scans for opportunities to offer advice, give information, or share one of our own experiences.

Instead, try this experiment, suggested by Jonathan M. Kramer, Ph.D., a clinical psychologist and marriage and family therapist in La Jolla, California, and author of *Why Men Don't Get Enough Sex and Women Don't Get Enough Love*: "Turn off your male conversational radar, take slow, full breaths to relax, and just let yourself be with your woman in conversation. Draw her out. Listen to what she's trying to say. Let her know you understand by paraphrasing what she says. Add whatever seems relevant, but keep the focus on her."

How Women Communicate

Better Than You, Buddy

You knew women were a breed apart from us; you just had no idea to what extent that was true. It's not just breasts, soft skin, and quarts of estrogen that make the difference between the genders. For instance, language skills come more easily to women than men.

This explains why conversations with your woman may have left you in the dust on occasion.

If you're going to hold your own in the arena of verbal communication, it pays to study the tactics of the other side. One of the best ways to learn how to talk to women is to listen to them talk among themselves.

Talking Her Talk

We know you're not about to go and eavesdrop on your partner's next gabfest with her girlfriends. After all, your goal is to understand her better, not bore yourself to death. So, we did the eavesdropping for you. Here are a few key ways that women make conversation. Incorporate these ways into your communication arsenal, and you may find yourself that rarest breed of men—the guy who, according to his woman, "really listens, really understands me."

Show her you're still alive. At regular intervals, let her know (or at least, let her

think) you're listening by nodding or saying "mm-hm." "Better yet," says clinical psychologist and marriage and family therapist Dr. Jonathan M. Kramer, "try paraphrasing what you think she said. Don't parrot. Rephrase what you heard with an 'Are you saying...?'" If you got it right, she'll be amazed that you really heard her. And if you didn't, she'll clarify what she meant and will be glad that you're sincerely trying to listen and understand her.

Offer support. After she has vented, you have a choice of offering her two things: advice or sympathy. If she asks for advice, give it. If she doesn't—or you're not sure how she wants you to respond—choose support and sympathy. In conversation, women try hard to gauge what the speaker needs and then offer it to them. Women also ask questions; they don't search for the answer. This gets the other person to open up more.

Praise unconditionally. Women tend to hear criticism, not praise. So when you say, "You looked better in that green dress than in the blue dress," they hear, "He doesn't think I look good in the blue dress." When giving praise, leave out the "buts" and any other conditionals. "Look for something positive to say," advises Dr. Kramer. "The blue in that dress goes great with your eyes. The green one makes you look 21."

Controlling Conversation

It's all well and good to understand how women communicate. But what happens when you're in a certain conversational situation with your woman and she starts crying? Or nagging? Or criticizing? Or, worst of all, what if she's winning the argument? Relax. Whatever scenario you find yourself in, here's how you can talk your way out of it.

She wants to talk. The words men dread the most: "Honey, we have to talk." If your partner says this, your personal defenses may switch to red alert. But before that happens, take a deep breath and ask yourself, "Do I want to talk?" If the answer is yes, great. If it's no, there is no law against telling her you're not in the mood but that you'll be ready in a half-hour (or two hours, after the game). But you have to be prepared to keep your word and talk, says Appalachian State University's Dr. Dan Jones.

She's babbling. One minute she's talking about the hard day she had at work; the next she's blathering about fat knees and wondering why her best friend hasn't sent her a birthday card. When that's the case, take the pressure off yourself. You don't have to solve a problem or offer advice. Just listen.

She's crying. Good rule of thumb: When she clearly shows an emotional response, respond to the emotion, not the words. "It would be ridiculous to walk away from someone who says she's fine if there are tears streaming down her face," says Dr. Jones. "Respond to the tears by holding her or saying something soothing. You don't necessarily have to force her to make sense of her feelings right in the moment."

She's nagging. Sorry to tell you this, but studies have shown that women "nag" more than men because we tend not to respond as readily to requests as our female counterparts. Get in the habit of stating specifically when you'll perform a task. For instance, the first time she asks you to take out the garbage, say, "I'll do it right after dinner." And, of course, stick to your promise.

Top 10 Things Women Should Never Say to Men

When it comes to conversation, there are a few choice sentences that should never be uttered in a man's presence. You don't have to clue her in; we'll tell her for you. Copy this page and leave it on her pillow. She'll get the hint.

10. "Here's how my last boyfriend did it."

9. "His car/boat/house is bigger than yours."

8. "At least after we're married, I won't have to worry about money."

7. "What are you looking at?"

6. "What are you thinking?"

5. "Deeper."

4. "Does this happen a lot?"

3. "Are you done yet?"

2. "Did you put on deodorant?"

And the number one thing a woman should never say to a man:

1. "Are you sure you know what you're doing?"

She's winning. As we mentioned earlier, women are better at conversation than men are. When you're fighting, that fact can be darn frustrating. Scary, too. Often, instances of violence in a home can be traced to moments where men feel frustrated at their inability to adequately defend themselves verbally in an argument, says Dr. Jones. To make sure that you never even get close to that kind of breaking point, don't be afraid to tell her to slow down, right there in the middle of the fight. Tell her that she has lost you and you can't keep up. Or maybe you can tell her that you need time to think about what she said and figure out what you really think and feel, says Dr. Kramer.

Communicating with Each Other

Keeping the Two-Way Street Open

Communication researchers call it the "beam-me-up-Scotty response." It's that moment when a man feels so overwhelmed by his partner's endless tirade about whatever that he looks up to the heavens, hoping an intergalactic rescue squad will transport him to someplace more pleasant. Say, perhaps, a planet of Amazon-like women in formfitting uniforms.

But odds are that those Amazon babes would speak a different language, and the poor guy is already having enough trouble communicating with this woman he happens to love right here on Planet Earth.

Communication. All the love, compatibility, and good intentions in the world can't make up for two people who can't get through to each other.

"When there's good communication, both people are staying centered within the conversation," says Sherod Miller, Ph.D., chairman of Interpersonal Communication Programs and co-developer of the Couple Communication program in Denver. "These skills aren't something we're born with, however. You have to learn them, whether you're doing the talking or the listening."

Rules of Engagement

"Successful communication depends on three things: knowing what you want to say, saying it in an effective way, and then giving someone a chance to respond honestly," Dr. Miller says.

This description of successful communication holds true for "low-ticket" chats ("Who's picking up the dry cleaning?") as well as "high-ticket" discussions ("Why were you staring at that woman?"). Both types of conversations require you to follow the same set of rules.

Observe the speed limit. You discover that your partner has bounced two checks, and without thinking, you call her up at work and demand to know how she could be so irresponsible. In the heat of the moment, you've forgotten that not only does your wife take care of two children and have a job but she has never before overdrawn on your joint account. There's a good chance that your words don't match what you mean.

"We often react so quickly and unconsciously to a situation that we never stop to ask ourselves how we really feel before we blurt out words that we don't really mean," Dr. Miller says.

In order to say what you want to say effectively, you need to learn to check your feelings and identify your thoughts. "People need to communicate in the 20 to 80 miles-per-hour zone," says Dr. Miller. "It's difficult to feel your feelings and edit yourself at the same time."

Choose your words carefully. "There are remarks that sow and remarks that reap," said the Austrian philosopher Ludwig Wittgenstein.

So let's say your wife did bounce two checks. You know that she is generally a responsible person, so she probably doesn't even realize it happened. What should you say?

There are basically three choices, says

clinical psychologist and marriage and family therapist Dr. Jonathan M. Kramer. You could say nothing and simply let it go, or you could open with a statement that provides information ("The bank sent us a letter saying two checks have bounced"). Or you could broach the topic with emotion, as in a question that demands information ("How come you bounced two checks?"). It's clear that one sentence conveys feeling and judgment, while the other doesn't.

The distinction may seem subtle, but the responses from your partner are likely to be very different. The nonjudgmental opening probably would elicit "Really? Which two? What happened?" The judgmental, emotional version would likely draw a defense: "I did? How do you know it was me? Maybe it was you."

If you've checked your emotions before speaking, it will be a lot easier to choose your words carefully. If you're not sure what you want to say, take the time you need to figure it out before opening your mouth, Dr. Kramer says.

Show her you're listening. It sounds simple, but to be an effective listener, you must demonstrate to the other person that you really hear what they're saying. This can vary from a simple nod of acknowledgment, to paraphrasing what was said, to advice-giving. "In general, you can respond in a warm or cold manner to something another person says," Dr. Miller says. "Cold responses will rarely get communication off the ground."

If your partner has complained that you don't listen to her, ask yourself if it's true. Perhaps you're preoccupied with your own thoughts. Or maybe you're not responding verbally or even smiling when she's finished talking. This spells double trouble for men because women need this kind of feedback and are used to receiving it from their female friends. That means that men often appear even more distant to women than they realize. Remember, unless you're hanging around the female version of the Amazing Kreskin, there's no reason to assume that another person can read your mind. Let her know that you heard what she said, or give a supportive comment

Why She Calls You Stud Muffin

It's a whole lot more embarrassing than the pig Latin you and Stinky Peterman muttered back in fifth grade, but it meets the same objective: When you and your partner speak a secret language, it cements the bond between you.

"Couples have a private language just like twins, prisoners, and fraternity brothers," says Mark L. Knapp, Ph.D., professor in the department of speech communication at the University of Texas at Austin and author of *Interpersonal Communication and Human Relationships*. "It helps solidify the bond between two people, especially during the early years of a relationship."

Using a secret language usually starts by the creation of pet names, such as "Tiger" or "Slim," then builds to include code names for other people, such as "Rick Drunk" for his buddy down at the bar or "The Great Big No" for a certain mother-in-law. Finally, the secret language fills up with special phrases. "Isn't it time to walk the dog?" can mean "Let's split this party, go home, and make monkey love."

Just like pig Latin, uttering secret phrases and pet words allows the two of you to create a world of your own. "Pet names and inside jokes usually fade away after six years or so," says Dr. Knapp, "especially after a relationship gains some stability."

("That must have been hard"). Somehow let her know that you're there with her and that what she says matters to you.

If you ever find yourself turning away from your partner without any sort of active response to her attempts at communication, at least raise your head and look into her eyes. In the end, a cold shoulder is the loudest message of all.

Interpreting Body Language

How to Read Her Like a Book

When a male herring gull wants to mate with his female companion, he repeatedly flips his bill up and down. If she's interested, the lady herring flips hers right back.

The mating ritual is enviably straightforward. The male herring doesn't wonder whether his lady bird is stretching her neck, teasing him, or, uh, flipping him the bird. No, her head bob means only one thing. He gets her drift. And the two get down to business.

And then we have human body language. We ask her if she's in the mood. She waits a few seconds, shrugs and nods, and doesn't smile. Well, is she in the mood or isn't she? We can only guess. And often we guess wrong.

Every Move She Makes

Women sure aren't easy creatures to figure out. In fact, women, more often than men, send mixed messages, says Anita L. Vangelisti, Ph.D., associate professor of communication at the University of Texas in Austin and co-author of *Interpersonal Communication and Human Relationships*. They say yes when they mean no. They say nothing's wrong when they're mad as hell.

There are numerous reasons that your partner won't tell you what's on her mind, says Cathleen Gray, Ph.D., associate professor of social work at the Catholic University of America in Washington, D.C. Maybe she

doesn't want to hurt your feelings. Or maybe she's fearful of your rejection or afraid you'll be mad. For whatever reason, she'll tell you "Yeah, it's okay if your mother comes this weekend" when she really wishes your mother would visit, say, Iceland instead.

One key to decoding such confusing messages is to listen to her body, not her words. Most people are pretty good at saying something to mask their feelings. Few people, however, can control the pitch of their voice, their facial expressions, or their posture when they're feeling strong emotions, says Chris Segrin, Ph.D., associate professor of communication studies at the University of Kansas in Lawrence.

According to research on this subject, couples who read each other's nonverbal cues correctly are usually happier than couples who either don't notice or misinterpret each other's body language. So get in touch with her unspoken language. Here's how.

See the whole picture. Body language is a complicated web of signals. You'll only be able to understand them if you take in all of the signals rather than zeroing in on individual expressions. So before jumping to conclusions, note the following nonverbal cues as a package, not as individual clues.

- The pitch of her voice
- Her posture
- Her facial expression
- The speed of her speech
  - What she's doing with her arms and legs

Only when you add up all of those aspects will you get a stronger picture of the message she's trying to send, Dr. Vangelisti says.

Always ask. When you realize that your partner has sent you a mixed message, you may think, "Aha, I have her figured out" and then spring to action. Don't. If you are wrong, you could escalate the fight. Instead, first verify your suspicion by questioning her. Then let her start talking, Dr. Vangelisti says. And keep in mind that she may have mixed feelings, which may explain why you're getting a mixed message.

Read emotions, not thoughts. You can't tell exactly what's running through her mind by watching her body language. But you can tell how she feels about what's running through her mind, says Dr. Segrin. For instance, if she looks elated, she probably is. But you have no way of knowing if she's elated because she's thinking about a past lover, about you, or about something else. Ultimately, you have to ask.

What She Really Means

Body language can be hard to accurately read—unless you're very astute and know the other person well. Of course, before you even attempt to decipher her body language, you need a quick vocabulary lesson. Here are a few of the more common messages women send using body language and nonverbal cues.

"I really don't believe you." You can tell whether your woman bought the story about the car breaking down on the way home by checking out her facial expression. She may verbally say, "Really, honey? And then what happened?" But if her head cocks to one side and slightly forward and one corner of her mouth pulls back, she probably thinks you're feeding her a load of manure, says Dr. Segrin.

"I really mean 'no.'" You ask her if she wouldn't mind cooking dinner. She says no. But she really doesn't want to and will resent it later. How to tell? She'll hesitate before saying yes. The tone of her voice may be less enthusiastic than other times when she really did mean yes, Dr. Segrin says. Finally, you might catch a

---

Her Lying Eyes

She said she was out with the girls. But somehow, it doesn't ring true. How can you tell for sure?

Not by watching her eyes. Most of us at some point were told that a liar doesn't make eye contact. Not true. Just like making up a false story, eye contact is one of the easier feats to pull off, says Dr. Chris Segrin of the University of Kansas in Lawrence. "The number one thing people do when instructed to lie is increase their eye contact with the other person," Dr. Segrin says.

So how can you spot a lie? Listen to the pitch of her voice; it's one of the hardest things to control when nerves or fear sets in. Her pitch will rise if she's fibbing. Also, listen for hesitation and stuttering, Dr. Segrin says.

But keep in mind that reading body language can be tricky. If you're not sure what she really thinks or feels or does, ask.

---

micro-expression—a very fast rolling of the eyes or scowl that she quickly replaces with a fake smile.

"I really don't want to have sex, but I'm giving in anyway." She'd rather scrub the bathroom floors than have sex, but she doesn't tell you. You can take her hint by noticing her blank facial expression and nervous laugh when she verbally says "okay" to your sexual advances. Also, see if she stiffens up when you touch her. Most likely, a woman who really doesn't want to have sex won't reciprocate your advances and may even turn away, Dr. Vangelisti says.

"I really do want sex—right now." You're both thinking the same thing if she smiles back, moves toward you, and reciprocates your advances. And if she walks up to you and starts biting the back of your neck as she places your hand on her breast...well, that's body language that needs no translation.

When to Talk

Getting the Ball Rolling

There's a time for talking and a time for doing. As men, the builders of civilizations, the shapers of worlds, we have the "doing" part of life down pat. When action is called for, we're up like a shot, ready to do our bit for God and country. When the time to talk comes, though, most men suddenly find themselves, well, at a loss for words. We know something needs to be said, but we can't quite...don't quite...aren't, uh...aw heck, we're just not sure what to say, or how to say it. And so many of us keep our mouths shut, which is the worst mistake we could make.

"Don't ever stay silent when an issue is important to you," says Harriet Lerner, Ph.D., clinical psychologist at the Menninger Clinic in Topeka, Kansas, and author of *Life Preservers.* "The cost will be that you end up feeling bitter, resentful, or unhappy. More important, however, you will be selling yourself short by not taking a stand on something that matters to you."

Mr. Fix-It

One of the reasons that many men are uncomfortable talking about problems is that they think they need to find solutions in every conversation. That's not true.

"Talking doesn't always have to solve a problem," says Howard Markman, Ph.D., co-director of the Center for Marital and Family Studies at the University of Denver and co-

author of *Fighting for Your Marriage.* "Sometimes it's enough for two people to simply explore a situation together."

There are some warning signs you may have been missing or ignoring that indicate when it's time to have a serious talk. Among the most common are:

Little things mean a lot. "Often, couples fight about small, petty stuff to avoid talking about the bigger issue behind it," says Scott Stanley, Ph.D., co-director of the Center for Marital and Family Studies at the University of Denver and co-author of *Fighting for Your Marriage.* Try to see past the moment, and you may be able to get at the real issue the two of you can solve. "And often, simply finding the real issue is helpful in itself. Couples feel like they've come closer together just because they've gotten to the root of something," says Dr. Stanley.

You feel threatened. A guy finds a photo in his wife's dresser drawer. It's a picture of another guy—tall, slender, making goo-goo eyes at the camera. The guy thinks, "Who is this man in my wife's drawers?" He's dying to know, but he can't bring himself to ask her.

In this circumstance, we cite Alexander Pope, who said, "A little knowledge is a dangerous thing." If you're faced with a situation that you're afraid to know more about, then what little information you have is only going to gnaw at you. Let's be realistic about this: If you ignore a problem, you know full well it's not going to go away. If anything, it'll get worse. And just because you might not like the answer doesn't mean that you should blind yourself to the issue. Instead, tackle it head-on, suggests clinical psychologist and marriage and family therapist Dr. Jonathan M. Kramer.

When in doubt, ask. It's more likely that you'll find the

problem isn't as bad as you feared. After all, it might just be a picture of her cousin.

You're keeping score. You find yourself looking for proof that she doesn't appreciate you or wants to control you. Worse, you find yourself looking for reasons to leave. That's called scorekeeping. "It means that you're looking for signs that something is wrong in your relationship," Dr. Lerner says. The problem is that if you already believe there's trouble, you usually can find ample evidence to support your case. Instead of keeping score privately, tell your partner the score—before the game ends for good. Talk about your level of satisfaction or dissatisfaction within the relationship, and you'll be a step closer to satisfying yourself and getting your needs met.

When the world gets you. Tattoo this to your forehead: No man is an island. If you're having problems on your own and need a little comfort, that's an important time to talk, too. As you might have noticed, women seem to know how to ask for comfort, but it's something that most men haven't mastered. You've had a crappy day. You come home. She asks what's wrong. You mutter, "Nothing," and start channel-surfing. But you really don't feel better, do you? And neither does she. (What, you didn't actually think she believed you, did you?) So forget about being the strong, silent type. Tell her you had a crappy day. Vent. What a scam: You get to moan and groan, and at the end of it all she hugs you for it. Why on earth were you keeping your mouth shut?

You feel like whooping it up. Men are their own worst editors. Sometimes, when we're up, when crazy thoughts rip through our minds, when we're struck by the wonder and

Small-Talk Secrets

Not every discussion has to be of the earth-shaking variety. It's possible to have small talk with your honey, too. The trouble is that when there's not a problem to discuss, you can't think of a thing to say to her. What's going on here?

"Men don't have trouble talking to their friends about any old thing," says Appalachian State University's Dr. Dan Jones. "They should try to talk to their wives about any old thing, too."

We're not saying that you have to interrogate her, but you can start the conversation rolling with a few questions. May we suggest:

- What did she dream about last night?
- What was her favorite thing to do on summer nights when she was a kid?
- If she could go anywhere in the world, where would it be?
- If she could be anyone for a day, who would she be?
- Clint Eastwood or John Wayne? Paul or John? Robin Williams or Billy Crystal?
- What's her idea of a great romantic evening?
- What's her favorite vacation spot?
- Best book or movie she has ever read or seen?
- What's her favorite fantasy about the two of you?

joy of life, we feel that impulse to blurt our thoughts and feelings out, but then some sort of safety valve kicks in. *Don't say that!* an inner voice cautions. *You want to look like the world's biggest sap?* Well, sometimes, why not? If you're in the mood for fun, for sex, for flirting, for loosing your wild yawp just for the pure hell of it, don't let us—or anyone else—stop you.

When Not to Talk

Actions Speak Louder

It seems like every time you turn on the TV or pick up a magazine, some expert is telling you to talk. About your feelings. About your fears. About your dreams. About your pain. About everything.

Sometimes you wish they would just shut up. And you know something? Sometimes they should—and so should you.

"Although people love to talk about their feelings, conversations don't necessarily solve problems, and the wrong words can make any situation worse," says Michele Weiner-Davis, a marriage and family therapist and author of *Divorce Busting: A Step-by-Step Approach to Making Your Marriage Loving Again.*

Among the times when silence truly is golden, according to Appalachian State University's Dr. Dan Jones, are when:

- You're going to say the wrong thing. Disagreements often turn into fights when one person can't resist the witty but cutting comment that's going to escalate the conversation from a mild misunderstanding to an all-out battle.
- You can't think of anything nice to say. Even in the middle of a fight, two people who love each other should be able to remember something good about the relationship. Some couples can even laugh while they fight. If you're so angry that you can't

think of a positive thing to say, take a cue from the NBA and call a time-out.

- Your partner is busy. You're fixing a leaky faucet, or she's fixing dinner, yet the other one feels compelled to start a serious conversation about this year's taxes. Bad idea. There's nothing wrong with saying, "I'm in the middle of something, but I realize you have something important to discuss. Can we do it in a half-hour?"

Make Change

Like they say, talk is cheap (unless you're talking with Bambi on a 1-900 line). There are times when words simply will not do, when one of you just has to take action to break a logjam. Since a lot of guys are better at doing stuff than talking about stuff, this should come fairly naturally. Except that some of the stuff you might have to do involves changing your ways—often not one of our strong points.

"Most of us find something we don't like in our relationships, blame our partners for it, and then tell them they need to change," Weiner-Davis says. "But blame is unproductive. It leaves you feeling powerless and your mate feeling defensive. So, if words aren't working, it's time to take responsibility.

"Actions speak louder than words," she says. "Your partner will know you mean business when you change your own actions and responses rather than waiting for her to do it." So what do you need to do? Here are some steps she suggests.

Set a specific goal. Not having enough sex? Don't just complain about it. Determine how much sex you want to have and brainstorm ways to make it happen, such as romantic dates once a week, shutting off the TV earlier every night and spending time together, or giving each other massages. Getting aggravated every time she nags you to clean up the bedroom? Find out exactly what she wants you to do. For example, does she want you to pick up your socks every day or to vacuum once a week? And keep in mind that there is no one solution to fit every couple. Figure out what works best for you and your partner.

"After you pick a specific goal, come up with an action plan to reach it," Weiner-Davis says. "Arguments are usually very vague, but problem-solving has to be specific. That's the only way to see results."

Go back to the future. One of the best ways to solve a problem is to think back to the time when it didn't exist. Why did you used to have sex more often? What behaviors and actions contributed to that happening? You may identify something you did—or didn't do—that is directly linked to the problem at hand.

Be positive. Catch your partner in the act of doing something right and then praise her for it. Remember that people respond better to praise than to criticism, however constructive you think it is. In order for someone to be open to accepting change, they have to know that you're on their side. Therefore, it's very important to make sure that you let your partner know how much you appreciate the times that work between you. If you only talk about the negative things, you'll sound like a critic, not a lover.

Let her follow. "If it works, don't fix it; if it doesn't work, do something different," suggests Weiner-Davis. Once you make a noticeable change, she will change in response.

Peace and Quiet

"Is something wrong?"

"What are you thinking about?"

"Can't you just say something?"

We've all endured these annoying questions, whether it's during a long car ride listening to a tape of our favorite tunes or while sitting engrossed in our favorite TV show. Unfortunately, this quality quiet time seems to make our partners very uncomfortable. What's going on here?

"She's not trying to bug you; she's trying to connect with you," says Appalachian State University's Dr. Dan Jones. For her, if you're not talking together, there *is* something wrong. Her need for sharing and closeness may be unmet.

Of course, there is the possibility that she senses that there really is a problem between the two of you and she's trying to fix it. "Since women take responsibility for the health of the relationship, they're often the first ones to bring up issues," Dr. Jones says.

How about those couples who sit silently together in restaurants, looking as if they'd rather have needles stuck in their eyes than have a conversation? These are the ones Dr. Jones calls married for life, but not for lunch.

If the silence bugs one of you, somebody should say something. If it doesn't, enjoy the peace and quiet. It's a rare commodity these days.

"Each of our actions has a ripple effect on the people around us," Weiner-Davis says. "So if you're the first person to instigate change, it can only change the way your partner responds to you. If you take a positive step, she probably will, too."

Communication Breakdowns

Solutions for Every Scenario

The loudest silence you'll ever hear is two people who aren't speaking to each other. You can see it in restaurants and in cars. You can even imagine it behind the front doors of some of the houses in your neighborhood. You've almost certainly experienced it a few times yourself. The quiet is deafening.

Not all communication breakdowns sound like silence, says Dr. Harriet Lerner of the Menninger Clinic and author of *Dance of Anger.* Some of the most damaging impasses can occur when two people look as if they're communicating—because they're talking or spending time together—but, in truth, they really aren't engaged in meaningful conversation at all.

Breaking Down the Breakdowns

Like a complex machine with a lot of moving parts, communication can break down for many reasons. Each of these reasons has a remedy, but you have to know enough about the machine and its parts to spot the problem and get some glimmer of an idea how to fix it.

Consider this chapter your fix-it manual. Here, we'll show you some of the many scenarios in which communication breaks down between two people. The good news is that hidden in each of the scenarios is a workable solution.

You're tuning her out. You don't need an expert to tell you that this is one of the most common breakdowns. You're sitting there, minding your own business (in this case, a Packers game), when suddenly she appears and starts in on you, talking about any one of a dozen topics troubling her. Or maybe it's nothing so stereotypical. Maybe you've just come home from a rough day at the office and you want nothing more than to relax. But she has that we-need-to-talk look in her eye and you just know you're not up for it. Your facial muscles go lax; you get that glazed look that your dog gets whenever you talk to him. Or maybe you simply get up and walk away. But no matter what you do, she spots a tune-out for what it is, and it can lead to a tense situation and conflict.

"During times of anxiety, some people pursue an issue, while others try to distance themselves from it," says Dr. Lerner. Pursuers feel rejected and take it personally when their partner needs a little space, while distancers open up more freely when they aren't pushed or pursued. As you can imagine, these differences can create an ugly chain of events.

Solution: Both people in this scenario need to give a little. It's impossible to withdraw completely from a stressful situation without creating a permanent breakdown. It's also difficult to remain calm and speak with intelligence in the middle of a high-stress moment.

To ease up on both people, it's best for the distancer to reassure the pursuer that he still loves her, but that he needs some time to think or relax. In fact, he should give her an exact time when they can talk—and then stick to it. Meanwhile, the pursuer needs to back off. If she feels anxious, she should find a way to relieve the stress that doesn't involve talking to her partner—maybe she could tape his picture up on the dartboard and play a few rounds until he's ready to talk. Or maybe she could call a close friend and talk it over.

You shout, she cries. When something really gets to you—regardless of whether she's responsible—you feel your temper rising, frustration building. As you start to talk, you find yourself getting more worked up. Your heart races, your mouth opens wider, your voice gets louder. And louder. Rrrraaaarrrr! You're the lion leading the pack, the bull elephant bellowing to the herd. And just when you start to feel some catharsis, you notice that your mate is tuning you out. Or worse, she's crying. So much for expressing yourself.

The problem here is that you each have differing communication styles, and they can rub up against each other as uncomfortably as two porcupines in heat.

Solution: Differing communication styles are exactly the sort of thing that needs to be discussed and resolved almost before a conversation, or even a marriage, starts, says the University of Denver's Dr. Howard Markman. If, for example, you know how your shouting affects your partner, then you may be able to reassure her—even while you're yelling—that you're not angry with her, and that the volume of your voice doesn't reflect any negative feelings you have about her. Unless, of course, you really are angry with her.

In either event, work on lowering your voice a little. Bear in mind that sometimes partners try to force the other one to love them by punishing them, insulting them, beating on them emotionally and physically, says psychologist Harville Hendrix, Ph.D., author of *Getting the Love You Want* and *Keeping the Love You Find.* You can do that, but it doesn't work. Okay?

When Violence Invades

Words are hurtful enough, but if a disagreement deteriorates into a hitting, shoving, or throwing match, then you and she have a major problem on your hands.

At any sign of violence, you both ought to seek the help of a professional marriage counselor because you're in a downward spiraling relationship. And if the relationship goes down with violence, the rest of your life might follow.

"A man needs to know that—even if his partner is the one to hit, throw something, or push him first—if he retaliates, there's a good chance he'll pay more of a price than she will," says Anne P. Mitchell, an attorney-at-law and advocate for fathers in Santa Clara, California. There's no denying the fact that most men can overpower most women, but even when she might instigate it or even have the upper hand (if she's wielding, say, a Louisville Slugger), women are still more likely to be seen as victims in domestic violence.

Unfortunately, it's sometimes difficult for highly stressed couples to know where to draw lines during an intense argument, as when someone says something cruel, breaks a dish, or slaps the other person. But Mitchell advises you to always be the one to take a stand against escalating a fight. Just as you learned when you got in fights as a kid and got separated by a parent or teacher, nobody cares who started it.

The best thing you can do when things get hot, when you feel the urge to retaliate physically, is to take a time-out. "Walk out of the house and start exercising," says Mitchell. "Walk until you don't feel your adrenaline pumping anymore." Let her know that you're leaving for both of your sakes so that things won't get even more out of hand. And that you'll be back when you cool down (however long that takes).

You don't mean what you say. You want your partner to pay a little more physical attention to you. But instead of being specific about it, you open your mouth and out falls a sweeping generalization. "You never want to do it," you blurt. She gets hurt. You don't talk for the rest of the week.

Solution: Far too often, we don't deal straight on with sensitive and even less-sensitive matters, notes psychologist Arthur Wassmer, Ph.D., author of *Making Contact* and other books. If you want your partner to do something for you, come right out and say it. And always try to be as specific as possible. You know what you need and want. Your partner knows what she needs and wants. She can help you get what you need, and you can help her get what she needs. But only if you let each other know specifically what it is, says Dr. Wassmer. Politely. Positively. Encouragingly.

You must communicate what you need and what you like in a positive, encouraging manner if you truly want a positive response, notes Polly Young-Eisendrath, Ph.D., clinical associate professor in psychiatry at the University of Vermont College of Medicine in Burlington and author of *You're Not What I Expected.*

Say, "I really like it when you lay your head on my shoulder, or when you hug me and stroke my body." It doesn't hurt to add how it makes you feel, says Dr. Wassmer. For instance, "It makes me feel loved and appreciated."

You assume she knows. So you've had a bad day. Or you want to be alone. Or you want to talk about something, but darn it, she should be the one to bring it up. So you don't say anything. And your resentment grows until you finally have a big fight. And you learn that she was waiting for you to bring a topic up. If this isn't an impasse, then there's no such thing.

Speaking and Listening

Sometimes you need specific rules to make sure that you're each being heard by the other partner. That's where the Speaker/Listener technique comes in handy.

Used by many marriage educators to help smooth conflict, the Speaker/Listener technique provides couples with guidelines on how to communicate successfully, says the University of Denver's Dr. Howard Markman. The rules for this technique aren't hard. "Eventually, you won't need to refer back to the instructions because you'll be in the habit of listening and repeating back what you've heard your partner say," says Dr. Markman.

Keep in mind that this technique does not aim exclusively at helping you solve problems. It can also help you have more effective conversations overall. Then you'll be able to express your own feelings and really hear the feelings of your partner.

Rules for the Speaker
- Speak for yourself. Don't mind-read or put words in your partner's mouth.
- Keep statements brief.
- Stop to let the listener paraphrase.

Rules for the Listener
- Focus on the speaker's message.

Solution: Too often we expect our partners to be mind readers, the counselors say. And too often we read our partners' minds—incorrectly. That's another form of miscommunication.

"We make assumptions about what the other person is thinking or feeling," says Wendy Fader, Ph.D., a licensed psychologist and certified sex therapist in private practice in Boca Raton, Florida. "But I don't care how good you are, you can't read the other person's mind." So we end up misjudging what certain behaviors,

- **Paraphrase what you hear. This shows that you are, in fact, listening.**

Rules for Both
- **The speaker has the floor. No interrupting.**
- **The speaker keeps the floor while the listener paraphrases what he or she has heard.**
- **Share the floor.**

When Dr. Markman and his co-workers teach couples the Speaker/Listener technique, they often have the person who is "speaker" hold an object, such as a piece of tile. It sounds a bit goofy, but that object can have talismanic effect, helping both speaker and listener to focus on following the rules of the conversation. Meanwhile, the listener is practicing a technique called active listening, explains Dr. Markman. All this means is that you're listening so well that you can repeat back everything your partner says in your own words—not just the last three words.

Of course, every good conversation is a dialogue, so the listener and speaker should switch roles as desired (and should exchange the pieces of tile, if necessary). Eventually, you might just reach a resolution that ends the argument.

cues, and signals mean. Again, if something's bugging you, you have to open your mouth and say so.

I'm right; you're wrong. Effective communication can really only occur when each person lets go of trying to change the other or trying to prove that they're right. But all too often, one or both people in the relationship proceed from an overwhelming sense of correctness—that they must be right, and the other person must therefore be wrong. You can see how this might lead to a communi-

cation breakdown, can't you?

Solution: Keep an open mind to other concepts, including the revolutionary idea that your way might not be the only right way. That's one of the keys to developing and enhancing a relationship, teaches Richard Cohn, Ph.D., a sexologist, family therapist, and adjunct professor of psychology at Pepperdine University in Malibu, California, and National University in Los Angeles. "A man needs to take the attitude: 'I don't know everything. And I accept that I don't know everything,'" says Dr. Cohn.

Another cure is to see the truth in each of your positions. When you do this, you build a bridge of understanding that brings you closer.

You're spinning your wheels. What does it mean when you start spinning your wheels in an argument? Picture two five-year-olds fighting in the backyard. "Did, too!" "Did not!" "Did, too!" "Did not!" If your fights start to take on that same shrill aspect of accusation and counter-accusation, you're spinning, pal.

"We've all had these ridiculous conversations, sometimes with our spouses, sometimes with our kids," says marriage and family therapist Michele Weiner-Davis. "It's fun until you realize that you're both repeating the same thing over and over again, and neither one of you is getting through to the other."

Solution: Communication will only begin when one of you stops spinning and shifts gears. Instead of blindly insisting on your point ("Did so!"), which only triggers her counter-accusation ("Did not!"), switch to a different tack. Try backing up and explaining your original point and how her reaction to it has made you feel, or try telling her what you think she said and ask her what she thinks you said. Then clarify your positions so that you both feel understood.

Fighting Fairly

The Relationship Rule Book

When a couple has a fight, there is no real winner.

Oh, one of you might make your point—or manage to score points off the other. But it's a hollow victory at best. Ultimately, when a couple fights, they're not solving problems; they're creating them.

"Fighting is a way to express yourself," says Verdi Lethermon, Ph.D., a staff psychologist for the Houston Police Department. But according to Dr. Lethermon, until you fully express yourself emotionally, it will be difficult to shift to problem-solving mode.

Don't misunderstand—while we're against fighting, there's nothing wrong with conflict. "Conflict is natural when two people live closely and try to communicate their points of view," says clinical psychologist and marriage and family therapist Dr. Jonathan M. Kramer. "While successful conflict allows each person to air their opinions and grievances, fighting tends to deteriorate into ugly behavior that can be hurtful and destructive."

In Fair Territory

"Even those of us with the very best intentions and the very best communication skills end up fighting. In fact, one of the most reassuring things you'll ever hear a therapist or marriage educator say is that everyone argues, everyone has misunderstandings—even therapists who know all the rules for resolving conflict fairly," acknowledges Dr. Kramer.

That said, if you're having a dispute, you ought to follow some basic guidelines. Consider the following a Geneva Convention of couple warfare. Follow it, and you will be more likely to stay focused on the issues that need to be hashed out now and then while avoiding doing any lasting damage to one another or your relationship.

Accept the inevitable. First, you and your partner have to acknowledge the truth of the situation—everyone fights. If that's so, you'd best accept it so that you can learn to fight fairly. "One of the great obstacles couples have to overcome is the fear of disagreement," says Dr. Scott Stanley of the University of Denver. "They think that if they fight, it's a sign that they're not meant to be together. But, in fact, arguing about things—fairly, honestly, with respect for one another—is healthy. It prevents frustration and resentment from building up, and it's one of the best ways couples can come to a resolution about the issues that concern them." If something bothers you, don't bury it, don't explode, but do come right out and say it. Be specific and always come at a touchy issue from the viewpoint of how it makes you feel. Don't attack her by saying, "You are the most anal-retentive woman on the planet!" Say, "When you tell me I have to arrange the shoes in my closet according to color and style, I feel confined and controlled."

"Explaining how an action makes you feel, rather than resorting to a general comment about your partner's behavior, is always more constructive and will ultimately be more satisfying," says Dr. Stanley.

Know when to compromise. "In marriage, everything is a compromise. It's not a bad thing," says Dr. Stanley. While you may have been brought up to always win at everything you do, you'll find that a compromising attitude, not a winning one, will serve you in good stead in a relationship. "If you feel like you're always doing things her way, or vice versa, one of you is going to be unhappy and feel frustrated in the relationship. And that's going to come back on the other person. But the more you can work to meet each other halfway on various issues, the more balanced the relationship will be," says Dr. Stanley.

Don't put her down. And don't denigrate her actions or feelings. This does not mean that you cannot disagree, says psychologist Dr. Harville Hendrix. It means that you learn to disagree while respecting your partner's feelings and positions as being as valid as your own. You can do this by practicing "I" statements instead of "you" statements. That is, "I am angry that you didn't pick me up after work like you said you would," instead of, "You are an inconsiderate, self-centered, undependable airhead." See the difference?

The first approach, notes Daniel Beaver, director of the Relationship Counseling Center in Walnut Creek, California, and author of *Beyond the Marriage Fantasy* and *More Than Just Sex*, tells your partner how you feel. The second attacks her character. Expressing feelings, as in the first approach, invites and leads to intimacy, he says. Attacking character destroys it and pushes the person away.

Learn her language. Men have a tendency to respond to the words being spoken rather than to what feelings are being communicated, says Beaver. Often, though, words are window dressing and the feelings are the point, he says. We need to make an effort to zero in on feelings and comment on them rather than on the words and concepts being communicated, he advises.

For example, "you sound angry" will probably yield a quicker under-

Beware Make-Up Sex

You're having a big fight. Dishes are hurled. Doors are slammed. Suddenly, amidst the yelling and screaming, you find yourself turned on. Instead of ripping into each other, you and your honey start ripping at each other's clothes. Before you know it, you've had make-up sex. Fight's over, right?

Not really. The truth is that having sex doesn't mean that you've resolved any problems.

"You can get really turned on during a fight because your adrenaline is surging, which gives you a real thrill factor," says Don Fernando Azevedo, Ph.D., clinical psychologist at the Psychological Resource Center in Cary, North Carolina. "Then, when you begin to have sex, you feel a huge amount of relief and gratitude. It's almost as if you're in a new relationship."

Lovemaking comes with its own set of hormones, which can make the two of you feel closer and more bonded than you did before, certainly more than while you were fighting.

"But if you haven't resolved the issue or learned to fight fairly, ugly arguments will keep reoccurring," says Dr. Azevedo. "Then fighting and having sex can become an addictive cycle."

While this cycle is passionate—and certainly has its temporary reward—in the end it creates another hazard in the relationship. For instance, "a man might think that he can continue a certain behavior once he's convinced he'll still be able to have sex with his partner," Dr. Azevedo explains. "Eventually, however, she'll really think he's a jerk if he keeps doing something she doesn't like over and over again—and keeps expecting to have sex." Soon enough, she'll feel used—and make-up sex becomes nothing of the kind.

standing and more positive resolution than "you've totally misinterpreted what I said." Why? Because "you sound angry" acknowledges a feeling, while "you've totally misinterpreted" escalates conflict through argument and attacks the other person's reasoning abilities.

Be an active listener. One important way to keep an argument focused and avoid escalation is to make it clear that you're listening to what your partner says. One way to do that, marriage educators suggest, is to employ a technique called active listening. When your partner says something, repeat it or paraphrase it as best you can and ask if you got it right, advises Dr. Hendrix. Don't argue about it or challenge how your partner feels, he says. Understand how your partner feels and acknowledge its validity.

Active listening may feel a little weird at first, and it will certainly require some discipline. In other words, you have to learn to keep your mouth shut and your mind focused while your partner is talking. Don't interrupt. Don't start silently rehearsing your rebuttal. Listen. And then prove that you have heard and understood what was said by restating it—without prejudice.

Don't be a fixer-upper. If you're debating an issue, your job at that moment is to listen, not to figure out how to solve the problem yourself. Women hate it when we try to be a Mr. Fix-It, says John Gray, Ph.D., author of *Men Are from Mars, Women Are from Venus* and other books. They take this attitude as a sign that we aren't listening (and we probably aren't). What they really want is empathy, he says. They want to know that we understand what they are going through. They usually don't want advice. And if there is a problem that needs fixing, your goal is to work on fixing it together.

No zoning out. Many men (and women) have a tough time handling conflict and want to escape by stalking out the door or switching on the TV. Do your best to hang in there and make a good-faith effort at resolving the situation at hand.

All too often, men reach a point where they just "don't want to hear it," and so they stonewall their partner, shutting down and refusing to listen anymore. Put yourself in your partner's shoes and try to imagine what a sign of contempt that is. If someone pulled that on you, you'd probably want to punch them in the mouth. Well, maybe that's how she feels when you short-circuit the conflict before you've reached a resolution.

The exception to this rule is if you've been fighting for what seems like hours, and you seem to have reached an impasse. Or if one of you is so angry that you can no longer control yourself or muster a coherent sentence, it's all right to take a breather. Announce that you need a little time to collect yourself, then go for a walk or retreat to your own private space. No slamming or thrashing as you go. And, at the risk of repeating ourselves, no fair doing this five minutes into the argument.

Embracing Conflict

People often fear conflict. They sense anger or disappointment and become afraid that their partner doesn't care for them anymore. In fact, just the opposite is true. The clearest sign of potential danger in a relationship isn't feeling or showing intense emotion, but apathy—feeling nothing at all. In fact, when she stops fighting with you or telling you how she feels, that's something to fear.

People make an assumption that happy couples don't fight, but that's not true, says the University of Denver's Dr. Howard Markman. In reality, every couple has disagreements, but happy and thriving couples learn how to handle conflict in a positive way. Handling these conflicts successfully—using specific rules of engagement—means that you and your partner look at disagreements not as an indicator of trouble but as a sign that it's time to start working together as a team.

Broaching Sensitive Topics

A Step-by-Step Guide to Conversation

Bringing up a touchy subject is a lot like defusing a bomb. Unless you want it to blow up in your face, you need to approach the thing with a mix of patience, caution, and gentleness. It's also vital to have the proper tools on hand. On the bomb squad, you'd have wire cutters and radio-controlled robots. To broach a sensitive topic with your partner, you need a specific set of communication skills to help avoid an explosive situation.

When it comes to discussing sensitive, difficult, or potentially painful topics, our usual policy is to let sleeping dogs lie. But sometimes, curiosity, guilt, or the simple need to put something to rest overwhelms us. We know it's time to broach the subject. But how to do it?

Be Prepared

The first step to talking about sensitive issues is to figure out your own motives for bringing the subject up, says Bonnie Jacobson, Ph.D., director of the New York Institute for Psychological Change in New York City and author of *If Only You Would Listen.* What do you want to get out of the conversation? Do you want to make a good relationship better by clearing the air about something, or do you just want to get something off your chest, even

though it may make your partner feel bad or even harm the relationship? If it's the former, you're on pretty solid ground for broaching the subject. But if you're trying to assuage a guilty conscience, or feel that bringing up the topic might ultimately do more harm than good, then you need to think long and hard before plunging ahead.

For the purposes of this chapter, we'll assume that you do have the best of intentions, which, you may have noticed, doesn't make bringing up a sensitive topic any easier. Relax. Take a deep breath. The following preconversation steps are comparable to taking warm-up swings before you go to bat. They'll loosen you up and help you relax.

Picture a happy ending. Fear—and the resultant urge to keep our mouths shut—usually strikes us when we imagine a worst-case scenario as an ending to a conversation on a touchy subject. So instead, keep your eye on the likely outcome, especially one you hope for. "When you use logic, you'll see that the ending will probably be something you can live with," Dr. Jacobson says.

Similarly, you need to imagine what will happen to your relationship if you don't say anything. "Not addressing something that's important to you will create resentment," says Dr. Jacobson. "And that just adds more fuel to the fire."

Save face. "The most unloving thing a person can do is make someone feel ashamed of who they are," Dr. Jacobson says. "The last thing you want to do when you bring up a sensitive subject is embarrass your partner." Unfortunately, that's not always easy to avoid because, well, some subjects are downright embarrassing. Bad breath, bad kissing, bad cooking...is there a nice way to bring this stuff up? To avoid humiliating the one you love, Dr. Jacobson advises that you stick to the "ask questions first, give your opinion later" rule.

For the sake of illustration, let's say that she has bad breath. You can try saying something like, "Have you ever noticed that some people can't tell when they have bad breath?" or "How's that cavity in your back tooth? Is it causing any side effects?" or "Is your stomach upset?" Of course, eventually you're going to wind up telling her that her breath isn't very appealing these days, which will probably hurt. However, backing into the subject this way, you may avoid making your partner feel embarrassed.

Say "I." When most people are upset about something—as might be the case when discussing a touchy subject—they accuse the other person. This is extremely ineffective and somewhat unfair. "The most important rule to remember when you're trying to talk about something important to you is that all of your sentences should begin with 'I,'" says clinical psychologist Dr. Don Fernando Azevedo, an instructor with PAIRS International, a course that teaches couples relationship skills.

For example, if you say "You never want to have sex anymore!" then you are making an assumption and accusing your partner of something that may not be true. (She may want to have sex but may be angry or sad or sick.) However, if instead of accusing her, you tell her how you feel, then she has less chance to get defensive and you're on more solid ground since feelings are valid, while accusations may not be. So in the above instance, saying something like "I notice that whenever I try to get close to you, you pull away" will have far less of an accusing sting.

Sentence Starters

Sometimes you need extra help to broach difficult subjects and keep them from spinning out of control. There is a great method for accomplishing just that, says Dr. Azevedo.

"In PAIRS, we give men and women a list of sentence stems, which are phrases—almost like opening lines—that give people a way to start communicating about their sensitive subjects," he says.

It sounds a tad contrived, but these opening lines can be highly effective at getting to the heart of a sensitive subject. The PAIRS list goes in a specific order. One partner is supposed to go down the entire list, finishing every sentence, while the other person listens. After each sentence the one partner shares, the other partner shares back what he heard. These sentence stems aren't meant to elicit particular responses, only listening. In fact, this isn't a problem-solving tool. Instead, you're using the list to help express feelings that are hard for you to express on your own. You could even write the list down, finishing each sentence on your own, and then give it to your spouse to read.

"Try not to skip a sentence stem," says Dr. Azevedo. "The whole list is important because it states the problem, helps you explain why the problem is so difficult for you, and then allows you to express love, appreciation, and hope to your partner." In fact, when a person wants to skip a stem, it's usually the ones he most needs to explore.

Here are the sentence stems PAIRS gives to its clients. For the sake of illustration, we've plugged in a hypothetical situation—a man who feels his wife doesn't want to have sex as often as he does—to show you how the process works.

"I notice..." that whenever I come into bed at night you're already asleep.

"I assume this means..." that you don't want to have sex with me.

"I wonder..." if you're withholding sex for some reason.

"I suspect..." that you're still upset about that fight we had last week.

"I believe..." that I still love you and want to be close to you, even when we disagree.

"I resent..." that you hold one argument against me for so long and try to get even in the bedroom.

"I am puzzled by..." why you do this because I know how much it means to you when we're intimate.

"I am hurt by..." this because it makes me feel like you don't love me anymore or find me attractive.

"I regret..." not handling this sooner.

"I am afraid of..." this escalating into something that could permanently damage our relationship.

"I am frustrated by..." your refusal to talk about this or do anything to fix it.

"I am happier when..." we're close and when I know that you're here for me.

"I want..." us to work things out even if it means staying up all night long.

"I expect..." that we'll fight sometimes, but I also expect us to work it out.

"I appreciate..." that you're still angry and obviously still need to tell me what's bothering you.

"I realize..." that you can't be happy with this standoff either.

"I hope..." that we can work this out and it results in bringing us even closer together.

What is your partner doing while you're pouring your heart out to her? Listening and then repeating back to you what she has heard you say, Dr. Azevedo says.

It Ain't Over...

So, when is a gut-spilling talk over? Whenever you both say it is.

"When you feel comfortable about the subject, then ask her if she feels comfortable,"

Timing Is Everything

Now that you know what to say, you also need to know when to say it.

"You should always ask your partner if she's able to listen to you now or to suggest a good time," says clinical psychologist Dr. Don Fernando Azevedo. "Don't attack someone with your emotions if she's not prepared to respond. It won't help either of you communicate well."

You shouldn't broach a sensitive topic when:

- Your emotions are out of control
- There are distractions
- Alcohol or drugs are involved
- One of you is driving
- The person listening says she can't do it right now

"Think of emotional conversations as equal to making a million-dollar deal in your business," says Dr. Azevedo. "You should at least be face-to-face."

Ultimately, the perfect time to broach a sensitive topic is when your partner says she's ready to listen. And if she's never ready to listen, then you just found out what your first topic of conversation should be.

Dr. Jacobson says. "If you're both feeling fine, then reassure her that the topic can come up again, if need be, but that now it's time to celebrate your closeness."

Hopefully, the conversation has created a more strengthened sense of togetherness between the two of you. "It's time for the movies or making love or some other fun pastime," says Dr. Jacobson. "You want to let her know that you're not angry and that, in fact, you feel better than ever about your relationship."

Reaching Decisions

How Everybody Can Win

You might not realize it, but the same process you and your partner go through to resolve small issues, such as "Chinese or Italian tonight?," is just as effective to resolve larger issues, like "Should we buy a house, or rent for another year?" When it comes to making a decision, it's not the size of the decision but the way you and your partner arrive at it that matters the most.

All too often, though, people assume that because they feel one way about a decision, their partner is automatically going to take an opposing viewpoint. Suddenly, their lover and best friend transforms from a teammate to a rival.

This is not how decision-making should be at all, says clinical psychologist and marriage and family therapist Dr. Jonathan M. Kramer. Instead of setting up a destructive win/lose situation in your mind, recognize decision-making for what it is—a means to an end. And if you should disagree about an issue, that's not necessarily cause for a fight.

Deciding to Decide

It's productive to think of a decision that needs to be made by you and your partner as an assignment you might get at work. First, you have to determine what your goals are. Second, try writing a list that includes each of your major and minor wants and needs. Third, there should be discussion to

see what resources are available and what potential costs are involved. Fourth, talk about how each of you feels about each option. Then it's time to resolve things.

Here are some successful strategies for making good decisions in a timely and thoughtful way, says Dr. Kramer.

Talk and listen. Before you attempt to reach a decision, make sure that both you and your partner have expressed all of your thoughts about it. Remember, you can't make choices and express your feelings at the same time, so if one of you is upset or anxious, deal with the emotions first. Before you go on to step two, each of you should be able to comfortably say, "My partner understands what's important to me."

Set an agenda. Now it's time to agree on exactly what the decision is and what problems stand in the way of making it.

For instance, let's say that you ended up having a fight about which family you'll be spending the holidays with. During the argument, she may have said one or two things about your parents that you didn't want to hear. Likewise, you may have come out with a dig against her good-for-nothing brother. See how easy it is to get sidetracked from the actual decision? An agenda can keep you on the straight and narrow.

Brainstorm. If you're at an impasse with a particular decision, break through it with a brainstorming session. Start tossing out all possible ideas for resolving an issue—even the really absurd or illegal ones. While you know many of these solutions won't be valid, just voicing them may put you on a train of thought that will help you arrive at something workable. The only rule with a brainstorming session is that there are no bad ideas.

Indeed, it's far more likely that you'll come up with a lot of great ideas and even some compromises that would work out far better than either of you could have imagined. For example, on the holiday you might see one family for lunch and the other for dinner. Or you might have both families to your house, or take turns on different holidays. Suddenly, a situation that seemed to be at an impasse becomes rife with possibility.

Create a win/win situation.
Now you have lots of ideas that have the potential to work for both of you. First, rule out any plan that one of you is strictly opposed to. Then, see which of the ideas, or parts of ideas, are left that you both find appealing.

For instance, let's say that your favorite part of the holidays is having your mom's homemade pie. You may find out that your partner doesn't want to miss her father carving the holiday roast. He always makes a beautiful speech that brings tears to her eyes. Your solution is to have dinner with her folks and dessert with yours. See, you *can* have your pie and eat it, too.

Make sure that you're sure.
A solution will only work if the two of you have honestly, and without pressure, decided on it together. If one of you is saying yes halfheartedly, believe us, the issue will come up again. Keep in mind that it's the nature of compromise that you're only partially satisfied—which means that you're going to be partially dissatisfied. That's because you both had to give in a little for each others' sakes.

Know when to ask for help.
Some conflicts may simply be too big for you to resolve on your own, especially if you find yourselves at a perpetual impasse, or if your arguments turn into personal attacks or possibly even physical violence. "Don't wait until it is an emergency situation," suggests Shirley Zussman, Ed.D., a certified sex

---

Decision-Making Aids

What? After all the great advice in this chapter, you still can't make up your minds? Then it's time to use a decision-making tool. We've listed several below. They're not the most elegant or scientifically valid, we grant you, but they're all guaranteed to break a decision-making deadlock—so long as you agree to abide by the results.

Flip for it. Hey, if a coin toss is good enough for the Super Bowl, then it's good enough for the two of you. And you have a 50-50 chance of having the decision go your way.

Draw! Shuffle a deck of cards, then set it on a table. Let her draw from the deck (ladies first!), then you draw. High card wins.

Let the dog decide. We saw this in an old Disney movie. Stand at opposite ends of the room and put your dog (or any household pet with legs) in the middle. Then you both call to your pet; whomever he goes to wins. No fair putting ground chuck in your pocket.

Call on the spirits. Break out the Ouija board and ask it to make a decision. Phrase your question in a "yes" or "no" format—it takes too long for the spirits to spell words out. Be warned, though: We think this is how all the trouble started in *The Exorcist*.

If none of these work, you have one last option.

Ask the eight ball. In the known universe, the Magic 8-Ball toy is regarded as the last word on any decision. Don't believe us? Ask it yourself.

---

and marital therapist in private practice in New York City. Instead, if you find yourselves unable to reach a workable decision, be smart enough to seek professional counseling to work through the issue.

Giving and Accepting Praise and Criticism

It's Money in the Bank

In a perfect world, we would only praise one another. We'd tell each other how good we look, how smart we are, how generous, how resourceful, how perfect. We'd all feel great.

But in the real world and in real relationships, we all criticize and get criticized, too. That's why learning when to criticize or praise—and to accept both—is vital to the health of any relationship. Here we'll talk about how to keep your criticisms constructive, how to accept praise graciously, and how to make sure that, in the great balance sheet of your relationship, the sum of praise far outstrips the sum of criticism.

Praise the Woman

To extend the financial metaphor a little, think of praise as money in your relationship's bank account. The more praise you give, the wealthier your relationship is, says Clifford I. Notarius, Ph.D., who runs a couples therapy private practice and serves as professor of psychology and director of the Center for Family Psychology at the Catholic University of America in Washington, D.C.

The problem is that sometimes we intend to compli-ment our partners but somehow hurt their feelings instead. You can avoid such pitfalls by following this advice.

Banish "but" from your vocabulary. Saying, "Honey, dinner tasted great, but next time let's have chicken," won't win you points with your partner. When you feel the urge to put your lips together for that three-letter word, stop yourself, says Dr. Notarius. Odds are that anything you say after "but" isn't going to be good, but that's the part of the sentence she's most likely to remember.

Know the right answer. Women often search for praise indirectly, says Dr. Cathleen Gray of the Catholic University of America. Often as not, she'll phrase her search in the form of a trick question. When that happens, always respond with an answer that is true and will make her feel better. If she asks, "Do you like this dress?" say "I think it fits you beautifully" or "That's a good color for you." Of course, if it's really unattractive, she'd probably rather be told—as long as it's said diplomatically, such as "That dress doesn't do you justice" or "You look prettier in some of your other dresses."

Soothe her sensitive spots. Many women have specific insecurities where they need consistent reassurance and compliments. "Whatever her sensitive area is—her looks, her mothering—she's going to be looking for more praise," says Dr. Gray. Just choose your words carefully. When you hit on a sensitive area,

women are pretty good at confusing the best-intended praise for criticism. For instance, if she's sensitive about her weight, she might interpret "You look fine in those shorts" as "Wow, you look fat in those shorts." If she truly looks fine, then give her the reassurance she craves, urges clinical psychologist and marriage and family therapist Dr. Jonathan M. Kramer. Tell her, "I mean it.

You look good in those shorts." If she does look too heavy, don't lie and mislead her. Tell her she looks better in some of her other clothes. And make sure that you let her know that you find her desirable and lovable—the real point of it all for her.

Letting Praise Go to Your Head

For a healthy relationship, you need to hear compliments from your partner just as much as she needs to hear them from you. But according to Randall B. Davis, a marriage and family counselor in Corona, California, most men are so bad at accepting praise that we actually discourage our partners from complimenting us ever again.

To help you get more praise and accept that praise graciously, follow these guidelines.

Acknowledge your strengths. Too often, when our partners tell us something nice, we argue the point. For instance, she tells you that your haircut looks wonderful. You complain how the barber cut off too much. She marvels at how well you painted the house. You say that you could have done a better job at it. Maybe you are being too self-critical and need to learn to accentuate the positive about yourself.

Instead of arguing, just say "thank you," says Davis. Acknowledging your strengths doesn't mean that you have a big head. Besides, showing how flattered you feel encourages her to compliment you again, he says.

Refrain from criticizing her. Sometimes when she has withheld

How to Handle an Insult

To find out how to take an insult well, we went to a guy who grins and bares it for a living. His name is John Sweeney, the public editor, correction writer, and chief complaint-taker for the *News Journal*, the leading newspaper in Delaware. On a bad day, Sweeney weathers nearly 100 insults on behalf of his paper. Here's his strategy for taking criticism unflappably.

Bury your emotion. Responding to an angry caller with anger only makes the angry caller angrier, says Sweeney. "If you call and complain about something and I respond defensively, that notches you up. You end up listening to the tone of my voice rather than the content of what I'm saying. And I end up listening to the tone of your voice rather than the content of what you are saying," says Sweeney. "We end up arguing about something that has nothing to do with the true complaint." Instead, Sweeney drains all emotion from his voice.

Avoid side issues. Disgruntled readers have accused Sweeney of plenty of untruths. For instance, one irate reader once called Sweeney a draft dodger. Sweeney served four years in the military, but he bit his tongue. Resisting the urge to stick up for himself, he instead searched for the true issue by asking, "What do you mean by that?" Turns out the reader was annoyed at the paper's editorial stance against the military, not at Sweeney.

Politely hang up. Some conflicts can't get resolved. When someone calls cursing and screaming and Sweeney can't make heads or tails of the situation, he politely thanks the caller for his opinion and gets off the phone.

praise for a long time and finally compliments us, we begrudgingly shoot back: "It's about time you said something nice!" Guess what? "That's the quickest way for her to never compliment you again," says Davis. By complimenting you, she's giving you a gift; don't throw it back in her face.

Let the sun shine in. Men often have a tough time handling all the mushy feelings that come along with graciously accepting praise. "It's okay to have feelings," says Davis. "They don't make you a wuss." When she says something nice, don't brush off the compliment emotionally. Let yourself feel the pride and love and satisfaction. After all, you probably deserve it.

Dishing Out Criticism

Now back to that bank account. If praise serves as your deposit, then criticism counts as a withdrawal. But praise and criticism don't match up dollar for emotional dollar. Each critical remark withdraws more funds than each compliment deposits.

"If you have a healthy balance, then you can make a withdrawal and consider it an investment for the future," says Dr. Notarius. "However, if you are running in the red, criticism is very risky. It's much more difficult to request change when there isn't a sufficient balance." If your relationship account is low, you'll want to think twice before complaining about her bras hanging on the doorknob. But even if you decide that you have sufficient funds, it still pays to remove as much sting from your remarks as possible. The following suggestions will help.

Butter her up. Both men and women pay close attention to the beginnings and endings of sentences and paragraphs, says Dr. Kramer. So to effectively cushion a criticism, try sandwiching it between two compliments to soften the blow. A nice compliment before

and after a critical statement can make it far less hurtful than a bare-bones gripe. "Thanks for getting my stuff at the dry cleaner's. I'd sure appreciate it if you'd try harder to put your shoes away. Oh yeah, I meant to tell you how much I appreciate your cleaning out the closet."

Phrase your request as a compliment. Praise motivates people. So if you want your wife to stop leaving her shoes on the floor, say "Gee, I love it when you put your shoes away" instead of "I wish you wouldn't leave your shoes on the floor," says Dr. Gray.

Provide specifics. Before confronting her, take some time to figure out exactly what's bothering you, says Dr. Anita L. Vangelisti of the University of Texas. Saying "You always leave your stuff lying around everywhere" begs an argument. Everywhere? Really? She's going to disagree wholeheartedly, and she'll be right. Instead of resorting to hyperbole, say exactly what's bothering you, such as, "I wish you wouldn't leave dirty drinking glasses on the nightstand."

Focus on the behavior, not the woman. As a corollary to the above, if you're going to criticize, it's important to comment on her behavior, not insult her as a person. Saying "I don't like it when you make fun of me in front of my boss" is better—and a lot more accurate—than blurting "You're such a loudmouth," says Dr. Vangelisti.

Use the alphabet formula. Criticism packs the least sting if you phrase it in what's called an XYZ statement. "When you do X in situation Y, it makes me feel Z," says Dr. Notarius.

The XYZ statement works for three reasons. First, it forces you to focus specifically on one situation that the person being criticized can do something about. Second, it shifts the blame from her as a human being to a specific behavior. And finally, it lets her know how you feel, which is something she can't argue about. So instead of saying "You're always squandering our money on trivial purchases," say "When you spend money to buy expensive hand lotion, I worry that we won't have enough money to pay the mortgage."

Licking Your Wounds

Men usually respond to criticism in one of three very unproductive ways, says Dr. Vangelisti. We take flight—we slam the door and lock ourselves in the garage. We fight—we criticize her right back. Or we shut down emotionally and sling sarcastic remarks that we'll almost certainly regret later, such as, "It must be your time of the month again!"

None of those responses will get you anywhere except into the doghouse. Instead, try the following suggestions for dealing with criticism.

Start a countdown. When your partner criticizes you, your instincts will scream for you to make an immediate response. Ignore that impulse. Instead, take a deep breath, count to 10, and genuinely ponder what she just told you, says Dr. Vangelisti.

You can think and feel whatever you want, adds Dr. Kramer. Just keep it to yourself.

Tell her how you feel. If you still feel defensive after counting to 10, tell her so. You'll do better to tell her you feel threatened or insulted than to sling back insults, says Dr. Vangelisti.

Kill her with curiosity. Once you've calmed down, ask for more information. You want to find out exactly what's bothering your partner. For instance, if she complains "You don't act like you love me," say "I'm not sure what you mean by that. Can you explain?" This

---

Critical Issues

Criticizing is dangerous business no matter how you slice it, but there are some subjects where you want to tread extra carefully—unless you want your criticisms to blow up in your face. What are the sorest subjects? We asked Dr. Bonnie Jacobson of the New York Institute for Psychological Change to rank them starting with the most sensitive. Here's how they stack up. Take care when either of you starts criticizing the other about:

1. Handling money
2. Sexual performance
3. Family (yours or hers)
4. Kids (how they're disciplined or raised)
5. Weight

Does that mean you need to be really careful telling her she spends too much money, but you can tell her with impunity that she needs to drop a few pounds? You know better than that. Proceed carefully with each topic, but tread ever more gingerly as you get closer to the top of the list.

---

will help her relax and get to the point, says Dr. Vangelisti.

Cultivate optimism. You'll both feel less threatened if you both expect to work things out, says Dr. Notarius. "It's similar to sports," says Dr. Notarius. "If you expect that you can do it, you're more likely to be able to do it." You can nurture your sense of optimism by talking to one another about your fears of getting criticized. Find ways to reduce those fears as a couple. For instance, once a day you might tell each other, or at least tell yourself, "We can always work any problem out."

Making Time to Talk

Words, Then Deeds

Consider it the biggest catch-22 in the relationship between men and women: Guys feel close to their partners when they have sex. We gain intimacy by doing.

For women, though, talk has to come first. It's words, not deeds, that matter most to them. And until they get that verbal intimacy, they won't feel in the mood for physical intimacy, says Dr. Cathleen Gray of the Catholic University of America.

This means, of course, that if we ever want to make love, we have to first make time for talk. But you should never think of that as a chore, says Dr. Gray. It may feel like one, but you have to remember why you're doing it. Talking is good medicine for couples. Regularly setting aside time for the two of you to share thoughts, feelings, and gripes will bring you closer—and help you fight less, says Dr. Gray. Further, our partners often are the only people we feel comfortable with to talk about our innermost fears, dreams, and thoughts, says Dr. Gray. That makes her an invaluable resource for you, man.

"We are brought up to be tough and strong," says marriage and family counselor Randall B. Davis. "But men need to learn that strength is not handling everything all by yourself. Strength is knowing when to ask for help. Reach out." Strength also lies in simply sharing and being close with another person.

As we indicated earlier, if we trust, admire, respect, and generally think our partner is the one for us, making time to talk shouldn't be a problem but a priority. "And if your relationship is a priority, then you'll invest in it," says Linda Acitelli, Ph.D., associate professor of psychology at the University of Houston.

Close Encounters with Womankind

A lot of us, though, feel uncomfortable or downright scared about increasing the intimacy level. And we're not really sure what "investing" further in a relationship means—or how to do it. If that's the case with you, you might want to try some of the following ways to make the most of your time together.

Pencil her in. Set aside a time to talk each day or once a week—even if you have no gripes.

"Scheduling time is simple and easy, yet almost no couple does it," says Merrill Douglass, president of the Time Management Center in Marietta, Georgia. "The couples who schedule time always seem to have time to talk. The couples who don't never have time to talk."

During your set time, give each other 10 uninterrupted minutes to talk—even if at first you feel you have nothing to say. Usually after a few minutes of quiet, issues will pop up, says Lynn Lott, a marriage and family therapist and co-author of *Together and Liking It.*

Sweat the small stuff. Usually, men avoid talking until something goes awry. Then they try to play Mr. Fix-It with the relationship. But we could save a lot of emotional wear and tear if we performed a little preventive maintenance and dealt with molehill nuisances before they grew into mountainous issues, says Dr. Acitelli. If little things come up and she wants to talk about them, deal with them then and there, as much as you can. You'll likely avoid a major breakdown later on.

Watch the clock. All-nighters are for college students, not committed partners. Don't cram every single problem into one talk. Instead, treat any talk time with your spouse like you would a meeting at work. Make sure that you have a start time, an end time, and an agenda, says Davis.

Or simply be aware when you're running out of steam, says clinical psychologist and marriage and family therapist Dr. Jonathan M. Kramer. He suggests saying something like, "I'd like to keep talking, but I'm tired and having trouble really concentrating. Could we continue it tomorrow?"

Edit her request. If your partner tends to go on and on, try to get her to focus on the problem at hand. Ask her to tell you what's on her mind in 10 words or less, suggests Lott. Just make it clear to her that you're trying to understand the problem, not cut her off.

Tell all. With all this talking going on, you might think that you'd run out of things to say to one another. If that happens, try letting all of your thoughts spill out of your mouth, says Davis. We all have brilliant schemes and wacky notions that we keep to ourselves. Stop editing yourself. Tell her all the crazy thoughts that come to mind. You may surprise yourself—and her. And you might find that you enjoy talking more than you thought you would.

Don't talk it to death. Finally, we'd like to assure you that there's a time to talk, but also a time not to talk. Recent studies have shown that endlessly talking about

---

Fear No Talk

If a guy is scared of killing cockroaches, we call him a wimp. If a guy doesn't play touch football because he's afraid that he'll skin a knee or elbow, we call him a hopeless wimp. But if a guy's neck hair stands on end every time his partner says "We need to talk," we call him normal.

"When a woman tells a man she wants to talk about their relationship, he thinks, 'What have I done wrong now?'" says Dr. Linda Acitelli of the University of Houston. But talking need not drain the color from your knuckles. Here are a couple of ways to make talk time easier on you.

Ask her to say "we." Explain to your partner that if she would phrase her concerns with "we" instead of "you" or "I," you would feel less defensive. For instance, "We have a problem" sounds better than "I have a problem." Another example: "We need to work on this" versus "You need to work on this." The pronoun shifts the emphasis away from you as the person at fault and instead focuses the issue on how you interact as a couple. Better yet...

Beat her to the punch. Listen and watch for small signals that something's wrong. Then initiate the talk instead of waiting for her to do so, says Dr. Clifford I. Notarius of the Catholic University of America. If you ignore it, the problem will not go away; it will get worse. Now that's something to dread.

---

relationships can actually contribute to women having higher levels of depression. If she feels the need to "have a talk" every single day, don't be afraid to preempt the talk once in a while and do something your way. Get her to take a walk or play a game with you. That might just get her mind off her problems enough so that they don't bother her—or you—anymore.

Counseling

When to Seek Help

Marriage therapists have found that couples wait an average of six years before going to see a professional about a problem they're having within their relationship. That can mean six years of no sex. Six years of constant bickering. Six years of hell.

"Men are especially less likely to seek help if they feel that there's a problem in their relationship," says Appalachian State University's Dr. Dan Jones. "They don't want to talk about negative feelings, and they believe going to a therapist is a sign of weakness."

In reality, seeing a therapist is similar to hiring a consultant for your business, says Dr. Jones. "If the vice president of a bank wants to boost morale, he doesn't think twice about hiring a team-building expert. If he needed someone to set up a computer network, he'd hire an expert. Therapy and counselors do the same thing for your relationship that consultants do for your business," Dr. Jones says.

But before a couple seeks professional help, there are two things they need to know: when it's time to use a marriage therapist, and how to find the right person for their situation and personalities.

According to Diane Sollee, director of the Coalition for Marriage, Family, and Couples Education in Washington, D.C., it's time to see a professional when you:

- Have been feeling discouraged or disappointed about your relationship for a while
- Think that you must have married the wrong person
- Lust after other women

- Fantasize about ending the relationship and wonder how much a divorce will cost or where the kids will go

Beyond that, of course, most of us intuitively know when something is wrong with our relationships. We may feel uncomfortable around our partner or avoid talking with her. So recognizing the existence of a problem is the first step in solving the problem, while finding someone you can trust and learn from is the second step.

Who Should Counsel You?

Okay, you've decided you need professional guidance to help steer your relationship off the shoals and back into those calm waters you once enjoyed. Here are some things you should consider when choosing a therapist.

Don't go it alone. It might seem like a good idea to fly solo first, to seek counseling for yourself before involving your partner. It's not.

"Don't go into individual therapy if you want to save your marriage," Dr. Jones says. "Individual therapy can be harmful to your marriage." Indeed, going it alone will most likely lead to divorce. That's because an individual therapist is interested only in helping you—that's his or her job—not helping your relationship.

Individual counseling is more appropriate for a person who has an individual problem that interferes with his ability to have a relationship, is trying to heal after a divorce, or is struggling to identify exactly what he wants from life. Couples who have relationship issues, on the other hand, need to work on their marriage together.

Counsel as a couple. The point of therapy should be to resolve your problems, not dwell on them, Sollee says.

That's why instead of individual therapy, you're better off seeing either a marriage counselor or a therapist who specializes in couples and family issues. Couples therapists also deal with sexual issues as well as broader relationship issues, says Dr. Scott Stanley of the University of Denver.

A marriage counselor will focus on ways to help the two of you learn how to get through the typical difficulties couples face—without feeling guilt or shame, says Dr. Jones.

Seek new skills. One increasingly popular option for couples is enrolling in a skills-based program. These are often a series of seminars—held over a weekend or several days—that teach couples how to interact better with each other, identify problems, and deal with them in a healthy way.

Skills-based programs may be especially appealing to men because they focus on the "how-tos," not on the "whys" of problems, says Sollee.

Many therapists lead marriage education classes, but these are counselors who believe in action-oriented work rather than using long-term psychology to explore human interaction. If the how-to approach is more your style, then it pays to ask a counselor if their program is "solution-based," or if they've studied such programs as PAIRS, PREP, or PREPARE/ENRICH—all successful skills-based counseling programs, according to David M. Schnarch, Ph.D., co-founder of the Marriage and Family Health Center in Evergreen, Colorado, and author of *Passionate Marriage.*

Seek divine guidance. Many clergypeople have taken marriage education classes to better assist people who come to them. "To get the best help available, you have to ask your pastor or rabbi if they've studied marriage education," Sollee says.

Although some churches and temples have stayed current with mar-

Passionate Sex

Most marriage education courses focus on communication skills, with some discussion of sex, commitment, and other aspects of relationships. But Dr. David M. Schnarch, of the Marriage and Family Health Center and author of *Passionate Marriage*, takes a different approach.

"I think all of this stuff about effective communication skills and learning how to validate each other can really hurt an adult sexual relationship," Dr. Schnarch says. "In fact, I think individuals should look to themselves, rather than their partner, for validation."

Encouraging partners to play the role of best friend/cheerleader takes away much of the possibility for having good sex, says Dr. Schnarch. "Your partner doesn't have to agree with you or even make you feel better about yourself to create feelings of warmth and intimacy," he says. "Passion doesn't come from validation; it comes from being able to stay centered in the face of your partner's emotions." Dr. Schnarch calls this process differentiation.

A Passionate Marriage retreat, which can last either four or nine days, uses sex as the vehicle through which to teach the skills of being a grown-up. "Sex is a strong motivator," Dr. Schnarch says. "You can learn a tremendous amount about sexual intimacy with your clothes on and your feet on the floor."

When the two of you have an adult relationship, based on the integrity you each feel within yourselves, your sex life will explode. "Once you're strong enough to be completely open and honest with your partner, you'll be able to have eyes-open orgasms," Dr. Schnarch says.

Resources for Marriage Education

The organizations listed below offer marriage education classes, which teach relationship skills rather than focusing on traditional therapy methods. Most of the organizations will work with either one couple at a time or with groups, depending on your preference.

Retrouvaille
"A Lifeline for Troubled Marriages"
Weekend and follow-up meetings for marriages at the breaking point. Taught around the United States.
P. O. Box 25, Kelton, PA 19346
http://www.retrouvaille.org

PAIRS
"Practical Application of Intimate Relationship Skills"
One-day weekend and semester-long programs offered by trained leaders throughout North America.
1152 North University Drive, Pembroke, FL 33024
http://www.pairs.com

Passionate Marriage Retreats
Couples enrichment workshops and other services. Contact the Marriage and Family Health Center, Suite 310, 2922 Evergreen Parkway, Evergreen, CO 80439
http://www.passionatemarriage.com

PREP
"Prevention and Relationship Enhancement Program"
Weekend version, or one weekend day and two weekend evenings, as well as audiotapes and videos. Led by counselors, clergy, and laypeople around the United States.
P. O. Box 102530, Denver, CO 80250-2530
http://members.aol.com/prepinc

Couple Communication
Four two-hour or six 90-minute sessions. Taught around the United States.
Interpersonal Communications Programs, 7201 South Broadway, Suite 210, Littleton, CO 80122
Email: icp@comskills.com

Coalition for Marriage, Family, and Couples Education
Can recommend marriage educators in your area. Their Web site is particularly helpful and informative.
5310 Belt Road NW, Washington, DC 20015-1961
http://www.smartmarriages.com

riage counseling over the last few years, others have continued to take a traditional view of marriage. This doesn't always help couples cope with contemporary issues or problems, Sollee says.

Look on the sunny side. Having problems doesn't mean that your relationship has failed. It goes with the matrimonial territory, Sollee says. Working with a professional to acquire the skills to help you work through problems not only will save your marriage but also will save you a world of hurt. Remember that the vow is "for better or worse." If the relationship has gotten worse, get help to make it better.

"Sometimes I want to shout from the rooftops about all that we've learned," says Sollee. "We understand so much about relationships and what helps them bloom. It's a shame that more people don't look into the programs that are offered."

Most marriage education groups emphasize information on conflict resolution and communication skills. There are often accompanying sessions on keeping the romance alive, being friends, and raising children.

Part Three

Keeping Sex Sizzling

Charting Your Own Lovemap

The Course of True Love...

Ever stop and wonder just how you got to this point in your sexual journey? You started off embarrassingly (sometimes rigidly) excited by the sight of a training bra strap two rows over. Then, after groping your way through the awkward physical initiations, you probably wandered through fields of wild oats until you got sidetracked by that special someone. But even with her by your side, you still get lost. If you knew sex was going to be such a long, strange trip, you would have brought a map.

Ah, but you did.

Imprinted somewhere deep in your brain circuitry is your very own, custom-made, personally monogrammed lovemap, and it has been guiding you since the days when you thought girls were yucky. Years in the making, your lovemap predisposes you to certain sexual choices and pretty much decides what turns you on, who you fantasize about, and who you fall in love with.

Making a List

When it comes to deciphering the love you feel in this life, and the women you feel that love for, about the only thing you have to help you is your lovemap, says Helen Fisher, Ph.D., research associate in the department of anthropology at Rutgers University in New Brunswick, New Jersey, and author of *Anatomy of Love.* "It's a very sophisticated  list of things you're looking for in a sexual partner, and it determines what arouses you sexually."

That word *sophisticated* is key here. While some features on your lovemap might be obvious to you—your preference for, say, perky blondes with tight behinds and hair-trigger laughs—many others are almost invisibly subtle. Your brain is capable of keeping track of sexual details you only wish you knew about.

Its names are as numerous as the theoretical slants that the psychology camps give it. You can call it your "core erotic theme," your "dream lover," your "search image," your "sexual script," or your "lovemap." Call it what you will, you're talking about a powerful internal steering system that pretty much calls the sexual shots.

One would assume that such an imposing piece of mental programming would be designed by the finest talents that your mind can muster. In fact, your lovemap is the work of a child.

"By the time you get to your teen years, you already have a strongly developed dream-lover image," says Polly Young-Eisendrath, Ph.D., clinical associate professor in psychiatry at the University of Vermont College of Medicine in Burlington and author of *You're Not What I Expected.*

Not only were you an underage erotic cartographer but you were also seriously unqualified to be forming tastes about women. After all, how many girls did you hang out with when you were eight?

In fact, little boys tend to keep their distance from girls more than the other way around, with predictable lovemap results that boldly influence your sexual journey. "Boys form a stronger fantasy life about girls because they're so isolated from the real thing," says Dr. Young-Eisendrath. In other words, the all-powerful lovemap that even today controls your sexual tastes and fantasies was forged by a crayon-pusher relying on nothing more than hearsay. But don't underestimate the richness of that hearsay. You build your dream lover not just from boy-talk, overheard man-talk, and your blooming imagination but also from emotional experiences with your family and the influence of the culture all around you.

Getting Oriented

What are the chances that this finely tuned and intricately woven lovemap of yours will find its match out there in the real world? Zero, of course. There will always be some discrepancies between your dream lover and your true lover. And you can count on those discrepancies defining many of the challenges you'll encounter as you advance deeper into the tunnel of love.

At this point, you have every right to ask a rude question: Just what good is this lovemap that I unwittingly created as an immature amateur, based mostly on messages from a sexually schizophrenic culture, when it won't even help me find Miss Perfect anyway?

But that's like asking what good it is to be left-handed. It's not good or bad, but it's sure useful to know about it. Same for lovemaps. You're not going to make any preferences go away—like all maps, your lovemap is impossible to fold back up once you start using it. But you can become the master of your own fate. Here's how.

Survey your attractions. So far, there's no cottage industry in

The Maid, the Mistress, and the Mother

There are as many individual lovemaps as there are individuals. But curiously, according to Dr. Polly Young-Eisendrath of the University of Vermont College of Medicine, many American men's dream lovers are identifiable types.

Here are the most common lovemap archetypes. Where does yours fit in?

Maiden Lover I—The Pure Young Thing. She's the budding flower who only needs your fertilizer to bloom. She's a waif who needs to be mentored by a man. She's sweet but uninformed, eager but in need of guidance. This maiden fantasy hovers over college classrooms, where the wise professor looks out over a host of ripe young things ready to be, ahem, tutored.

Maiden Lover II—The Amazon Superwoman. At the other end of the fantasy maiden spectrum, she's strong and independent but still in need of a man. And none of this mentoring stuff—what she needs him for is sex. Other than that, she's in control. You've seen her in fantasy/adventure movies. James Bond knows her well.

The Mistress. She's the nympho, the slut, and she can't get enough. "She's the kind of woman who's just wild for a man's body," Dr. Young-Eisendrath says. "She'll jump on him and rip his clothes off. She just wants sex." Most porn-movie actresses have played this fantasy character through miles of cheap celluloid.

The Great Mother. Think Harriet Nelson and June Cleaver, but sexier. Her reason for being is to take care of other people, and since it's your fantasy, she takes care of *you.* Not surprising, the prototype for this fantasy comes from a particularly supportive mother.

lovemap reading. So it's up to you to bring some of your dream lover's major traits to the surface where you can deal with them. It's not a mysterious process, says Louanne Cole Weston, Ph.D., a board-certified sex therapist, a marriage, family, and child counselor, and a sex columnist for the *San Francisco Examiner*. "Just look at the people you've been sexually involved with over the years, or sexually attracted to," she says. "Notice what seems to be common to them all." Chances are you'll find some traits they all have (tall? sad-eyed? nurturing? athletic? independent?). Even if you don't, the trip through your mental sexual scrapbook shouldn't be dull.

Write it out. Try to put a conscious spin on what was essentially an unconscious creation—your lovemap. "You can actually sit down and write on a sheet of paper what you're looking for in a mate," Dr. Fisher says. "Then you can write down the things in a mate that you could do without as well as those things you can't do without."

Negotiate with yourself. You may uncover some strict dream-lover requirements that limit your options, says Dr. Weston. To use a rather clichéd example, let's say you're only attracted to women with very large breasts. "That's no real problem," says Dr. Weston. "But you might be missing a good bet with somebody who's amply built, but not enormous." See if you can compromise with your lovemap, Dr. Weston suggests. Ask yourself if you can really live without this quality. But also be prepared for the possibility that an unyielding lovemap will have its way. Either way, at least you'll know.

Learn from your mistakes. A lovemap is a particularly good tool for not doing the same bad thing again, especially if your lovemap has been a little messed up, says Dr. Fisher. Say, for example, you've tended

Beware the Evil Stepmom

An evil presence may be lurking in your lovemap, men. Imprinted somewhere in your psyche, mixed in with the dream girls, is your worst nightmare.

She's the bitch, the witch, the nag, the hag. This is the evil-stepmother image that's as old as fairy tales. Called The Terrible Mother by Dr. Polly Young-Eisendrath of the University of Vermont College of Medicine, she, too, is one of the classic archetypes—maybe anti-archetype would be a better term—of the male lovemap.

But wait a sec. If your lovemap is the blueprint of your dream girl, who let this woman in? You did. Obviously, she's not somebody you intentionally fall in love with. "But I include her as a dream lover because she has a very strong presence in men's psyches," says Dr. Young-Eisendrath. "And she'll often emerge when you become disillusioned with your partner."

toward the needy type, perhaps going back to some family crisis in your childhood. And suppose that this needy type always ends up needing your alimony checks more than she needs you. After two bad relationships, you should finally realize that this part of your lovemap is not doing you any good, Fisher says.

Know your history. Be aware of your original family's qualities, both good and bad. The key to whom we pick as partners often comes from the relationships we had and saw when we were growing up, notes Jonathan M. Kramer, Ph.D., a clinical psychologist and marriage and family therapist in private practice in La Jolla, California, and author of *Losing the Weight of the World* and *Why Men Don't Get Enough Sex and Women Don't Get Enough Love*. Patterns tend to repeat themselves unless we make conscious, concerted efforts to do something new.

Young Love

Romance Knows No Age

The thing about being young and in love is you don't have to be young and you're often not exactly in love.

Youth has no monopoly on that heady, on-top-of-the-world, can't-get-enough-of-each-other euphoria that goes with a new relationship. "We're seeing more and more new love affairs in senior citizens homes," says Dr. Helen Fisher of Rutgers University. "It's the same deal."

But is it love? That's what we always call it. So does every romantic song ever written. But people who study these things will often put quotation marks around the word *love* when it's applied to the early stages of a relationship. There's a difference, they say, between the "passionate love" of the honeymoon and the "true love" that takes over down the road. This fleeting "infatuation" is not the same as the later, more profound "attachment." Early "romance" should not be confused with lasting "love."

But if it ain't love, it ain't bad. And the sex is usually great. "The initial period of bonding between two people is very intense, very erotic, and very sexy," says Timothy Perper, Ph.D., a Philadelphia biologist and independent sex researcher who wrote *Sex Signals: The Biology of Love* and numerous articles and presentations on human courtships.

There are lots of reasons for this feel-good phase. One is chemistry (which we explain more fully in Attraction on page 4). "When you're in love, you're under the influence of chemicals," says Dr. Fisher, with

refreshing bluntness. "That's what gives you those feelings of infatuation."

Another reason that good things happen at this stage is simply that many of the bad things don't. For example, love's little burdens, emotional and otherwise, can make intimacy an obstacle course in a long-term relationship. But they simply haven't had time to accumulate with a couple who's just starting out.

More important, you're not withholding your feelings, because the feelings so far are mostly good. "When you're first in a relationship, the 'arteries' between the two of you are wide open, so the flow of emotions is unhampered," says Daniel Beaver, director of the Relationship Counseling Center in Walnut Creek, California, and author of *Beyond the Marriage Fantasy* and *More Than Just Sex.* "Those emotions are generally what people judge as positive, such as excitement, anticipation, attraction, lust, romance."

Making an Early Investment

You know what's coming, so let's get right to it: It ends. That dizzy, dancing feeling doesn't last forever. The doctors give it three years, max. Often less. Cause of death? Natural causes.

"High-frequency, high-passion, high-newness sex is going to die of its own accord," says Barry McCarthy, Ph.D., a Washington, D.C., psychologist for the Washington Psychological Center and author of *Male Sexual Awareness.* "It's like when you put two chemicals together. You may get something that burns brightly, but it's unstable. It dies out fairly soon."

If this strikes you as a tragic fate—and the end of good sex with your chosen life partner—you're not alone. The seeds of sexual boredom are sown by a refusal to accept that infatuation is temporary. If your only definition of good sex is the yearning kind you have those first few years together, you can end up on the bad side of disappointment.

But if so, you're taking it all wrong. Your sex life can't stay on automatic pilot forever, and you wouldn't want it to. In fact, nothing is really dying here. Infatuation-based sex is simply evolving into a much more satisfying attachment-based sex.

That is, if you let it. "There's nothing wrong with passionate romantic-love sex as long as you understand that it's a phase," Dr. McCarthy says. "But you have to make the transition to more intimate sex. And you have to see that you're not losing anything, but rather gaining something valuable."

Admittedly, that's easier for sex experts to say than for blissed-out honeymooners to absorb. When you're young and in love, it's hard enough to believe that you won't always be young. Now you have to accept that you won't always be "in love"?

But it's precisely because you're so enchanted with your new relationship that it makes sense to invest in its future. Preparing for the transition into a new phase is just one of many investment tools. And the time to use them is now, when the market is overheated.

"Think of the beginning, head-in-the-clouds stage of your relationship as a jump start," says sex therapist Theresa Crenshaw, M.D., author of *The Alchemy of Love and Lust*. "Take advantage of it. Because if you just coast, you'll only go downhill." Here's how you can take advantage of your young love, no matter how old you are, and use it to help your future relationship.

Tales of Delusion

What is this crazy little thing called love? At the early "romance" stage, it may be just a big mistake.

Romance is basically you projecting the image of your perfect dream lover onto a member of the opposite sex, says Dr. Polly Young-Eisendrath of the University of Vermont College of Medicine. "You actually fall into your own fantasy."

In other words, though the object of your new affection may be a fine lady who'll make a great lifelong partner, she's not what you're convinced she is. You're seeing in her the image of your ideal woman and refusing to see much of who she really is. Love, as they say, is blind.

"Your capacity for self-delusion when infatuated is staggering," says Dr. Helen Fisher of Rutgers University. "You can ignore the fact that she's fat, ignore the fact that she's 10 years older than you, ignore the fact that she's married to somebody else. We all act irresponsibly when we're in love."

For example, it's common these days, says Dr. Young-Eisendrath, for a man to believe that he has fallen in love with a strong, independent woman because he has projected that image of unassailable strength and independence onto her. When she shows signs of weakness and need (that is, of being human), he feels betrayed.

"Eventually, reality surfaces, and you realize that this person is not what you expected," according to Dr. Young-

Take immediate control. Sex is not a gift, whatever the dime-store theologians say. It's your creation. "Start with the assumption that your sex life isn't going to keep itself going," says Robert Birch, Ph.D., a psychologist in Columbus, Ohio, who specializes in marriage

Eisendrath. "Every couple goes through this disillusionment."

So what do you do after your ideal image has been shattered? You project another one, but not nearly as nice. When you're disillusioned, you have a tendency to shift from projecting a positive image to a negative one, says Dr. Young-Eisendrath. So what you once saw as a sexual woman, you now might see as a deceptive seductress.

None of this sounds as pleasant as being young and in love. But think of it as a river of rough water between the initial euphoria and the promised land. Navigate the crossing, and it's going to be a lot easier to keep that sex smoldering for the next 50 to 60 years.

"The disillusionment phase is your first opportunity to form a real loving relationship," Dr. Young-Eisendrath says. "But many people give up at this time, men especially." That's why knowing about your image of the ideal woman, your lovemap, is so helpful. The best way to work through this disillusionment is to turn the projector around and see that your lovemap's traits are in you, not her. Think about what you imagined and wanted her to be. Now focus on all her traits that you find endearing, enjoyable, or lovable. By appreciating the other person's good qualities, you can allow yourselves to see each other as two different and acceptable people, with weaknesses as well as strengths, says Dr. Young-Eisendrath. "That's true intimacy and real love."

and sex therapy and is author of *Male Sexual Endurance*. "Make a commitment from the very beginning to nurture your sex life. Don't get lazy, don't take it for granted, and don't assume it's going to run on automatic forever."

Aim to please. When the sex is relatively new, and ergo hot and heavy, thinking about what you can do to please your partner may seem superfluous. It isn't, says Dr. Birch. "In the early passion stage, she may not notice that she's not well-satisfied because of her overwhelming love and lust," he says. "But at some point, she may realize that you're having all the fun and she's being left out." Don't let it come to that, Dr. Birch advises. "As soon as a relationship begins to become sexual, you need to keep asking her how you can please her, what works best for her," he says. "That ought to be done right from the beginning."

Open the dialogue. Start talking to each other about sex before problems force you to. "This will give you a language you can use later on," says Dr. Perper, "and a sense of security that comes from knowing that you can talk about sex openly with each other." Sexual communication while the sex is relatively new is more likely to be free of the guilt-assuming, blame-shifting misinterpretations that plague so many couples. "You have to be able to talk about sex without recrimination," Dr. Perper says. "And the best time to start is when you're in the passion period. Then there will be a carryover effect."

Feed your relationship. You don't feel like getting dressed up. She doesn't feel like going out. A perfect pair of reasons to stay home, right? Not always. If there's something about going out that will help your relationship—for example, you both know you've fallen into a stay-at-home rut—then you should go. Do it for the relationship. "You have to see the relationship as the third party that needs to be fed," Dr. Fisher says. "Make the relationship healthier, and you get less bored with it."

Evolving Sexual Needs

How to Last a Lifetime

Good loving is a moving target. Your sexual needs change over time. So do hers. So does the relationship.

This is good news, actually. So why don't we take it that way? Seems we'll do just about anything to bring new excitement into our sex life. But when nature does it for us, we hate it.

Still, change happens, and the best strategy is to get smart about it. Smart, as in not denying it. Smart, as in taking advantage of the benefits that sex at 45-plus has to offer instead of comparing it to sex at 25. And smart, as in knowing about the changes so they intrigue you instead of scare you.

Coming Together

The twenties is the traditional time to mate up for life. It's also the worst time, biologically speaking. "This is when men and women are more different sexually than in any other decade in their lives," says sex therapist Dr. Theresa Crenshaw. "It's the most difficult time to understand each other and get along."

That's mainly because your high testosterone levels, unbalanced by any real kind of maturity, are steering your sexual style. Essentially, you're a genitally driven, fast-paced, hard-thrusting, orgasm-obsessed tomcat who'd be on the prowl if he were single, as you once were. Your mind may be pure,

but your glands are working against it. "Testosterone has a real tough time settling down with one sexual partner," Dr. Crenshaw says.

At the same time, women are at the height of their "estrogen receptiveness," meaning they're eager to please you. But they're really much more fulfilled by being held and touched while penetrated than they are by your jackhammer act.

Your adult sexual development offers a built-in path to sexual success if you both stick it out. But there's no rule against taking shortcuts. Adopt a fortysomething sexual approach when you're still twentysomething, and you're way ahead of the game, says Dr. Barry McCarthy of the Washington Psychological Center.

"Even a 20-year-old can learn to enjoy the give-and-take of sex with a partner," Dr. McCarthy says. "Make requests for your own arousal and learn to get turned on by her arousal. If you do, you're going to inoculate yourself against sexual problems as you age."

You come around a bit in your thirties, as the testosterone backs off enough to let you see the merit in meeting her needs. You're just not too good at it yet.

The major sexual change in the thirties is hers. That once docile and receptive young thing wants her orgasm, and she wants it now. "The problem is that she's not necessarily very graceful about her new assertiveness," Dr. Crenshaw says. "She can get pretty prickly."

Meeting in Midlife

All things considered, then, men and women should embrace their 40th birthdays instead of fearing them. It's in your forties that you both become better, and more compatible, lovers. "Finally, biology isn't driving you apart," Dr. Crenshaw says. "In fact, you're becoming more and more alike."

Your testosterone levels have dropped—not much, but enough to change the nature of your sexuality to the good. You're less aggressive, less demanding, and less orgasm-driven.

Your mate, meanwhile, has come more than halfway to meet you. She's still eager for orgasm, but she has learned how to help herself instead of jumping all over your back about it. Still, you're more than able to do your part because (partly through some overall slowing, but mostly because you're more experienced) you now generally last longer before ejaculating.

Indeed, the biggest sexual challenges of your forties aren't physical but social. "In your forties, you're both burdened with a lot of responsibilities, like young children, old parents, mortgages, career crises—all that stuff," says Gina Ogden, Ph.D., a sex therapist and author of *Women Who Love Sex.* "How do you even have time to spend making love, let alone the energy or inclination?" To solve these and other tricky situations, follow these tips.

Know your hormones. Hormones, especially your testosterone and her estrogen, are powerful forces, but so are your good judgment and common sense. "Information is power," Dr. Crenshaw says. "Your hormones are on duty 24 hours a day. If you don't know what's going on, they will govern your life like tyrants."

"My hormones made me do it" won't cut it today. "You can influence your hormones by the choices you make and the behavior you choose to follow," Dr. Crenshaw says. "That's the difference between us and the lower animals."

Face the changes together. Privately brooding about your "slowing down" or secretly resenting her growing assertiveness is no way to deal with changing sexual needs in a relationship. You're in this together. "Negotiate these changes together, and your relationship

---

Man in Demand

Want your wife to appreciate you more in your golden years? Point out that if you were single as an older man, women would be eyeing you like chocoholics ogling a hot fudge sundae. When you were young, you may have had the sex appeal of Alfred E. Neuman. Now you have the allure of Paul Newman. Here's why.

- At age 65, there are 25 women for every 17 men.
- By age 75, there are only 14 men for every 25 women.
- At age 85, there are 2½ women for every man.
- There are nearly five times as many widows as widowers among people age 65 and up.

What this means, of course, is that if you live long enough, you start looking mighty good to women. The laws of supply and demand are on your side, and it's a feller's market.

---

will end up stronger and better," Dr. Crenshaw says. "If you don't work them through, they'll zap you upside the head or on some more tender spot."

You have an ally in all this, assuming that you're still in love. "During any of these stages, love bridges the broadest gaps," Dr. Crenshaw says.

The Golden Years

By your fifties, you can expect to start noticing new and significant changes in your sexual functioning. Simply put, your blood is flowing more slowly, and your nerve supply isn't as rich. That means slower-forming erections, less-firm erections, less-frequent ejaculations, less semen ejaculated, and longer refractory periods (intervals between ejaculations). "When you're 20, your refractory period may be 15 minutes," says Dudley Seth Danoff, M.D., senior attending urologist at Cedars-Sinai Medical Center in Los Angeles and author of *Superpotency*. "When you're 65, it might be 15 days."

But your sexual needs do change. You (and she) need more patience to wait for your slower-developing erection. You need more direct stimulation of your genitals to achieve that erection. And you need more time to reach ejaculation. Think about it: Don't such "needs" present more opportunities for pleasure than anything else?

Her change at this time, of course, is a big one. Menopause results in two immediate considerations for your sex life: possibly diminishing sexual desire on her part, and vaginal dryness. Hormone-replacement treatment can solve both those problems, but if she shuns that option, try water-based lubricants for the latter and patience for the former. Many women, in fact, find their sex drive zooms after the possibility of pregnancy disappears.

Face these challenges, and your fifties can be the best years of your sex life, according to Dr. Crenshaw. "For the first time in their lives, men and women are perfectly matched sexually and emotionally," she writes in her book *The Alchemy of Love and Lust*. "The fifties...hold great opportunities for relationships, whether two people have been together for decades or have just recently met." Here's how to take advantage of those opportunities.

Boost her self-esteem. It doesn't matter how well-adjusted and well-preserved she is, your partner is probably not reacting with joy to the loosenings and wrinklings and grayings that accompany the sixth decade and

Age Myths

Not so long ago, people under 60 assumed that people over 60 stopped having sex altogether. We've gotten smarter than that—even if Hollywood hasn't—but other myths of maturity prevail. To wit:

Myth: At a certain age, a man can no longer get an erection.

Fact: True, erectile dysfunction is increasingly a problem with age, but age itself isn't the culprit. If you can't get it up, something is keeping it down. That something can be anything from high blood pressure to diabetes to depression to medications.

"Erectile dysfunction should not be considered normal aging," says Fran E. Kaiser, M.D., director of the Sexual Dysfunction Clinic at St. Louis University's Health Sciences Center. "Things are slower when you're older, but a healthy man should be able to get erections till the day he dies."

Myth: Testosterone disappears with age and your erections go with it.

Fact: Testosterone levels do begin to drop in a man's forties, says clinical psychologist and marriage and family therapist Dr. Jonathan M. Kramer.

But "testosterone really does not diminish a great

beyond. That's where your charm comes in. "She needs a lot of stroking to feel she's still sexually attractive," says Wendy Fader, Ph.D., a licensed psychologist and certified sex therapist in private practice in Boca Raton, Florida. "Making her feel desired really goes a long way."

Prime the pump. Remember, blood flow to the penis is the key to mid- and late-life sex. So keep the blood flowing. How? By having sex, of course. The more sex you have in your

deal until the middle of the seventh decade," says Dr. Sandra Scantling of the University of Connecticut School of Medicine. "But even then, so what? Testosterone has very little to do with erections; it has more to do with desire."

Myth: Couples over 60 don't enjoy sex as much.

Fact: Studies in the 1990s have consistently pooh-poohed this poo-poo. Whatever changes happen after age 60, the sexual-satisfaction level isn't one of them. In fact, one of the studies concluded that the happiest men and women in America are married people who continue to have sex frequently after they are 60.

Myth: Older men risk heart attacks by having sex.

Fact: Sex may be good exercise, but it certainly is not strenuous enough to trigger a heart attack, even if you have a history of heart disease. "The chances of it happening during sex are infinitesimal," according to Dr. Kaiser.

Myth: Older men can't fall head-over-heels in love.

Fact: They can and they do. "An older man still has the brain chemistry for infatuation," says Dr. Helen Fisher of Rutgers University. "Infatuation is a basic human emotion and it can happen at any age."

your doctor about an exercise program.

Watch your medications. You're more likely to be taking medications in your fifties and sixties. And the medications are more likely to sabotage your sexual functioning. Hypertension drugs, ulcer medications, antidepressants—these treatments can be as bad as the diseases, sexually speaking. Don't shirk your medicines, but ask your doctor about their sexual effects.

Take erotic inventory. Your sexual druthers can be changing right along with your needs. It might not hurt for you to do a little re-evaluation of your turn-ons from time to time and share your discoveries with your mate. "Sensory preferences change over time," says Sandra Scantling, Psy.D., assistant clinical professor of psychiatry at the University of Connecticut School of Medicine in Farmington and creator of the video series *Ordinary Couples, Extraordinary Sex.* "The way you like to be touched now may be different than it was."

Stretch it out. If your erection is slower in coming than it used to be, take advantage of the time. "Use it for foreplay," says Dr. Fran E. Kaiser of St. Louis University's Health Sciences Center. "See it as a positive."

In fact, sometimes it might be best to forget about any erection. There's more to sex than genital intercourse. "A lot of couples are surprised to hear it, and most of the time the man doesn't believe it," says Karen Donahey, Ph.D., director of the sex and marital therapy program at Northwestern University Medical School in Chicago. "But being sexual doesn't depend on whether you have an erection. It means being there with her, kissing, touching, holding, even talking."

fifties, the more you'll have in your sixties and seventies. It's the old use-it-or-lose-it situation.

Stay healthy. Age doesn't, ahem, peter you out, but the illnesses that can come with age do. If you value your sex life, or just your life, now is the time to break the bad habits that you used to think you got away with. That means curbing excess alcohol, high-cholesterol eating habits, smoking, and what Dr. Crenshaw calls couch addiction. Get off your duff and see

Banishing Sexual Boredom

How to Take the Monotony Out of Monogamy

There is no reason to be sexually bored in a monogamous relationship. No reason, that is, except for a few million years of polygamous human evolution. And a brain constructed without any consideration for monogamy. And a natural human preference for sexual novelty and variety. And some subtle "permission" from society to fool around. And all the attendant pressures of just being in the same house with the same person every day.

Come to think of it, we should rephrase the question. Is there any reason not to be sexually bored in a monogamous relationship?

Yes, and it's worth it. The monotony monster is eminently slayable. The secret is the oldest battle strategy known to man: Know thy enemy, and you can whip it. In this case, your opponent is called biology.

The basic problem is simple. "You're fighting a genuine restlessness born from millennia of having sexual variety being part of basic human reproductive strategy," says Dr. Helen Fisher of Rutgers University. "I don't think the human animal was built to be with one person for the rest of his life," she says. "So the sexual boredom that can set in with monogamy is real."

It's not that we're evil or sinful or unable to make commitments, says Dr. Robert Birch, a psychologist who specializes in marriage and sex therapy. "It's just that we're struggling with our biology." Sex researchers agree that there's something about us that equates novelty with excitement. At the same time, the very definition of monogamy makes novelty impossible. Houston, we have a problem.

Nurturing Novelty

"If novelty weren't sexually exciting, how would Hugh Hefner have created his empire?" Dr. Birch says. Good point. One centerfold serves its purpose as well as any other, but it was the appearance of a new one every month that built the Playboy mansion.

And, let's face it, in the novelty competition, monogamy struggles to keep up. "Marital sex won't be as 'exciting' as an affair," says Dr. Birch. "A long-term relationship doesn't have the novelty, the risk, the danger, and the forbidden aspects of an affair. That's just reality."

But it's also reality that we don't live in nature. We may be animals, but we're not *animals.* We want monogamy; we just don't want it to be dull. Our evolutionary heritage is a challenge, not a sentence. If shortcomings in the novelty department are the problem with monogamy, there are ways to fight it. A good start: Take the monotony out of monogamy by putting novelty in, starting with these suggestions.

Bust the rut. Same time, same place, same way, every time. You're on the fast track to booorrrring. Routine guarantees monotony. But couples fall into routines as easily as they fell in love. And then they wonder why they're bored. "You have to do something to make it different and exciting," says Isadora Alman, a San Francisco sexologist who writes the syndicated sex and relationship advice column "Ask Isadora." "Even the most incredible lover imaginable has to be more than a one-trick pony."

So instead of poking this and rubbing that every Wednesday night during Letterman, try poking and rubbing on a

Tuesday night during Leno. Throw in a lick here or a nuzzle there while you're at it. Hey, it's a start.

Put sex in prime time. Rut happens. And time management is often the culprit. You have your work, she has hers; you both have the kids. Sex gets relegated to the back burner or gets taken off the stove entirely. That's boring. Re-arrange your priorities, says independent sex researcher Dr. Timothy Perper. "It's a ghastly cliché," he says, "but you have to set aside quality time for your sex life together."

And to qualify as "quality," this time has to be at least as prime (though maybe not as long) as what you give to your work, and, yes, to your kids. After midnight on exhausting days doesn't cut it. "How can you enjoy sex when you're in no condition to enjoy anything?" asks sex therapist Dr. Theresa Crenshaw. "You can't operate on burnout and expect sex to function."

Make it a project. Pay as much attention to your sexual relationship as you do to your work (or sports, or your car), and you'll fend off boredom, says Dr. Fisher. Approach it like a project. That means doing the research (books, tapes, videos), exploring the possibilities, identifying your needs, testing alternatives, practicing the technical tricks. In other words, everything you do when you buy a computer or join a fantasy baseball league.

"There are all kinds of ways to combat boredom, but you have to make the effort," Dr. Fisher says. "Too many men get caught like a mouse on a treadmill. They complain about how boring it is—but they never get off the wheel."

Don't *work* at your relationship. Yes, you read that right. True, you do have to make the effort to keep the zing in your sex life. But

So Who's Bored?

Monotony or no monotony, monogamy is far more emotionally and physically satisfying than playing the field. It's true—you can look it up.

Specifically, you could look it up in the landmark *Sex in America* survey conducted by the University of Chicago and the National Opinion Research Center. So if you're concerned that once you make the commitment, you're doomed to be Al Bundy, take heart from the following survey findings.

- *Monogamous men are the most satisfied.* About 50 percent of married men said that they were extremely physically and emotionally satisfied with their partners. The lowest satisfaction rates were among men neither married nor living with someone.

- *Monogamous men have more sex.* On average, cohabiting men have sex eight times a month, married men seven times, and noncohabiting men six times.

- *Monogamous men have steadier sex.* Almost half (48 percent) of noncohabiting men have sex either just a few times per year or not at all. Only 8 percent of cohabiting and 14 percent of married men fall into those categories.

- *Near-daily sex is not the norm.* The overwhelming majority (more than 75 percent) of monogamous men—be they married or cohabiting—have sex between a few times a month and two or three times a week. Single guys average much less.

if you think of it as work, you're losing the battle. In fact, that's a big reason why some couples throw in the towel, says Dr. Barry McCarthy of the Washington Psychological Center. "When couples stop having sex, it's almost always the man's call," he says. "He figures if it's going to be more of a hassle than a pleasure, then it's not worth it." So don't hassle.

Enjoy the process. Think of Operation Anti-monotony as an exploration, an adventure. "Sustaining the sexual chemistry isn't work," says Dr. Crenshaw. "It wasn't work when you were doing all those things to orchestrate special evenings with your conquest of the week. Keep that sense of pleasure."

Assume she'll cooperate. Don't short-circuit your anti-monotony efforts out of fear that she may not be in the spirit of things. Remember, she doesn't like ennui any more than you. And if you're bored, odds are she is, too. "People don't get bored by themselves; relationships get boring," Dr. Fisher says. "If you come up with a good idea, she'll probably go for it."

Hang in there. As you make that broken-field run toward sexual pay dirt within your relationship, you're going to have to dodge some temptations to give up. "You have all kinds of things set up for you to escape," says Kathleen Gill, Ph.D., a clinical psychologist, certified sex therapist, and adjunct professor of psychology at Harvard Medical School. "You have access to pornography, prostitutes, cybersex, affairs." The point, says Dr. Gill, isn't that these things are evil, but rather that our culture, by winking at transgressions by men, makes it easy to lose track of the larger goal.

Injecting novelty into your sex play is a useful ongoing pick-me-up, a proven boredom-killer. But you need to make a more fundamental change in your approach to sex if you want to weed out monotony at its roots.

How? Dr. McCarthy calls the answer interactive sex. It comes down to intimacy, to exploiting the arousal inherent in you, in her, and in the interaction between you. "If you buy only the notion that what makes sex hot is a new stimulant from

The Spice Rack

How do you spice up a bland sex life? The answer is in the question: Put some spice into it. If you've only been cooking with salt and pepper, here's a sampler of simple spices that will take the same-old out of your sex life. Remember, what follows isn't even the hot stuff (that's in upcoming chapters). Rather, it's a little list, garnered from experts we've interviewed, of easy-to-implement variations that will help get you out of that sexual routine.

Shift it. Stuck in the missionary position? So change positions. Turn it around, or upside-down, or inside-out. You can't claim ignorance in this era of the sex-manual-of-the-week. And even if you do have a repertoire, when's the last time you tried a brand-new pose?

Reschedule it. A set schedule is good for exercise. For sex, it's monotonous. There are 24 hours in a day, seven days in a week. That's 168 different time variations. That means you can do it three times a week for a year and never use the same hour of the same day twice.

Move it. The bedroom is the easiest place to have sex. It's the most convenient. Easy and convenient are boring. The living room, the kitchen, the bathroom, the laundry room—they're unusual and challenging. Unusual and challenging are not boring.

Take it outside. Got a backyard? A garden? A private rooftop? Add them to your list of sex venues. Strategically located flora or a moonless night can take care of any privacy requirements.

Take it away. A secluded glen off the main trail. A picnic basket. A blanket. Find private places in public

the outside, you wind up devaluing ongoing sex and de-eroticizing your partner," Dr. McCarthy says. "It's as if you don't own your own sexuality, that it's something external to

parks or wilderness areas. **Throw a little fresh air on your sex life from time to time.**

Get it wet. You sing in the shower. Why not make love in the shower? You can even do both at the same time. Sure, the logistics are limiting, but that's offset by the novelty of the thing. And if you like to wash afterward, think of the time you're saving.

Throw some light on it. Making love in the dark has one drawback—you can't see anything. It's amazing how much the atmosphere can change by illuminating the proceedings. Vary the wattage. And remember, light comes in lots of colors.

Make it fast. Quickies are underrated. What they lack in duration, they make up for in thrill-power. You need some mutual agreement here; no fair imposing a quickie when she's ready for a longie.

Approached right, a blink-and-you-miss-it session can be a nutritious sexual snack. And it's different, which is exactly what you're going for.

Make it last. A quickie is at one far end of the sexual intensity scale. A loving, intimate, two-hour, stare-into-each-other's-eyes encounter is at the other. They're both good, as is everything in between. Experiment with different levels of intensity in your lovemaking.

Abstain from it. It's an old favorite in the sex therapists' book of tricks. Occasionally, plan a romantic encounter but agree that it won't go to intercourse. Everything else, but no going all the way. One option may be closed, but many more present themselves.

you." So take responsibility for your own arousal instead of wondering why it doesn't "happen." Stop chasing lightning and build a fire instead.

Getting Intimate—Again

Sexual boredom is sometimes nothing more than a cave-in to intimacy overload, says sex therapist Dr. Louanne Cole Weston. "When you feel you're getting overloaded with all the intimacy that accumulates in a relationship, sex is the place where you turn it down."

Here are some ways to blast boredom and restore intimacy to your love life.

Get together. Connecting sexually is easier if it's just one more aspect of other kinds of intimacy. In case you haven't noticed, men and women are pretty busy these days, so it's important to set aside time to be together somewhere outside the bedroom. Alman calls it sweetheart time, but just pretend you never heard the term. The important thing is to do it. "It doesn't necessarily have to be time for sex," Alman says. "But if you build in sweetheart time, sex follows."

Share an adventure. While a woman's idea of intimacy is talking, a man's is doing. So try to get her to do things with you that tap your sense of intimacy. "Men love adventure," Dr. Fisher says. "A side-by-side adventure is intimacy for a man, just as it was on the grasslands of Africa a million years ago."

Try a long walk in the city with no set destination. Your prey? The unknown bookstore, the hidden park, the street you didn't know was there.

Soak her in. Okay, you've had your adventure together. Now try it her way. That means talk. "You have to recognize that face-to-face talking is intimacy to her," Dr. Fisher says. Find a conversation-conducive setting that holds out some other attractions and approach it in good faith. Try talking in the tub, for example.

Seduction

It's a Lifelong Process

Marital seduction...that's a contradiction in terms, right? Shouldn't you expect sex in a committed relationship? Isn't convenient, available sex one of the perks of tying the knot? Don't most societies consider it a wife's duty to deliver sex?

Well, sure, if you want expected, convenient, dutifully delivered sex. Why not just call for a pizza while you're at it?

If, on the other hand, you'd prefer to keep sex as thrilling and fulfilling during your relationship as it was before the commitment, keep your seduction kit in a handy place. You need it more than ever. Seduction is the ventilation that keeps the fire burning.

But let's be clear about this. By seduction, we mean *seduction.* As in courting, sparking, pitching woo—what a sex therapist might call pleasuring. But mostly, we're talking about making her feel wanted enough to consider giving in to your desire, and then making her feel confident enough to do more than just consider it.

So forget all those *Cosmo*-inspired clown acts that put her in Saran Wrap and you in a G-string and half a tuxedo. The fine art of romantic persuasion doesn't have to turn into some crazy caricature of itself. "I can't think of anything less exciting than coming home drag-ass tired and seeing my partner prancing about in some ridiculous getup," says sexologist Isadora Alman, who writes the syndicated sex and relationship advice column "Ask Isadora."

Don't get us wrong. Fun and games have their place. But seduction is something else,

something far more effective (not to mention more dignified) as a sex motivator on a daily basis. That's because continued courtship works. It works to get her in the mood. And it works to get you in the mood.

Building Anticipation

For one, it kindles that most delicious of all sexual feelings—anticipation. Sexual spontaneity may get all the good press, but anticipation, nurtured along by your seduction skills, is where the thrill is at. A delay between the idea and its fulfillment heightens the entire experience.

Believe it or not, that's even more true in a relationship (when you're pretty sure of a successful seduction) than it was back in your will-she-or-won't-she days. For that, you can thank something called the partner engagement theory.

"That's where the arousal builds because of who your partner is and what she means to you," says sex therapist Dr. Louanne Cole Weston. "It's why the mushy, romantic stuff is so important."

Also, by setting out to seduce your wife, you remind yourself that she's your ultimate sexual conquest. Admit it—you do tend to overlook that sometimes, don't you? Well, don't feel guilty. It's common in the best relationships.

"Men tend to 'neuter' their wives over time," says Dr. Robert Birch, a psychologist who specializes in marriage and sex therapy. "We see them as companions, as partners, as helpmates, as co-parents, as co-managers of the household, as every wonderful thing there is except sexual objects."

The key to availing yourself of seduction's sex-enhancing power is convincing yourself to do it. The rest is easy. There are a million and one seduction techniques, and we offer a mere fraction of those below.

Do it her way. Seduction may turn both of you on, but don't forget it's her you're trying to seduce. Remember, women place a lot of importance on the more tender signs of affection. She probably won't like it if you sneak up behind her to pinch a breast and bite an ear, and there's no way she's going to interpret that as seduction. On the other hand, a longer-then-usual goodbye kiss in the morning with a meaningful "I'll see you tonight"—now you're getting somewhere. "It has to be something that she can easily interpret and appreciate," Dr. Birch says. "Seduction has to be romantic."

Create the mood. Don't wait until one or both of you is "in the mood." That's cheating. Waiting is the opposite of seduction. The whole point is to create the mood, even if you're creating it in yourself as well as in her. Don't look for the conditions that will lead to the best sex. Plan them.

Start early. Women are more enthusiastic about lovemaking at night if they feel connected with you throughout the day. A little extra attention at the breakfast table, followed up by an afternoon I-love-you phone call, will pay big dividends come bedtime.

Take the hint. Women are even more into this seduction thing than you are, says Dr. Perper. After all, the romantic side of sex is their specialty. But their technique can be subtle, like leaving that sinful little negligee around someplace where you're sure to see it. So look alive and help her out. "She can be setting things up with sexy little hints," Dr. Perper says.

Do the little things. Seduction doesn't have to be a big production. Courtship behavior

Seduction Scenarios

A little rusty on your seduction techniques? In the world of woo, the tried and true still work the best. Here are some commonsense courtship ideas that will help get you both in the mood.

Bring home presents. And not just on her birthday. Little things, wrapped, get big results. It has always been that way and it always will.

Give her flowers. Especially when you're not trying to get her to forgive you for something. A time-honored tradition that women love. And anyway, when was the last time you brought her flowers?

Arrange a candlelight dinner. With soft music, champagne, the works. Cliché? Sure, because some pleasures are eternal. You cook, or the deal's off.

Send her a love note. It doesn't have to be a major opus. Just a Post-it note, slipped into her purse, reminding her how wonderful you think she is.

Make out in a parked car. And for more than 30 seconds. Long enough to hear a full side of a tape you both like. This is quintessential courtship behavior.

Watch an old romantic movie with her. Try to get into the spirit of the thing instead of reciting to her the names of all the minor character actors as they appear. Pay as much attention to the "with her" part as you do to the movie.

Listen to her. That's it. Just listen. Being listened to by a man she cares about is one of the great turn-ons for a woman. A couch. A quiet evening. Her mouth. Your ears. That's amore.

can consist of small touches. Literally. "Hold her hand," says Dr. Helen Fisher of Rutgers University. "A little extra touch here or there is very exciting to a woman."

Touch

Sensuality at Your Fingertips

So you can't plane a shelf or fix a broken light socket. There are other ways to use your hands that will do a lot more for your sex life.

Touch is an underused source of mutual pleasure in many relationships, sex experts say. It's underused during foreplay. It's underused during lovemaking. It's underused as an alternative to genital intercourse. And it's underused during the 23 or so hours of the day when you're not engaged in sex.

"Just a touch on the arm or on the back of the head can convey a lot," says Dr. Karen Donahey of the Northwestern University Medical School in Chicago. "It can mean 'I'm thinking about you' or 'I care about you.' Both men and women like that."

Hands On

Touch, then, is a powerful thing. That innocent-looking skin of hers is actually hot-wired with tactile receptors that sort out different types of touches. Those deemed pleasurable prompt her brain to send out a loud message to the rest of her body that sex may not be a bad idea in the near future.

Hence the ember-smoldering function of touching her and touching her often. Your relationship's temperature control is quite literally at your fingertips. Here's how to keep your hands on the thermostat.

Start early. The sooner you start the touching, the more time it has to work its seductive magic. "Sexual response begins long before you get into the bedroom," says sex therapist Dr. Gina Ogden. "Physical contact during the day is going to end up in more intimate sexuality later."

Vary your touching. Shun routine in your touches as you would in anything else in your relationship. That means, among other things, shifting the intensity of your touches as the occasion warrants. Touch intensities can even be correlated to car gears, according to Dr. Barry McCarthy of the Washington Psychological Center. First gear: affectionate touching, fully-clothed. Second gear: semi-sexual touching, semi-clothed. Third gear: playful sexual touching, clothing-optional. Fourth gear: sexual touching to orgasm. Overdrive: sexual touching during genital intercourse.

"Learn to value all five gears," advises Dr. McCarthy. No problem. Sounds as easy as driving a car.

Staying in Touch

Now that you're developing your touch-meister skills, keep them up during and beyond the flame-stoking phase. Sure, you already touch each other a lot during intercourse, if only to hang on for dear life. But touch can play a starring, not just supporting, role in sex.

That's because, while men tend to home in on the target like a heat-seeking missile, women prefer the whole-body approach to sex. "That's not to say women don't like intercourse," Dr. Donahey says. "But they view sex typically as involving a lot of things, including touch. Expand your definition of sex, and you'll see that there are other ways to give pleasure."

Just look at the mathematics of the thing. Instead of touching her in one place with one penis, touch her in a hundred places with 10 fingers—that's a 1,000-percent increase in pleasure possibilities. And there's a bonus: By concentrating on full-body tactile pleasure, you take the focus off the twin obsessions of erection and lubrication. "Forget the penis. Forget the vagina. Forget performance," says Rachel Copelan, Ph.D., a psychologist and sexologist who wrote *100 Ways to Make Sex Sensational and 100 Percent Safe.* "That's all a big issue over a little tissue. Just try sensuality for a while. Let the sex organs lose their anxiety."

Of course, an erection may present itself of its own volition. Let the feeling frenzy continue anyway. "Some men find they're having so much fun doing these other things that they decide to forget about intercourse," says Dr. Donahey.

In fact, according to Dr. Ogden, some women can be touched to orgasm without genital stimulation. That's not common enough for you to make it a realistic goal, by the way. But you should have plenty of fun trying. Here are some ways you can stay in touch with your woman.

Take it slow. If you're wearing a watch when your sensual session begins, take it off. You could scratch her. But worse, you might look at it.

The idea isn't to fill a cuddle quotient so you can move on to "real" sex. Like the song says, women want a man with a slow hand. Make that two hands. And make it very slow. "It should get to the point where she's asking for you to penetrate her and you still don't," Dr. Copelan says. "It's better for her to really want it than to be coaxed into it. And the way to do that is with a lot of touching."

Touch, her way. Remember, you aim to please. Sometimes those breasts seem to cry out for some serious kneading, but what she really wants may be feathery touches. Or firm but gentle stroking. Whatever she wants, obey the signals. And take them in the right spirit. "Women vocalize their desires about touch

Touch and Go

Her body—yours, too, for that matter—is mined with explosive pleasure points. Erogenous zones (body areas conducive to sexual arousal) aren't limited to the obvious. Why do you think Chinese women wore those high-necked dresses? Because the back of the neck is an important erogenous zone. So are ears, throats, hands, toes, inner thighs, feet, the backs of knees, lower backs...the list goes on.

But a checklist won't find you the buried pleasure. Not all zones are equally erogenous for all people. Besides, what are you supposed to do with a zone once you know about it? Rub it? Prod it? Lick it?

Better to just try everything, everywhere, says Dr. Ted McIlvenna of the Institute for Advanced Study of Human Sexuality. That's where massage comes in. There are two ways of going about giving sensual, erotic massages to your beloved. One is to get the books, buy the tapes, take the courses, and wait several months to become an expert amateur. The other? Just do it.

"Just start rubbing," says Dr. McIlvenna. "Touch her with affection all over the place."

more than men do," Dr. Donahey says. "That doesn't mean you're doing anything wrong. It's just that you can't be expected to know exactly what she wants." So let her tell you.

Practice your fingerwork. Touch marathons are for pleasure, not work. But like any neglected skill, pleasure-touching may require a bit of dedication at the outset. "People are not very good at touching each other," says Ted McIlvenna, Ph.D., president of the Institute for Advanced Study of Human Sexuality in San Francisco. "You have to practice. But enjoy the practice sessions."

Kissing

The Pathway to Passion

Why should you, a sexually adept veteran with a live-in squeeze, bother with kissing?

Short answer: Because kissing paves the pathway to passion, establishing the intimacy that leads to the best kind of sex.

Shorter answer: Because she wants you to bother.

In fact, she really wants you to.

"One of the biggest differences between men and women is that women want much more kissing in their relationships," says William Cane, a Boston College English professor who undertook extensive research on the subject for his book *Art of Kissing*. One of the most common queries from the typical woman, according to Cane, is "How do I get my man to kiss me more?"

One way might be to remind him that kissing is sexually exciting. Your lips, mouth, and teeth are, after all, erogenous zones. Kissing, quite simply, arouses her—and you.

A Kiss Is Just a Kiss?

Of course, we're not talking cheek-pecks at family gatherings. It's the deep, sexual kissing that's the instant turn-on for many women. But there is something in between, something perhaps lighter than your highest-intensity tongue warfare, but it still qualifies as heavy artillery in your sexual armory. That's the kind of kissing you do with her that's warm, intimate, loving, and yes, sexual—

but you're not fumbling at your buckle and her buttons to move the action along.

Here again, men and women part ways in their approach to kissing. Men see it as simply a prelude to intercourse; women see it as much more. "From a guy's point of view, it may seem strange to kiss just for the sake of kissing," Cane says. "But that's what women say they like."

Despite conducting countless surveys and interviews to come up with his compendium of osculation preferences, Cane came across very few guys who put kissing, in and of itself, high on their list of sexual pleasures. But that doesn't mean men aren't capable of enjoying smooch sessions for their own sake. "I definitely think men can enjoy kissing if they let themselves," Cane says.

Kissing = Sex

In their book *Men and Sex: Discovering Greater Love, Passion, and Intimacy with Your Wife*, Clifford L. Penner, Ph.D., and Joyce J. Penner, R.N., note that kissing is a "barometer to measure the degree of intimacy and passion between a couple." To keep the barometer readings the way you want them, their advice is straightforward and to the point: "Kiss daily. Kiss softly and tenderly. Kiss passionately and warmly. Kiss when you feel sad. Kiss when you feel happy."

"To get what you want, you have to understand what she wants," Cane says. "Women want kisses. Make the effort, and you'll get your payoff." We know you know how to kiss, but next time you start up a necking session with your honey, keep these pointers in the back of your mind.

Keep it up. Going through the motions just to get in enough required kissing time won't cut it with her. She can tell. Get into the spirit of the thing. Kiss her until you're sure that she has been thoroughly kissed. Then kiss her some more. "Remember, women like more kissing than men do," Cane says. "Once you've had enough doesn't necessarily mean that she has."

Watch your hands. It's almost an automatic reflex. Your lips go to her lips, your hand goes to her breast. Or her buttocks. Or somewhere very personal. That's fine at the right moment, but not every moment is the right moment. "Women often say that guys sexualize kissing too often," Cane says. "They like sex, too, but not every time they're kissed."

And if you're innocent? If you're putting your hands there because it feels good, not because you want intercourse right this minute? Doesn't matter. She'll usually interpret it as coercion anyway. So, Cane suggests, "stop your hands from wandering in such a way that makes her feel that she's being led into sex. Just keep it nice and romantic sometimes."

Find out what she likes. Kissing is supposed to be pleasure, so it should be pleasing to both of you. Each woman (and man) is unique, so pay attention to her physical and verbal messages to slow down, do more of that, or cut it out. This includes finding out how she wants to be kissed, and letting her know your own likes and dislikes.

Get around this by talking about your kissing preferences in a casual way when you're not kissing, suggests Cane. That way neither of you will feel you're being criticized for what you were just doing. And when you do bring it up, turn it into a fun thing. "Make it almost a game," he says.

How Not to Kiss

Women say they want us to kiss them more. Then they complain about how we do it. What's a guy to do? For starters, know what not to do. Here's a list of women's complaints.

"He always does the same thing." The "same thing" is actually two things: the basic puckered-lip press and the French kiss. "Women like French kissing," says William Cane, who researched American kissing habits for his book *Art of Kissing*. "But they complain that their guys don't know other types of kisses."

"His French kissing is uninspired." Just stuffing your tongue down her throat as you kiss is an insult to the French. Where do you think the word *finesse* comes from in the first place? Flick. Explore. Massage. Communicate with your tongue.

"He tries to suck my face off." Passion is wonderful. Disfiguration isn't. Control your animal instincts; this is kissing, not a feeding frenzy. Make sure your enthusiasm is in sync with hers.

"He slobbers all over me." Passionate soul-kissing may sometimes get a little sloppy. But if you're the only one spilling the soup, you're probably making her more angry than excited.

"I feel like I'm kissing a corpse." That's because your kisses are mushy, limp, dead. Where's the feeling? These limp kisses don't tell her you're gentle. They tell her that you're either squeamish or preoccupied with other things.

"His breath is bad." After a few years together, you may tend to get careless. It's just as annoying to her no matter how long you've been together. Where'd you leave that Listerine bottle?

"Like, 'I'll tell you what I like if you tell me what you like.' And then listen to her."

Make it one-way. Here's another way to communicate your kissing druthers—and it can be a major turn-on in and of itself, according to Cane. "Tell her not to kiss back for a minute or two or three while you kiss her the way you like to kiss," Cane says. "Then reverse the roles." The assertive role is exciting for the kisser, the holding back thrilling for the kissee. And in the bargain, you both get a living picture of the other's idea of great kissing.

Plan an ambush. "Spring new things on her," Cane also suggests. "Don't talk the subject up too much. It leads to too many expectations." In other words, communicating your kissing preferences is useful in the broad sense, but the best way to introduce new twists in your kissing is to just do it. Explaining what you're going to try and choreographing the entire operation turns it into a performance. That's not romantic.

"Try for variety in kissing," Cane says. "But try to introduce it smoothly into the context of the situation."

Vary the action. Use your imagination, says Cane. Tongue on tongue is nice, but you can also let the little fellow dance around her lips, her gums, even her teeth. Let it do a little exploring. Gently run it along the outside of her lips and inside her mouth, between her cheek and gums. Make swirling, spinning motions from one side to another. Try sucking on her lower lip while she sucks on your upper. While you're at it, see what moves turn her on. And ease off sometimes; vary your pace. Most specialists find that the change from intense to easy, from sexual to playful and back again, only heightens excitement and adds to your pleasure.

Kiss her neck. This is a winner, a Grade-A surefire partner-pleaser. "Women rave about being kissed on the neck," Cane says. "The statistics on it in my surveys were amazing."

Don't stop there. Cane also found that most women love kisses on the outer ear, the lobe, and its environs. Of course, there's no place on a clean body that isn't kissable during foreplay or "outercourse." But during your newly rediscovered kissing for kissing's sake, there's a universe of pleasure to be found from the neck up.

Kiss in public. "If you've never done it," says Cane, "it can be kind of exciting." A modest public kissing demonstration can strengthen your bond—it's the two of you alone against the world. Of course, some women are just plain uncomfortable showing private acts in public places. And even if she's okay kissing publicly, don't overdo it. You're not trying to create a spectacle. "It doesn't have to be intimate kissing," Cane says. "But everybody has a little bit of exhibitionism in them."

Kiss in cars. There must be something about the automobile that gets lips puckering. Just about everybody likes making out in cars. But there's also something about steady relationships that seems to make people forget how much they liked it. So try negotiating those bucket seats again.

By the way, part of the thrill of vehicular osculation, according to Cane, is that cars are only semi-private places. Thus, kissing inside of one falls under the category of quasi-public. But what have you got to hide?

Kiss as foreplay. All the encouragement you're getting to disassociate kissing from intercourse doesn't mean kissing has ceased to be a superb form of foreplay. "Especially if you prolong it a little," Cane says.

Kiss during sex. If you saw the movie *Pretty Woman*, you know that prostitutes usually don't kiss their clients. Why? Because it's part of what turns a physical act into intimate interaction. That's the last thing a self-respecting professional wants. Of course, there are some positions in which even contortionists couldn't reach each other's lips. But kiss when you can. "Kissing makes her feel that she's not there just for the sex," Cane says. Besides, when you're kissing her during sex, nobody can accuse you of using kissing as a mere appetizer. Then it's part of the main course.

Fulfilling Your Fantasies

Dare to Dream

Sexual fantasies are great, aren't they? How else could you break the record for consecutive simultaneous orgasms with all the Spice Girls and their older sisters? Is there any other way to turn that overbearing but well-built receptionist into a piece of warm putty who calls you King?

And the beauty of it is, you can do all that without feeling guilty. You don't even have to worry about safe sex. You know why? Because fantasies aren't real.

Well, duh, you're probably saying to yourself. But it's not so obvious to most men. "A lot of people are walking around with the notion that if they fantasize about something, it means they really would go out and do it," says Robert O. Hawkins, Ph.D., professor emeritus of health sciences at the State University of New York at Stony Brook. "Get rid of that notion."

And while you're at it, get rid of the notion that your daydream date with last night's waitress means you're losing interest in your full-time, real-world partner. Or that her closed-eyes encounters with Kevin Costner in his Robin Hood outfit reflect on your desirability to her. Fantasies don't work that way.

If they did, they wouldn't be very good fantasies. If Jenny McCarthy really invited you to her suite at the Beverly Hills Hotel, you'd probably spend more time worrying about your clothes or your breath or what to bring with you than what you were

going to do with her. Those concerns don't even exist in fantasies. "Nothing in fantasies relates to reality," Dr. Hawkins says. "In fantasies, you don't think about what you're wearing or how you smell. There's no concern for outcome."

Fantasy Follows Function

So if fantasies aren't real, what are they? Hold on, because you're going to love this answer. "Fantasies are designed to make sex more pleasurable," says Dr. Hawkins. "The reason we're even able to have fantasies is so we can use them to increase sexual pleasure."

In other words, fantasy sex doesn't lure you away from the real thing with your partner, as some fear. Quite the contrary. "Fantasies can motivate you," says Dr. Robert Birch, a psychologist who specializes in marriage and sex therapy. "Thinking about a fantasy during the day can help with your arousal in the evening."

And that arousal assistance can continue right on through the main act. You're not guilty of betraying your woman by thinking of someone else's buns while holding on to hers. "If it gets you off and you're not hurting anybody, why not?" says Dr. Wendy Fader, a licensed psychologist and certified sex therapist.

Besides, she could be doing the same thing. "Fantasies can trigger an orgasm for some women," Dr. Birch says. "She can get right to the brink, conjure up a stimulating fantasy, and she's over the edge."

Still, there's such a thing as overdoing it. As extra motivation and stimulation, fantasy can be a sexual relationship's best friend. As an escape clause, it's a potential enemy. "If you rely on fantasy every time you're with your partner, if you're never involved in the moment but always a thousand miles away, there could be a problem there," says Dr. Karen Donahey of the Northwestern University Medical School in Chicago.

And one more thing. Fantasies aren't mandatory. There are people who are perfectly happy without them, Dr. Hawkins says. "You shouldn't feel pressured to fantasize," he says.

Getting in the Act

By playing them in your mind, you've just begun to tap your fantasies' arousal power. Share some, and you've let the genie out of the bottle. Fulfill them with your partner, and you're on your way to making a million wishes come true.

"Fun" is an operative word in fantasy fulfillment. "Intimacy" and "pleasure" are two more. But "easy" isn't. "Fantasy enactment really takes a lot of courage," says sex therapist Dr. Louanne Cole Weston. "But it has the potential to strengthen a relationship by prompting more sexual creativity." Provided, of course, that you follow some commonsense guidelines for sharing or enacting your fantasies.

Share judiciously. "Some fantasies are better off remaining fantasies," Dr. Donahey says. It's easy to see her point. You can probably think of several fantasies on your playlist that she would either (a) not understand at all, (b) not appreciate in the least, (c) consider you a nutcase for, or (d) leave you as a result of. Rule of thumb: The closer your fantasy is to reality, the worse candidate it is for sharing with her. Extreme example? "Telling her you've been thinking about getting it on with her sister," says Dr. Birch. "That doesn't fly very well."

Enact judiciously. Be just as intelligent about which fantasies you select for fulfillment.

Her Fantasies

"Juliette DeMornay Brookington-Thorncastle, the young Duchess of Pleasantshire, stifled a scream as the brutal but handsome seafarer of questionable lineage and even more questionable occupation slung her trembling body over his strong shoulders. She knew her honor was in imminent danger, yet she felt a strange tingling in her delicate, heaving bosom and a curious desire to submit to his unbending..."

Enough. You get the idea. Sound familiar? Actually, we just made it up. But passages like that fill enough pages of enough romance novels, and they seem to revolve around one basic fantasy.

But what a fantasy. After a million years of evolution, several thousand years of civilization, and a few decades of modern feminism, women still fantasize about being taken against their will. They daydream about being dominated. What's going on here?

"It's about being desired," says Dr. Karen Donahey of the Northwestern University Medical School in Chicago. "It's about a man being so taken with her that he's willing to do anything to have her."

That ties in with the tendency of women's fantasies to run toward the romantic, while men's race toward the raw. But why does she need to be overpowered to feel desired?

Your imagination manufactures some complicated scenarios that you'd never want to act out, even in a role-playing style. A lot of these would-be major productions present insurmountable logistical problems anyway. Like, how do you know you can book the dwarfs, Donny and Marie Osmond, and the old barroom set from *Cheers* all on the same night? But even a lot of plausible ones can do more

"It eliminates the responsibility for being sexual," Dr. Donahey says. "Women are socialized to believe on some level that wanting sex means they're bad girls." In other words, if Brad Pitt ties her up and has his way with her, she hasn't done anything wrong, no matter how much she liked it.

It goes without saying, but we'll say it anyway—none of this reveals any real-world desire to be taken advantage of, nor any permission for men to do so. "If you ask women if they really want to be dragged away, they'll say 'of course not,'" Dr. Donahey says.

The *Sex in America* survey asked that very question and got the same answer. The percentage of women who found the idea of being forced to do something sexual as "very appealing" was a fat zero. Obviously, there's no real-world correlation.

But there are some interesting fantasy enactment possibilities, if both partners are willing. Imagine yourself as *the dashing Lord Powerman, he who must be obeyed, driven to obsession by your desire for the gentle but budding little milkmaid whose delicate, tender body could never resist the iron will of your yearning...*"

You two take it from there.

Get inspiration. You've talked about it and decided to go for it. Tonight, you're going to enact a fantasy. Tonight comes. Okay, honey, what shall we do? One huge silence. Two blank stares. Four shrugged shoulders. Time to hit the books.

"Using a book is a very nonthreatening approach to finding fantasies," Dr. Hawkins says. "It's a concrete, practical way of getting started." You won't have any trouble finding sources to steal from; forests have been felled for the printing of popular books on romance and sex fantasies. Some old classics that Dr. Hawkins recommends include Alex Comfort's *Joy of Sex* and, for her, Nancy Friday's *My Secret Garden*.

Nude photos and videos are a hot topic in more than one way. Tens of millions of men and women buy X-rated magazines and films that fire their imaginations and warm them everywhere else, says clinical psychologist and marriage and family therapist Dr. Jonathan M. Kramer. More men than women use naked visuals to enjoy sex, but what turns him on may turn her off. If your woman wants attention and affection and intimacy, try giving her that first—then bring out your monthly men's magazine and see if she's willing to join in. If not, let it go. At least for now.

Expand your definition. There are fantasies and there are fantasies. You may be primed for an evening of whipped cream, Led Zeppelin, and nurses' outfits, only to find that what she had in mind was for you to wear briefs to bed instead of boxers. Wrong reaction: "You call that a fantasy?" Right reaction: Do it. You're trying to fulfill her fantasies, not critique them. If it turns her on and makes the sex better, it's as good a fantasy

harm than good. Anything involving a third person, for example, deserves a red flag.

Keep some private stock. By all means, play out some fantasies with your partner, but not all of them. "If you have a particularly effective favorite fantasy, keep it to yourself," Dr. Hawkins suggests. "Hang on to some private stock, and accept that it's okay for her to do the same thing."

as any. You can take your stairway to heaven tomorrow.

"Some of us consider something like going to a hotel for a night to be a simple relief from everyday pressures," Dr. Hawkins says. "For others, it's a real fantasy come true."

Try, try again. Three times, to be precise. "If you don't like acting out the fantasy the first time, give it two more tries," Dr. Hawkins suggests. "Very often, the first time through you're both more focused on getting it right than on feelings and pleasure." If after the third time you still think it's a waste, it's reasonable to conclude that this particular fantasy is not for the two of you.

Finding Out Her Fantasies

You can't fulfill her fantasies if she won't tell you what they are. At the same time, her reluctance to confide her secret desires doesn't mean that she doesn't want them fulfilled by you. You have to coax them out of her and lead her to Fantasy Island.

It's not that she doesn't have it in her. For women, the context of the encounter, its romantic setting, its emotional currents (all of which are exploitable for fantasy scenarios, by the way) are essential to sex. In fact, sex therapist Dr. Gina Ogden found that many women can actually reach orgasm just by using their imaginations. "Thinking off," she calls it.

So while she may get carried away by her fantasy, at the same time, she's "supposed" to be sexually conservative. Sexual lust is for sluts, not wives. If she never gets past her straight-laced conservatism, you'll never get to the opening act of your Fantasy Follies. It's what you have to conquer.

His Fantasies

"We're all responsible for our own fantasies," says Dr. Helen Fisher of Rutgers University. Indeed, our imaginations can churn out some real custom-made stuff. On the other hand, there are several fantasy types that seem to be in the male public domain. Any of the following strike a chord?

You and another woman. This is number one on the hit parade. She can be somebody you had great sex with before, somebody with whom great sex is an intriguing possibility, or somebody with whom you could never have great sex—but the idea is tempting. She can be a friend, an ex, a movie star, or a purely fictional character. To repeat, it is not cheating to have this fantasy.

You dominating her. This one comes straight out of the reptilian brain you inherited, insists Dr. Fisher. Most male animals brook no nonsense out there in the wild. Again, this doesn't mean you're an insensitive brute in real life. In fact, this is one of the few fantasies on this list that has potential to be acted out, since it's the mirror image of the most common female fantasy.

But before you get started on the crusade to loosen her up, make sure the rest of your relationship is relatively healthy. You can't build fantasy castles on rotting foundations. "What gets in the way of sharing fantasies is a lousy relationship," Dr. Fader says. "If, for example, she sees you as a very controlling, demanding husband, and now you're talking about her getting dressed up in leather and a whip, she's not going to want to do it. It's not because she's prudish about it; it's because she sees it as another example of you trying to control her. Anger is a real sex-killer." Instead, try some different, nonthreatening approaches to

You and her...and her... **Taken two or more at a time—it's so easy in fantasyland—your imaginary sexual conquests can add up fast. It's the call of the wild, says Dr. Fisher. Male chimps go from one chimpette to another, and they're not fantasizing.**

You watching them. **Thank your relatives the chimpanzees again for this one. "When a male chimpanzee watches another pair copulate, his testosterone levels go up," Dr. Fisher says. "It spurs the sex drive." We have more civilized ways of taking advantage of this arouser than the Peeping Tom chimps do. We call them movies, videos, books, and magazines...and fantasies.**

Them watching you. **You can't say our fantasies aren't democratic. There's a little exhibitionism hidden in all of us.**

You and him. **We keep telling you, fantasies aren't real. "A lot of people get freaked out by erotic homosexual fantasies," says Dr. Wendy Fader, a licensed psychologist and certified sex therapist. "But they're common, and they don't mean you're gay."**

Be suggestive. Begin to draw those fantasies out of her by subtle suggestive references. Use props. A travel ad for a Caribbean resort could cue the question, "Hey, what do you think it would be like to make love on that beach?" Or a lingerie ad: "Would you feel sexy in something like that?" Just about any answer more substantial than "I don't know" can help get things rolling.

Prime her pump. "If she's having problems visualizing anything or is holding back, give her something to fantasize about," suggests psychologist and sexologist Dr. Rachel Copelan. And make it one she'll like. Example: "You know, I can see you as an exotic belly dancer, with guys just gushing all around you." She may pooh-pooh the image, but you can be pretty sure she'll think about it for a while.

Give her a challenge. Tell her you'll do anything she wants in the bedroom for one hour, suggests Dr. Helen Fisher of Rutgers University. Her response may be for you to paint the walls, but it also might get those wheels turning in her head. "Try it and find out what happens," Dr. Fisher says. "Most couples who are sexually bored probably know very little about each other's fantasies and how to play into them."

Compromise. Never imply that her hesitancy means she's intimidated or hung up, even if you think she is. Respect her feelings without caving in to them. She won't even go for making love with the lights on? Tell her that you understand her shyness—that you're a little self-conscious, too—but maybe you could just light a candle at the other end of the room. "Keep an atmosphere of goodwill between the two of you," Dr. Donahey says. "Work for a compromise."

get at her fantasies and make them come alive for her.

Take the initiative. Of course you want to be nice to her, but you can kill your sex life with kindness. Meekly accepting her reluctance to experiment sexually isn't doing either one of you any good. You need to nudge her out of her comfort zone, gently and positively, but also with determination. That doesn't mean badgering, but it does mean encouraging. "The philosophy of never making anybody mentally uncomfortable sexually is what causes monotony," Dr. Weston says. "If nobody is ever uncomfortable, nothing ever moves forward."

Overcoming Inhibitions

It's a Team Effort

Ever feel like punching a sex expert?

That's not recommended behavior, but if you're told "vary your sexual routine" one more time, you just may lose it. We hear you: You know there are other positions. You know there are other ways to do it. But it's not so simple. You want to try new things, but it's just that...well...you know...

We know. We know that even in the closest relationships, there can be something holding you back from breaking out of that routine. Those same sex experts you're so mad at say such inhibitions are common and conquerable.

They're also understandable. There are at least three good reasons why you tend to trod the tried-and-true.

It's easier. Your sex habits can behave like water running downhill, finding the course of least resistance. That's one reason why a lot of couples seldom stray from the missionary position. "You know why man-on-top intercourse is the most popular?" asks Dr. Barry McCarthy of the Washington Psychological Center. "Because it's easier."

It's more convenient. "The straight penis-vagina thing is really convenient for guys," says sex therapist Dr. Gina Ogden. "It's quick, it's efficient, it's right there, and it feels good. You don't even have to relate while you're doing it."

It's safer. As in emotionally safer. "Doing the same thing all the time is safe," says Daniel Beaver, director of the Relationship Counseling

Center. "Making things exciting by blazing a new trail is taking an emotional risk."

Birth of an Anxiety

Your inhibition has its childhood roots, of course, as you remember from Psychology 101. "If you weren't free to create, if you were told from the time your little ears could hear that you never were doing things right, you're going to lack confidence to pursue things," says psychologist and sexologist Dr. Rachel Copelan.

But it's also a cultural thing. "You get horrible messages from the culture," says Harvard Medical School's Dr. Kathleen Gill. "Like the idea that sex is dirty unless you save it for marriage. Even if you do save it for marriage, you still carry around with you the 'sex is dirty' part."

And it's a macho thing. "Men are supposed to know it all, and their bodies are supposed to always work," Dr. McCarthy says. "Inhibitions have to do with these unrealistic expectations."

That gets back to the position problem. Move out of the missionary, and you usually have to work with her to get things physically organized. This is a good thing, but your macho expectations may not see it that way. You don't want to lose control of the situation. "Penises tend to slip out of vaginas in many positions," says Dr. McCarthy. "Men tend to get anxious about that, so they just stay away from them."

But that's not a very good strategy for long-term sexual fulfillment in a relationship. Besides, anxiety comes with sex, according to Dr. Gill. "Anxiety is motivating," she says. "We don't do anything in life without it." And that includes (please don't hit us for saying it) varying your sexual routine. What follows are strategies to help you identify and conquer whatever inhibitions might be lying around in your mind.

Manage your anxiety. The trick, Dr. Gill says, is to learn to tolerate a certain amount of anxiety. "Avoiding anxiety is not the point," she says. "Learning to live with it is." In other words, somewhere between paralyzing fear and total apathy is a level of anxiety that you can work with. Find that level. "And then manage it well enough so that you can confront what really turns you on," Dr. Gill says.

Accept yourself. Recognize that what turns you on is simply a source of sexual pleasure for you, not some kind of cosmic comment on your worth as a human being. You don't need to feel embarrassed or personally rejected if she doesn't happen to share that particular turn-on. "Rather than depending on validation from your mate for what you think, give that validation to yourself," says sex therapist Dr. Louanne Cole Weston.

Example: You'd just love it if at certain impassioned points of the process, the love chatter between the two of you turned X-rated. But you'd never bring it up because you're afraid she might think you're a foul-mouthed fool. Hence, nothing ever happens. "That's the kind of inhibition that keeps you from being real about sex," Dr. Gill says. "You have to be able to say, 'Hey, it may not be politically correct, but it really floats my boat.'"

Let go of something. One way to loosen the logjam, suggests sexologist Isadora Alman, who writes the syndicated sex and relationship advice column "Ask Isadora," is to find within you just one long-held sexual secret that you can somehow tell her about. "That doesn't mean sharing all your secrets," Alman says. "Just let go of something that has been keeping you from being closer to her."

Using Your Tongue

Language, they say, is what separates us noble humans from the baser animals. But when it comes to sex, we're often no nobler than aardvarks. In fact, we can be pretty dumb about it.

If you're having trouble breaking out of those dull sex patterns, maybe your first order of business as a couple should be naming your nemesis. Like, what do you actually call things? Do you use medical terms like *coitus*? Common euphemisms like "making love"? Street talk? Humorous names? It doesn't matter as long as you have a working vocabulary, says independent sex researcher Dr. Timothy Perper. "Work out a language that's clear to both of you," Dr. Perper says. "It's your own private language. Nobody's listening."

The alternative to a language is a lifetime of uncommunicated desires. "If it's hard for people even to ask for routine sex, it's even more difficult to ask for something that's a change of style," says Dr. Robert Birch, a psychologist who specializes in marriage and sex therapy. "You need to break through that barrier."

Inhibited couples also tend to be too subtle with their sexual messages, says Dr. Birch. An example is a woman who takes a shower when she's in the mood for sex. "That's supposed to be his signal," Dr. Birch says. "That's crazy. People miss signals like that."

So you have to talk the talk. And while constructing your own private language is a good beginning, your healthiest option is to get to the point where you both can communicate your desires in plain English without being self-conscious about it. "Adult human beings should be able to say, 'I'm horny. How about you?'" Dr. Birch says. "If you want something, you have to ask for it."

A favorite one for women, Alman says, is "I always think that if you really knew me, you wouldn't love me." If she can get that out, you're more likely to say "Of course I would, honey," than "You're probably right." So if you can manage to blurt out, say, "I'm worried I'll keep slipping out of you if we try it spoon-style," you'll probably discover that she won't immediately file for divorce. She might even say, "So what? It feels good when we get it back in."

Jettison excess baggage. You don't have to keep carrying society's sex-is-dirty messages around with you. Liberate yourself from inhibiting notions about sex that were forced upon you when you didn't know any better. "Do some self-examination," advises Dr. Gill. "Get conscious about what those messages are, and get rid of the ones that aren't serving you."

Helping Her Along

Now that you're overcoming your own inhibitions, you still have hers to think about. Last we looked, it took two to perform most sex acts.

Take oral sex, for example. Yeah, we know, you'd be glad to. But will she provide it just as gladly? The *Sex in America* survey found that while a not-so-surprising 83 percent of men consider it appealing to receive oral sex, only 57 percent of women consider giving it appealing. What's more, almost a third of women (32 percent) don't even like receiving oral sex. There's a discrepancy here.

You don't need statistics to tell you if she's uptight about pursuing new paths to pleasure. But why? Take all the social messages you got about the evil of sexuality and multiply it many-fold for her.

"It goes back to the virgin thing," says Dr. Copelan. "Girls are told not to let anybody

Solo Sex Together

You can't exactly say men are inhibited about masturbation, since at least 60 percent of them do it, according to at least one survey. But try getting just about any guy to talk about his personal masturbation habits, and you'll get a pretty good idea about the queasiness still connected with it.

Which complicates the issue of masturbation in a relationship, doesn't it? Even if you've overcome the old taboos, your marital status may be throwing a whole new set of doubts at you. Am I betraying her by taking things into my own hands? Shouldn't I be saving it for her?

Researchers say that masturbation can be a godsend for overcoming inhibitions and developing better sex in your relationship, especially if you supplement your private activity with some joint sessions. There are two major variations on that theme for you to take hold of.

Mutual masturbation. Bringing each other to orgasm is foolproof birth control and about as safe as sex can get. For a steady couple, it has even more to recommend it. For one thing, it's an ongoing learning experience for both of you, the lesson being how to touch your partner with maximum effect. For another, it's decadently self-indulgent, which is good. A little bit of mutually agreed upon selfishness now and then helps takes some pressure

touch them. They're taught early not to respond sexually."

That sort of programming can lead to body hang-ups. Next thing you know, years have gone by and she still won't consider making love with the lights on. "Women have the same kind of head noises about measuring up as men do," Dr. Ogden says. "But with them, it's more like 'I'm too fat' or 'I'm too thin.'"

And, just like you, women can be wary of what enjoying certain sex acts might say about who they are. "Some women might shy

off a relationship. "It's often a good thing for both of you to concentrate on getting just one of you off," says Harold Litten, an author who has written about human sexuality for more than 30 years, including the titles *The Joy of Solo Sex* and *More Joy...An Advanced Guide to Solo Sex*. "Then the next day, or maybe the next hour, you concentrate on the other one. That's a nice change of pace."

Solo sex together. Sex therapists often recommend focusing on the masturbation taboo as a way of overcoming sexual inhibitions. You do that by masturbating yourself in front of her, while she does the same. Obvious drawback: A couple with cold feet about trying new things sexually may have frozen feet at the thought of it.

But that's just the point, says Dr. Robert O. Hawkins of the State University of New York. "It can be very threatening," Dr. Hawkins says. "But you have to look at it as a challenge. If you can do it with your partner, then you establish a very high trust level. That brings you closer together."

It's also even more educational than mutual masturbation. "It shows your partner what she can do to make things better for you," Dr. Hawkins says. "You each know best what pleases you, and masturbation is one way of showing it."

away from oral sex because of what it might uncover," Dr. Weston says. "It's not just that they might like it, but that they might even like it if you demand it in a demeaning way." Here are some suggestions for helping her confront and overcome her inhibitions.

Enlist in the battle. "Any woman can be helped," Dr. Copelan says. "You have to take charge and struggle to help her, if she wants you to." That means encouraging her to reveal her desires. How? Try asking. "You have to ask her what feels good, what she wants you to do," Dr. Copelan says.

Take it easy. Ask, but don't push too hard. "Have patience," Dr. Copelan says. "Don't overwhelm her with your desires and needs. Take your time." Remember, you have a lifetime (hers) of negative momentum to overcome. Go slowly. Start out a bit naughty and playful. Talk dirty. Get comfortable with your new sexual territory and lingo and keep experimenting.

Strike while the iron's hot. Ask her over coffee what she'd like you to do sexually, and she needs to answer in full, blushing sentences. Ask her if she likes what you're doing while you're doing it, and she can respond negatively or positively with a mere moan. "Do you like this?" is a lot more effective when the "this" is a real feeling instead of an abstract idea. "One of the best times to find out what your partner likes is during sex," says independent sex researcher Dr. Timothy Perper. "When you're in the throes, you can make personal requests of each other that at other times might horrify one of you."

Wash away the worries. One reason some women are shy about oral sex, according to Dr. Copelan, is because they think their sex organs are dirty. Or smelly. "There's a simple solution for that," she says. "Take a shower together. Take a bath together. Be clean together."

Be sexual friends. "The biggest secret to overcoming inhibitions is to think of each other as your intimate sexual friend," Dr. McCarthy says. "With a friend, you don't need to get defensive if something doesn't work."

The spirit should be camaraderie, not competition. Instead of judging each other, think of yourselves as partners in crime, of sorts. "When people back off from their adversarial ways, new solutions tend to rear their heads in funny, unpredictable ways," Dr. Weston says.

Expanding Your Sexual Horizons

Heading for the Frontier

Erotic.

It's a wonderful word, and it means a lot more than sexy. Think of eroticism as the thing that puts the meaning and richness into your sexual experiences. Without it, sex is nothing but urges and acts.

You have urges, and you like to do the acts, but chances are you and your significant other want more than that. And you can get more by broadening your sexual horizons, by which we mean heightening the erotic content of your sex sessions. "Eroticism is what makes hotter sex," says Dr. Barry McCarthy of the Washington Psychological Center. "It can be anything from playing out sexual fantasies to having sex in the shower to using different lotions." Or even more daring explorations involving sex toys, tying each other up, role-playing, and other highly eroticized scenarios.

We're not saying you have to do something that scares or disturbs either one of you. But somewhere between heavy bondage and dabs of rose petal cream, there ought to be something you and your partner can use as a wild, healthy, harmless horizon-expander. As you'll see, just about anything qualifies if you see it as erotic enhancement. All that matters is that you really want to do it.

Columbus in Bed

If you haven't been pushing a lot of envelopes in the bedroom lately, don't feel like you're pulling down the average. Good old-fashioned, no-frills loving is still the best loving.

"You ought to be a good sex partner first," says Dr. Ted McIlvenna of the Institute for Advanced Study of Human Sexuality. "Then sex doesn't need a hell of a lot of other stuff. There's something about lust and enthusiasm that does more than any 'extras.'"

But, Dr. McIlvenna adds, the lust and enthusiasm can use some help sometimes. That's where creating an elevated erotic context comes into the picture. Here are some suggestions to help get you started in a fun, nonthreatening way.

Do it your way. Okay, you're convinced. Erotic enhancement is just the ticket. Horizons, prepare to be broadened. Which way to the whips and chains department?

Whoa, boy. Forget the Top 10 List of Most Erotic Scenarios. Your new sex scenarios should be extensions of what the two of you find arousing, not impositions from outside sources. If she doesn't even like it when you pat her behind, how's she going to enjoy spanking?

"Don't do something that's bizarre just to bring in something new," advises Dr. McIlvenna. "Be creative, but if something doesn't follow from your established sexual patterns, it's going to do more harm than good. Build on who you are and what you want."

Be flexible. When it comes to erotic sex play, there's more than one way to play, especially when the two of you put your heads

together. But make sure that the two of you are in agreement when you set out, says Dr. Karen Donahey of the Northwestern University Medical School in Chicago. And don't feel rejected if she's not big on your idea of erotic. "It's a mistake to think that if she rejects your suggestion, the whole deal is broken. Expand the options." Sooner or later you'll find something you both like.

Get tickled pink. Many of the different erotic games people play often involve intense sensations—it's one of the reasons bondage and spanking have such a following. If you're curious about exploring the whole intense-sensation genre, start small. "Some people, because their bodies are quite sensitive to it, love tickling," Dr. McIlvenna says. "Others hate it." That pretty much sums up what intense sensation is all about as sex play, but those who love it rave about it. Especially tickling. Just punch up the word on an Internet search and you'll get the idea. Dr. McIlvenna doubts that many orgasms are reached by tickling alone. "But it makes them feel good," he says.

Start from the soles of the feet and tickle your way up, suggests psychologist and sexologist Dr. Rachel Copelan in her book *100 Ways to Make Sex Sensational and 100 Percent Safe*. "Sure, we struggle against the feeling at first," she writes, "but what seems like irritation will turn to ecstasy when you finally tickle the right places, in the right way."

Flash each other. As you know, visual stimulation is the penultimate erotic tool, and one of the reasons why some people wear outrageous costumes or play into different roles. It's also the reason that the Victoria's Secret catalog is so popular. You should absolutely incorporate visual stimuli into your sex games. One of the easiest ways is to strip for each other, an activity that requires no special skills (you already do it every day) and no expensive costumes. Consider: An overwhelming number of men (93 percent) and women (81 percent) love to watch their partners undress, according to the *Sex in America* survey.

You have lightning in a bottle there, but not enough couples take ad-

Love Is in the Air

Those who have done the deed at cruising altitude swear by the experience and claim membership in a loose and lighthearted organization known as the Mile High Club.

But for average mortals, in-flight coupling used to mean negotiating those tiny commercial airline bathrooms that aren't even big enough for one person sitting still, let alone two in various postures of gyration. This is not a comfortable or sufficiently private venue for airborne antics.

Enter Nick Edgar, a licensed southern California pilot whose Mile High Adventures service offers couples private pleasure flights for $450. The "pleasure" part is just what you're thinking it is. "A lot of people fantasize about making love in an airplane," Edgar says. "This is a way to experience it in a more romantic setting."

Romantic it is. "The combination of making love in an airplane on a down-filled feather bed with your favorite lover, surrounded by romantic music, champagne, and chocolate-covered strawberries in complete privacy creates an event that's out of this world," Edgar says.

Right now Mile High Adventures is only flying out of Van Nuys Airport. So unless you're a Los Angeles–area resident, you'll have to consider squeezing in your fantasy flight between Universal Studios and the Walk of Fame on your next California trip.

The estimated 25 couples a month who fly Edgar's friendly skies are apparently performing with admirable zest. Indeed, airport-area residents have complained about the noise from the ever-increasing number of flights that take off and land at Van Nuys airport.

vantage of the potential it offers for erotic scenarios, according to Dr. Robert Birch, a psychologist who specializes in marriage and sex therapy. "Try to catch her from a different angle," he says. "Encourage her to let you catch a peek here and there, as if she didn't know you were looking." Flashing and the striptease scenario are there for the exploiting. So why settle for just kicking off your clothes as though you were in a locker room? "Keep the excitement alive," says Dr. Birch.

Go public...discreetly. If the fear-of-getting-caught scenario is your bag or you just have some exhibitionist tendencies as a couple, consider playing it out in ways that will get you excited—but not caught. Touching each other under the water in a crowded pool or at the beach is a reasonable (and thrilling) compromise, according to Harold Litten, an author who has written about human sexuality for more than 30 years. Or wandering fingers under an ample tablecloth at a packed restaurant can embellish the menu. "It's really pseudo-exhibitionism," Litten says. "It's the unexpectedness, the freshness, that makes it a hot experience."

Rings and Things

Anne Semans, co-owner of Good Vibrations, a sex accessory store in San Francisco, took the phone call: It was from a man in his seventies, wondering if Semans could help. "My Mrs. and I are looking for something in rubber and leather," he explained.

Sex toys are among the most used, and often most effective, methods of expanding one's sexual boundaries. Often, Semans says, couples are looking for something to re-ignite their sexual fires, and sex toys can really fit the

Blue Movie Dates

There's little doubt among sex researchers and therapists that explicit sex on videotape can tune up your skills while it turns you on. "If you want to learn to do things, you do better by watching," says Dr. Robert Birch, a psychologist who specializes in marriage and sex therapy.

And in addition to their educational value, or perhaps because of it, a growing proportion of triple-X viewers are couples. Blue movies are no longer just a guy thing. They're the media age horizon-broadeners for couples.

As a result of all this, sex movies, even some good ones, are easily available, sanctioned by most sex therapists, and not very expensive to rent. But it's not like you're running down to the 7-Eleven for nachos and sour cream. Porn videos are still controversial. And they can be controversial in your home. "There are a lot of women who'll throw you out of the house if you bring one home," Dr. Birch says. So proceed on your stay-at-home movie date with caution.

Make sure she wants it. Cueing up *Monty Python and the Holy Grail* after you told her you were bringing home a "British historical epic" might work as a funny shtick. But promising her a "romantic classic" and surprising her with *Debbie Does Dallas* can backfire something terrible (even though you were technically telling the truth). "You have to communicate with her on this," Dr. Birch says. "Every woman is unique, with different appetites and desires."

Make sure you want it. It doesn't matter how sea-

bill. Toys perhaps qualify more as sensation-intensifiers than as erotic scenario props, although your creative imagination can meld the categories. At any rate, they pass the extend-your-regular-pattern test since they basi-

soned a porn veteran you may be. Seeing it with the one you love (and live with) is a whole different ball of wax. "There are times where embarrassment takes over and the guy can't do anything," warns Dr. Robert O. Hawkins of the State University of New York. So it's not just for her sake that you need to talk about the whole experience beforehand.

Find one she'll go for. Most X-rated videos—in fact, until recently, all X-rated movies—cater to men's tastes, and not necessarily our most civilized ones. But some are produced with women or couples in mind. A few are even made by and for women (although with the whimsical pseudonyms prevalent in the business, it's hard to tell who's what). At any rate, it's your challenge to find the appropriate genre, even if it means asking the guy behind the counter. "You need to be discerning," Dr. Hawkins says. "Don't assume that what you find stimulating will be equally stimulating to her."

Get educational. It's pretty hard to find a plot in a sex movie anyway, so why not try the how-to kind? "There are some great sex-ed videos available that are introduced by sex therapists," says sex therapist Dr. Gina Ogden. "They're terrific teaching tools." And they teach what you want to learn—positions, techniques, and so on—not just biology. The reputable ones include the *Better Sex* series and Dr. Sandra Scantling's *Ordinary Couples, Extraordinary Sex* videos. Oh, and don't let the "educational" tag fool you. This is stimulating stuff.

cally accomplish what you're usually trying to do—stimulate each other's genitals. These days, they're easily and discretely available by mail. Two of the more reputable suppliers are Good Vibrations and the Xandria Collection in Brisbane, California. If you decide to go toy shopping, here's an idea of the sort of products you'll find.

Vibrators. Whether it's an innocent "self-massage" unit or a phallic-shaped pulsating object, this is far and away the most popular category of sex toy. The average price for a basic, battery-powered novelty item can be less than $10. Big electric massage unit/vibrators come with multiple attachments for different sensations and can cost as much as $60.

Dildos. Not to be confused with vibrators, dildos usually don't pulsate, but they're typically phallic-shaped and are meant to be inserted in your partner's vagina (much smaller ones can be used for anal pleasuring and are known as anal plugs). Some are even quite arty—shaped like whales and dolphins. The best dildos are made of silicone, which cleans easily and retains body heat, so they don't feel so cold when they're used. Prices can range anywhere from $10 to $65.

Constrictor rings. When placed on the base of the penis, the ring (often called a cock ring) traps blood in the erectile chamber, making you harder longer. Some of them also have tiny vibrators attached, so that during intercourse, women feel that sensation. "And it's sort of the male equivalent of lingerie," Semans says. "It adds kind of a visual element to sex play." Just make sure that you don't wear one for longer than 20 minutes at a time because rings cut off blood flow to the penis. If fresh blood doesn't get pumped in there, you could be looking at tissue damage. Stick with rings that are easier to take off like elastic or latex rings, or try a leather ring with snaps or a Velcro release. Typical cost: $3.50 to $20.

Lubricants. These are great sensation-enhancers for both of you, but especially for her. As women get older, they lubricate less and it takes them longer to become aroused. Luckily, there are many commercial lubricants to choose from that mimic the properties of a woman's natural fluids. Astroglide and K-Y Jelly are two examples.

A lot of couples are embarrassed to buy sex toys and aids, acknowledges Semans. "But there definitely are plenty of people out there who take that leap and try something new." Maybe you could be one of them.

Of Human Bondage

Once you've explored some basic erotic scenarios or toyed with the toys, your mind may start to turn toward other forms of sex play. We're talking about what you thought we were talking about when you first started reading this chapter: bondage, dominance/submission, spanking. In short, the supercharged erotic stuff you always thought of as being at the edge of your sexual horizon.

One look at the back of the classifieds confirms it. Sometimes it seems like half the country is into dominance, the other half submission.

Popular as it is, the notion persists that the dominance/submission scene is a back-alley phenomenon that has no place in a solid relationship. *Au contraire*, says Dr. Hawkins. A relationship is the best place to engage in this kind of erotic behavior if you're so inclined.

Why? Because, Dr. Hawkins says, it relates to couples' fantasies—her romance-novel ravishment, his call of the wild. Because it's a potential mine of mutual pleasure that couples can help each other explore. And, if it includes bondage, because it's most safely done in a relationship.

"If it's a situation where you're going to be tied up or restrained in any way, don't do it with a stranger," says Dr. Hawkins. "That's too dangerous. You do something like that with somebody you're connected with."

Letting one partner dominate the other in an exaggerated way can be a popular form of sex play among couples because it taps into a key element of their sex lives, says sex therapist Dr. Louanne Cole Weston. When you think about it, says Dr. Weston, little mini-dominations go on all the time while you're having sex. Somebody decides we're going to stop kissing now. Somebody decides we're going to roll over this way. "All these things have to do with who's in charge, who's running things at the moment," Dr. Weston says.

Pull that little thread of thought, and you have a long string that can lead to a dominant/submissive scenario. Maybe you like it when you do most of the leading. Maybe sometimes it's nice when she does all of the leading. Maybe one day you just lie back while she does whatever she wants to you. Then vice versa. By then, maybe a little cord around the wrists and the bedposts is just the next step.

Which doesn't, by the way, lead to harder stuff. The point of light bondage within a marriage is to increase sexual pleasure by exaggerating (with the aid of knots) the role of do-er and done-to, even to the point of imposing "discipline." But that doesn't mean the next thing you know you have a Harley-Davidson on your king-size and a wife in jackboots. "The whips-and-chains thing is an extreme version with a particular look to it," says Dr. Weston. "That's not what it's all about."

A lot of people, perhaps assuming that all that kinky stuff is the same, confuse sexual spanking with the discipline aspect of some dominant/submissive behavior. "Spanking is very different from bondage," Dr. Hawkins says. "People who are into spanking basically really like the spanking itself. There's seldom any bondage or discipline attached to it."

Again, spanking is a turn-on for some couples because it grows out of what they like to do in their "normal" sex life. Some fanny-slapping during intercourse—he to her in the rear-entry position, she to him in the missionary—seems almost natural and very pleasant to a lot of people.

Turning one another over the knee is just formalizing the issue. If you're interested in pursuing this form of erotic play, proceed carefully. To keep it fun and safe for both of you, here are some ground rules.

Find a starting point. Don't dive right into the deep end, suggests Dr. Weston. Test the shallow waters first. It's not like you have to be tied up tonight. "If you're looking for that feeling of being dominated or dominating, you can find an easy place to start and work your way from there," she says. That could mean clasping the headboard with untied hands instead of tying yourself to it, or adding a few extra slaps during intercourse instead of full-fledged spanking.

Tie it lightly. Many couples find that light tying with ribbons is all they really need for dominant/submissive pleasure. "It's the symbolism that counts," Dr. Weston says. "Tying somebody up with ribbons is not going to keep them tied up. But it makes it clear who's in charge and who's receiving."

In fact, she says, you can do it with nothing but thread, which is hard not to break during sex. Then turn it around by threatening to stop what you're doing if she breaks the thread.

Keep it fun. Even if she's not against it, the idea of an offbeat scenario can be intimidating to your partner. How would you feel if somebody bigger than you told you out of the blue that he'd like to spank you? Don't let things sound frightening to her. Try the humor route, suggests Dr. Copelan, as well as switching the initial spanker and spankee. "It's less offensive to her," she says. "Say, 'You know, I've been a bad boy and I'd like you to spank me.' She might have a lot of fun doing it."

A Sampler of Kiss Types

One of the quickest ways to broaden your sexual horizons is simply by varying an old theme. Kissing, for instance. To help you get started, here are some offbeat kisses that have already been created for you.

The hummer. Add a little vibration to your osculation by humming as you press her lips. Talk about a buzz. You can work your way up from a monotone hum through a melody you both like and on to Beethoven's Ninth. And by the way, the humming is even more titillating when the venue is moved further south on the body map.

The vacuum. It's the Coneheads' favorite. Tone it down a bit, though, and you have yourself a slightly silly but very sexy kissing riff. What you do is (gently, nicely, slowly) suck some of the air out of your lover's mouth as you kiss. Don't laugh until you've tried it.

The upside-downer. Nothing like a new angle to change your view of what a kiss should be. You can do it by leaning over her from behind while she's sitting and you're standing. Or lie on a bed with her feet facing east and yours west. The point is that top lips are touching bottom lips.

The shocker. This one was big in the 1930s and 1940s. Rub your feet back and forth on a rug to build up a static charge before you move in for the smacker. It's a great way to put the spark back in your kissing. For the record, rug-rubbing is the safe way to do it. We won't even mention what those prewar teenagers did with battery cable clips and wall sockets.

The sweet thing. You may even have tried this one in your teens. All you do is pass a piece of candy back and forth as you smooch. Why should it just be kid stuff? It never hurts a relationship to be more sharing. Mints and hard candy drops work best.

Overcoming Roadblocks

How to Make Time for Sex

Back in those heady first days of courtship, you never thought your love life would come to this. The long, lusty afternoons that melted into passionate nights. Staying up to greet the sunrise as you held each other close. But before you get too rapturous, Romeo, let's fast-forward to the present. To a dual-career marriage, kids, mortgage—the works. And those red-hot, marathon lovemaking sessions? Truth be told, nowadays they're often replaced by something very different.

What we're talking about here is hurried, harried, beat-the-clock lovemaking. Trying to steal a few minutes under the covers, with one eye on the bedroom door, praying that your three-year-old will stay tuned to the "Alphabet Song" just a little while longer.

Or maybe the specialty of your house is *Nightline* sex: Your wife, vainly trying to wait up until you get home from yet another business trip, conks out in bed as Ted Koppel drones sweet nothings in her ear.

The numbers back up the frustrations we're feeling. A study by Runzheimer International, a consulting firm in Rochester, Wisconsin, found that the average business traveler spends 51 days a year on the road—with some respondents away from home as many as 150 days. That's a lot of opportunities for missed anniversaries and belated birthdays. In your role as breadwinner, you're also losing something in the deal.

Most of us need to face some tough questions, according to Rich C. Moore, a counselor and seminar leader in St. Louis.

"Have we adjusted our lifestyles to meet our desired incomes? Is climbing the corporate ladder worth the possible damage to our relationships? It all comes down to the choices we make," Moore says.

Dueling Schedules

It can be tough to unleash your sensuality if the object of your desire is usually backing out of the driveway as you pull in, and vice versa. Fortunately, there are some things you can do to keep the passion alive when your schedules just don't jibe.

Keep in touch. Be affectionate with each other. Give hugs and kisses, hold hands, put your arm around her shoulders—even if it's only in passing. This ongoing contact keeps the flame of passion turned on and is more likely to lead to closeness and sex, says clinical psychologist and marriage and family therapist Dr. Jonathan M. Kramer.

Do the write thing. "You simply can't talk enough," says Ab Jackson, a management consultant, seminar leader, and author of the audiocassette program *Organize Your Life and Get Rid of Clutter.* "If you can't be together, use phone calls, voice mail, the fax machine, a letter under the pillow. The more the better."

The power of the Post-it note for reaching out and touching someone is lauded  by Moore. A sexy message, silly poem, or a simple "I love you" can really make someone's day.

Steal away. We all need to blow off our duties every once in a while for a little R and R. Relationships can benefit enormously from this tactic, Moore believes. And don't bother feeling guilty about abandoning your post either. If you're like most of us, he says, you're probably working far more than 40 hours a week. So getting away from the office every now and then should be no problem. Moore's personal favorite? A midweek matinee, just you and your wife, munching on Gummy Bears and popcorn while the rest of civilization toils away at its labors.

Sacrifice some Zzzs. Spouses who work different shifts have an especially tough row to hoe. But if each of you is willing to give up a little sleep, you can snag some quality time together, says Diane Dashner, clinical director of Family and Community Services in Burlington, New Jersey.

"Your wife picks a night to stay up and watch Letterman with you while you unwind from work; maybe you share a bottle of wine. Conversely, you get up early one morning with her and relax together over coffee. By planning in advance, it gives both partners something to look forward to," Dashner says.

Make a date. "One night a week, without fail, my wife and I have a scheduled date night," says Moore. "It can be as simple as window-shopping at the mall, or as elaborate as an overnight stay at a bed-and-breakfast." The point, he says, is to stick to it faithfully. You don't indiscriminately skip out on appointments and meetings at work just because you're feeling jammed up, so don't cancel your dates either.

The Sunday Night Fights

Is there a relationship scenario tougher to deal with than the commuter marriage? Charlie Brown Jr., Ph.D., a family psychologist in private practice in Charlotte, North Carolina, can't think of one.

"When a husband and wife are separated by the miles and see each other only on the weekend, this can place a whole new set of stresses on a marriage," Dr. Brown says.

A phenomenon observed by Dr. Brown in his years of counseling couples in this situation is something he's dubbed the Sunday Night Fights.

"Just as there's more pressure to have a good time when you don't see each other often, so too does the anxiety build as you get closer to the time of separation," Dr. Brown explains. "Ironically, many people find it easier to part if they start a fight. Somehow it's less emotionally wrenching to leave in the wake of a disagreement."

Rather than lacing up the gloves come Sunday afternoon or evening, Dr. Brown recommends that you and your partner begin planning a "gentle exit" the night before. "By starting to 'check out' mentally and emotionally well in advance of the actual parting, you'll find it much easier to pull it off without a lot of tension," he says.

And your time together will be that much more enjoyable if you're both not dreading the witching hour.

Family Man

Let's face facts: Those beautiful little cherubs gobble up a lot of your time and attention. Here's how to make it through the years of diapers, dolls, and driving lessons with the flames of desire still burning.

Send them to bed. For tired bodies and frayed nerves, you can't beat the end of the day. Thankfully, you and your partner can get some precious time alone in the evening, provided you control your youngsters' bedtimes. Sounds like obvious commonsense advice, but lots of families don't do it.

"There's a temptation, especially in very busy households, to let the kids stay up later so the family can spend time together," says

Norman Epstein, Ph.D., professor of family studies at the University of Maryland in College Park and a marriage and family therapist. "But setting a regular, reasonable bedtime hour for the kids gives parents much-needed quiet time together at the end of a long day."

Get help. Ask Moore for the most important advice he has for couples with children and he'll answer, without hesitation, "Hire a babysitter." But this isn't always feasible, especially for young couples who perhaps can't afford a sitter as often as they'd like.

If that's the case, Dashner recommends setting up a cooperative nightcare among your neighbors and friends.

Let the kids pitch in. Rather than looking to isolate yourselves from the kids, you can enlist them to help you enjoy a cozy candlelight dinner at home, suggests family psychologist Dr. Charlie Brown Jr. "Depending on their ages, they can set the table, light the candles, even serve the food. Kids enjoy pitching in to protect Mom and Dad's privacy, so they can also screen phone calls so that you're not interrupted," Dr. Brown says.

At-Home Vacations

We all dream about vacationing in exotic locales, but in reality, the best place for you to really unwind may be your own home. This is an especially good ploy if both you and your wife have jobs that require travel, says family psychologist Dr. Charlie Brown Jr.

But it's important to keep your respite-from-the-road a secret, at least from certain people. "If your boss, the in-laws, or anyone else who might intrude upon your privacy asks if you'll be in town, simply tell them, 'We have plans and won't be available until whenever,'" he advises.

The key is to treat yourselves to a true vacation by doing only those things that are relaxing and bring you pleasure. (Here's a built-in advantage to get you started: no need to do any dreaded packing.) "Take a long, slow bike ride followed by a mid-afternoon nap; prepare a gourmet meal together and crack open a bottle of good wine; get fresh-squeezed orange juice and flowers for Sunday morning. Just flat-out pamper yourselves," Dr. Brown says. "This can also include putzing around the house or yard, but I encourage staying away from major projects. The goal is relaxation."

Travelin' Man

You're away from home so much that your wife is threatening to put your face on a milk carton, eh? Then you need some tips for keeping it together on the road.

Write it down. Jackson leaves his itinerary behind whenever he goes on the road. "I want my wife to know where I am and what I'm doing at all times," he says. "This also makes staying in touch a two-way street since she can reach me as easily as I can reach her."

Rather than spending the wee small hours of the morning alone in a hotel lounge listening to, well, "In the Wee Small Hours of the Morning," take a cue from Jackson and bring your wife along on the occasional business trip. Hint: She'd probably enjoy Montreal a bit more than Peoria.

Phone home—twice. When you call from the road, try to phone once earlier in the day when you can talk to the kids and give them your full attention, suggests Dashner. Then when you call to talk to your wife in the evening, "you can have a decent conversation without the children pulling on Mom's skirt and interrupting because they want to talk to Daddy."

Part Four

Sharing Your Lives

Marriage vs. Living Together

What You Need to Know

If you marry, you will regret it. If you do not marry, you will also regret it.
—Danish philosopher Søren Kierkegaard

You're in love and in a quandary. The woman you've been seeing is pretty, smart, funny, and makes a wicked jambalaya. Heck, she even has a good income. And yet the thought of proposing marriage puts a knot in your stomach like the one you got in grade school on the day report cards came out.

The dilemma is this: You don't know if your relationship will be the sweet real-life equivalent of Paul Reiser and Helen Hunt on *Mad about You* or the nightmare of bickering Michael Douglas and Kathleen Turner in *The War of the Roses.*

"Marriages are made in heaven," says one proverb.

"Marriage is a noose," wrote Cervantes in *Don Quixote.*

Conflicting messages are everywhere. And so, you think, maybe we ought to live together first, as a sort of trial run before the main event.

Living Together

Is living together a good idea? A way to dip one's toe into the matrimonial waters without actually taking the plunge?

For those who believe that premarital sex and living together before marriage are morally wrong, it's a moot question. But for those who are not

sure, the advice from experts is mixed.

"I'm a big proponent of it," says Jonathan M. Kramer, Ph.D., a clinical psychologist and marriage and family therapist in La Jolla, California, and author of *Losing the Weight of the World* and *Why Men Don't Get Enough Sex and Women Don't Get Enough Love.* "I think of the living together part as a warmup to marriage, when you find out if you're really meant for each other. My wife and I lived together for more than five years before we got married."

Living together enables a couple to see beyond the honeymoon or infatuation phase, says Dr. Kramer, who has been married for 18 years. "The best way to find out who somebody is is by living day-to-day with that person. That's how you get to know the person more fully."

Couples today are far more likely to live together before marriage than were their parents. The authors of *Sex in America* found that 94 percent of women and 85 percent of men born between 1933 and 1942 got married before ever living with their partners. But only 35 percent of women and 34 percent of men born between 1963 and 1974 got married without living with their partners first.

Living together, however, is not necessarily a good way to prepare for marriage, cautions David Olson, Ph.D., professor of family social science at the University of Minnesota in St. Paul. A couple may share a bedroom, but they may not work through various issues that a married couple would be more inclined to tackle, he says.

"They don't cohabit like a married couple; they often play at living together," Dr. Olson says. "Living together helps you become more aware of some of the things you don't like. But couples need to learn to resolve their differences."

In fact, couples who marry after living together have higher divorce rates than those who don't. A nationwide study conducted in part by Larry Bumpass, Ph.D., sociology professor at the University of Wisconsin in Madison, found that the number of couples separating or divorcing within 10 years was one-third higher among those who lived together before marriage than among those who did not.

"My feeling is that it's one of those examples where statistics lie," says Dr. Kramer. "I bet that there are zillions of people who didn't get married because they lived together and realized that they were incompatible, and it saved them from getting a divorce later on."

But Dr. Bumpass says the higher divorce rate among those who first lived together makes sense. "Those who hold the least traditional views are more likely to be accepting of cohabitation and more likely to be accepting of divorce as a solution," he says. "Put differently, those who would never think of cohabiting would never think of divorcing."

Couples also often live together because they hope to resolve uncertainty about their relationships, whereas those who marry right away are less apt to be plagued by such doubts, adds Dr. Bumpass.

Dr. Kramer agrees with Dr. Olson that living together first does not by itself ensure wedded bliss. "Whether you succeed, I think, is unrelated to whether you live together," he says. "There are other issues that are important: the ability to communicate, to see things from the other person's perspective, to do problem-solving—all those other kinds of skills come into play then."

Dr. Olson has developed PREPARE/ENRICH, a counseling program that includes questionnaires for premarital and married couples, respectively. Based on their responses to

Marriage Stats

When it comes to marrying and divorcing, Nevada is the nation's hub of happiness and heartbreak. No other state comes close. This is among the snapshots of our marital health gleaned from recent statistics collected by the U.S. government.

- There were more than six times as many marriages in Nevada per thousand population as the next highest state, Hawaii. The state with the least marrying people? Pennsylvania, followed closely by West Virginia.

- Nevada also was easily the most divorce-prone state. Massachusetts residents were most likely to remain hitched.

- People married at a greater clip in the West and the South than in other regions of the country.

- More couples were married in June than any other month. January had the fewest marriages.

- Nearly 1 out of 6 brides marrying for the first time was a teenager. In 1970, nearly 4 out of 10 were teens.

- Almost one divorce out of three involved couples married one to four years. About one in eight occurred in marriages of 20 years or longer.

- Alabama led the nation in divorces occurring in marriages of less than one year, while Virginia had the fewest such quickie dissolutions.

- The wife was awarded custody of the children 72 percent of the time in divorce cases where this was an issue. Husbands got custody in 9 percent, while there was joint custody 16 percent of the time.

the PREPARE questionnaire, Dr. Olson says that whether couples will divorce can be predicted with 80 to 85 percent accuracy regardless of whether they live together.

Is there a downside to living together? "I suppose it takes some of the glamour and mystery out of marriage," Dr. Kramer says. "The traditional system was that you didn't know each other really well beforehand. Then you got together at your wedding, and you got to know each other and grew together and learned about each other sexually and in all other ways after the marriage. I don't know that that works in our era. How many people are saving themselves for marriage? I don't think it's a lot in modern society. So I don't know that the mystery element is there anyway."

About 90 percent of young people surveyed in *Sex in America* had intercourse by the time they were 22. "Since the average age of marriage is now in the mid-twenties, few Americans wait until they marry to have sex," the authors concluded.

More recently, however, the federal government released figures showing a decline in the number of young women and men who had intercourse between the ages of 15 and 19. This trend may mean that more people are waiting until they're married to have sex.

Present and Accounted For

Who among us hasn't witnessed this sorry sight: A guy at his fiancée's bridal shower, smiling gamely while his bride-to-be opens yet another box of towels or a set of linens.

Now, these are things men need and use, too, but we give them about five seconds of thought. Women, however, can become downright giddy about the color and weight of a bath mat. Many of them even believe fervently that it must match the bathroom decor.

It's no wonder that one guy we know asked for and received a 1956 Sandy Koufax baseball card from a buddy for a wedding present so that he'd have one gift that he would really relish.

Happily, this state of affairs is changing. The reason? Guys are becoming more actively involved in all aspects of their weddings. On the Internet, Black & Decker now has a site in which the company suggests wedding gifts of its

Getting Married

You've probably heard it said many times: Marriage is simply a piece of paper. Why bother? In fact, it is much more.

"Somehow, when you make a legal contract, it's a statement in front of society that you don't walk away so easily," Dr. Kramer says. "If you're just living together and you're fighting and it's not working out, you can say, 'I'm out of here' and it's pretty easy to do. You don't do that when you're married. There's much more of a feeling of being bonded together and committed. Then you're forced to deal with things you might not otherwise deal with if you were just living together."

Being married also carries considerable financial obligations. You and your wife probably pool your financial resources and make joint decisions on how to spend money. But you and your live-in girlfriend quite possibly keep your funds separate and spend as you please. And if you marry and divorce, you may well be ordered to pay alimony or child support, or both. It's something to consider, since half of the marriages in America end in divorce—the highest rate in the world.

Prenuptial Paperwork

Nobody likes to dwell on it, especially if they're about to be married, but there's a lot at stake financially if your marriage fails. Some

own products, which include such manly wares as circular saws, sanders, and workstations for storing tools. The site address is http://www.blackanddecker.com/bridal.

"We have noticed a trend," says Denise Ryan, Black & Decker's director of marketing communications. "You find more and more couples putting together their gift lists and including his and her type of products."

And that's not all. Janet Renner's Royal Hawaiian Weddings helps plan about 250 nuptials a year—everything from what food to serve, what music to play, and which photographer to hire. "In probably 50 to 75 percent of the weddings, men work jointly with the brides in making the decisions," Renner says.

Men tend to become most involved in the overall cost of the ceremony and reception, especially if the couple is paying for their own wedding, Renner says. "The thing they get involved in least is the flowers," Renner adds.

men, and a few women, insist on prenuptial agreements. A prenup typically spells out how your property will be divided and whether alimony will be paid, including how much and for how long, if you divorce. Inheritance rights often are addressed, and sometimes child support, but not visitation or custody issues.

Family law attorneys say men about to embark on their second or third marriage are the most likely to seek a prenup. That's because they felt fleeced after earlier marriages ended in divorce, or they have children and want to protect their inheritances.

Both the prospective bride and groom should hire lawyers when a prenup is at issue, advises Eric D. Turner, an attorney specializing in matrimonial and family law in

Media, Pennsylvania. "It's not mandatory, but it's highly advisable," he says. "A lot of lawsuits about prenuptial agreements have to do with the fact that one person didn't have a lawyer and claims that 'you just jammed it down my throat' or 'I was pregnant and desperate to get married, and you made me sign this agreement.'"

Couples often are concerned that prenups imply that their marriages will fail or that they don't trust one another, lawyers say. And they complain that it makes a romantic event little more than a business transaction.

"This is the most difficult thing we face in doing prenuptial agreements. On the one hand, the parties are in love and wanting to get married, and on the other hand, the nasty lawyers are arguing already about what's going to happen when they get divorced," Turner says.

"There's no getting around the fact that it does take the shine off the romantic idea of marriage," adds Thomas Railsback, a family law attorney in Dallas. "That's why I see few people in first marriages do prenuptials."

If you are going to ask the woman you love to sign a prenuptial agreement before you marry, it's not the sort of thing you want to spring on her at the last minute. "I think any way you can present that topic as an aside or in a what-do-you-think-about-it manner is a whole lot better than at the time of proposal," Railsback says. "I doubt that a proposal is going to be very well received if it's followed with a caveat: 'By the way, I want a prenup.'"

And while the subject of a prenuptial pact is sensitive, it probably won't scuttle your marriage plans if it's handled tactfully, Turner says. "What usually winds up happening is that the dependent spouse-to-be caves in and signs what she's asked to sign," he says.

A Healthy Marriage

It's the great tug-of-war: Men don't want to commit. Women want them to commit. A lot of guys—maybe even you—view marriage as warily as a trip to Las Vegas: You might get lucky, but you also could end up broke and brokenhearted. It's a gamble. Yet men who do marry are generally happier than the women so anxious to get them to the altar. What's going on here?

"I think men are more dependent on women emotionally and socially," Dr. Kramer says. "I think our needs are met more by women, and women are in certain ways able to fend for themselves better."

So, tough guy, still skeptical that marriage will make you healthier and happier? Still busting a gut when you hear the old joke that one of the most dangerous foods known to mankind is wedding cake? Then consider this.

- Married men report greater satisfaction with their lives than single guys.
- Men on low-fat diets who have the support of their wives are up to five times more likely to meet their weight goals than men who got the least support, according to researchers at the University of Washington.
- Prostate cancer was 80 percent more likely to be diagnosed at an early stage in married men than never-married men, a study in New York concluded.
- Middle-age men who live alone or with somebody other than spouses are twice as likely to die within 10 years as men of the same age who live with their wives, according to a University of California at San Francisco study.

And then there's this benefit: While cohabiting and married couples have sex a lot more than folks not living with a lover, those who are hitched report the most satisfying sex, physically and emotionally.

Making Marriage Work

Even though studies show that guys thrive while married, the popular perception remains that a married man is a harried man. "American women expect to find in their husbands a perfection that English women only hope to find in their butlers," the British author William Somerset Maugham once said.

Actually, both partners may bring to marriage a template for how each ought to behave based on how their own parents interacted, says Mel Krantzler, Ph.D., director of the Creative Divorce, Love, and Marriage Counseling Center in San Rafael, California, and co-author with his wife, Pat, of *The Seven Marriages of Your Marriage*, *The New Creative Divorce*, and *Learning to Love Again*. "The more that expectations clash about what a good wife or husband must be like, the more diminished each becomes in the other's eyes," Dr. Krantzler says.

Here are some ways to avoid falling into that trap.

Get a history lesson. Couples need to tell each other in detail their family backgrounds, so each can better understand and tolerate the differences between them, Dr. Krantzler contends. It's also a good way to build intimacy since you're getting to know each other that much better.

Banish the boss. For a guy who grew up in the traditional family where Dad was the sole or principal breadwinner and mom took care of the house and kids, marriage to a modern woman can be an especially tough adjustment.

"I've heard a lot of women say, especially in the last five years, that as they have become more successful in their careers, they're less and less dependent upon men economically," says Dr. Kramer. "If they're not treated right, a lot of women are saying, 'What do I need marriage for?' So I think the pressure is being turned up on guys to be better partners than they had to be in the past, when they could say, 'I'm supporting you. I'm bringing home my paycheck. Isn't that enough?'

"Well, I don't think it is enough anymore."

Know your math. The key element to a good marriage is not that couples always agree, but that they find a way to resolve conflicts that works for them, says John Gottman, Ph.D., professor of psychology at the University of Washington in Seattle, who has studied married couples for more than 20 years. Ultimately, it all comes down to a simple mathematical formula, says Dr. Gottman in his book *Why Marriages Succeed or Fail.* A couple must have at least five times as many positive as negative moments together if their marriage is to be stable.

The hard work that goes into making a marriage work is worth it, say those who study such matters. "Married men live longer, and their general level of happiness and life satisfaction is significantly higher," Dr. Kramer says. "They eat better and have better habits. They're more connected with others."

"Marriage offers the opportunity of maximizing one's sense of achievement," adds Dr. Krantzler. "Two equal people joined together help each other actualize their own individual potential as well as the couple potential. With marriage, you are better able to prevail over difficulties rather than to cop out of them."

So should you marry the woman you love? Perhaps the advice of Socrates still applies today: "By all means marry; if you get a good wife, you'll become happy; if you get a bad one, you'll become a philosopher."

Common Law

If you're like a lot of us, you grew up hearing that if you live with a woman, she becomes your common-law wife after seven years of sharing a home. But length of time together has nothing to do with it, says Eric D. Turner, an attorney specializing in matrimonial and family law.

In order for you to have a common-law marriage, Turner says, you must consider yourselves married and represent yourself as husband and wife to the community. The distinction can be important.

"Common-law marriage is a true marriage," says family law attorney Thomas Railsback. "All the benefits that flow from a common-law marriage are exactly the same as those that exist in a ceremonial marriage." In other words, the woman you live with may be entitled to money if you split up or if you die.

Determining if a couple had a common-law marriage when this is in dispute can be tricky business. Certain circumstances, such as owning a house and other property jointly and listing each other as beneficiaries on life insurance policies can imply such a relationship existed, says Railsback.

"If they filed a federal income tax return together, many judges are going to say these folks are married because they represented themselves to the federal government as married," Railsback says.

A man living with a woman out of wedlock might consider getting her to sign a cohabitation agreement, spelling out all the rights and obligations of the couple's living arrangement, Turner says. In Texas, however, such a pact wouldn't be recognized by the courts, Railsback says. He advises men to learn what the laws say regarding cohabitation in the states in which they live.

Setting Up House

Harmony on the Home Front

Want to put a relationship to the test? Try decorating a room together. Or sharing a bathroom each and every day. Or a refrigerator, for that matter. And yet, there is little choice. If you are to be long-term lovers, ultimately, you are going to live together, which means you must get over the challenges of sharing a living space. The thing is that home decorating not only can spark disagreements about taste but it also can cause feelings of being suffocated, stifled, and confined—particularly if either or both of you previously lived on your own.

These differences can be especially delicate if one partner is moving into the home of the other, rather than the two of them looking for a neutral site, says Riley K. Smith, a marriage and family counselor and co-author of *True Partners: A Workbook for Building a Lasting, Intimate Relationship.* That's because the partner into whose home the other is moving already has his things on shelves and walls as well as his own way of doing things, making his mate feel like it's not her home, too.

"It's a very important difference," Smith says. "Unless people sit down and talk about this stuff, it can get really weird."

People usually have pre-existing notions about cohabitation that stem from sharing a house with parents and siblings while growing up, Smith notes. In some cases, individuals want to emulate their old homestead; in other cases, they want the exact opposite. Either way,

these unspoken "rules" emerge when you move in with somebody.

Indeed, there is "an enormous code of secrecy surrounding the newlywed year," Samuel L. Pauker, M.D., and Miriam Arond wrote in *The First Year of Marriage: What to Expect, What to Accept, and What You Can Change for a Lasting Marriage.* Perhaps that goes for the first year of any living-together arrangement.

Couples tend to idealize each other during courtship, say Dr. Pauker and Arond. They are drawn together by what they have in common, but they overlook each others' faults. Once they're married, those faults become more evident, and they become disappointed in their partners and often more critical of them.

Working It Out

Domestic skirmishes needn't escalate into full-fledged battles if you simply show some empathy and courtesy. Give peace a chance and preserve your domestic tranquillity with these strategies.

Negotiate and compromise. Discuss the problem before it becomes emotionally charged. Most of your differences can be worked out through a little give-and-take, Smith says. So if your partner feels strongly that the dishes ought to be washed right after dinner, and you feel just as strongly that they can wait, you might suggest that she wash them in return for your doing one of her daily chores.

Seek common ground. Try not to take a partner's behavior personally, urge Dr. Pauker and Arond. You know, for example, that leaving the toilet seat up is an old habit that has nothing to do with her. So why take it so personally when she absentmindedly moves the TV remote from your designated spot? Instead, focus on what the two of you have in common, and gently work out the small details.

Be reasonable. Discuss differences in a spirit of goodwill rather than when you are angry, Smith says. You can do this by stressing that you aren't trying to autocratically impose your tastes or standards, but rather reach a mutually satisfying decision. Often, the person objecting to something the partner wants isn't really opposed to it, but wants to know that his or her wants are of equal importance. "One person gives in, or both people give in a little, and they come up with an accommodation that neither of them particularly likes but they're willing to live with," Smith says.

Pick your battles. You can avoid conflicts by arguing only for those things that truly matter to you.

Smith did just that with an abstract painting featuring buttocks that he loves but his wife doesn't. "There was a value judgment going on that turned into a real battle," he recalls. "She compromised. She's still not altogether happy about it. I insisted it was very important to me. We hung the painting."

Mark your territory. Smith and his wife agree on most household furnishings, but to avoid conflicts, they came up with a plan in which each gets something. Decorating decisions in some rooms of their house, such as his office, are made by Smith. Other rooms, including the living room, fall under the aesthetic jurisdiction of his wife. And some rooms, such as the family room, are joint decisions. "That has worked out really well for us," he says.

Don't nag. Finally, there are times when you're just going to hit a brick wall. When a compromise isn't possible, agree to disagree, and make a conscious effort to stop pestering your mate to change.

Sentimental Journey

You and your partner each have a television, a stereo, a set of dishes, works of art—and not enough room in your new home for them all. One of you can place your possessions in storage, sell them, or loan them to a friend or relative. But which partner should make the sacrifice?

"I recommend that you sit down and decide what style you want," says Melinda Sechrist, owner of an interior design company in Seattle. "Then you look at what you have. You go through it and keep the best stuff."

Sechrist has these words of caution, however, for the person with the best stuff. "When one person has a sentimental thing that he or she wants to keep, the other person really has to try to understand that, even if it's the ugliest thing you've ever seen. It could be something like a rocking chair that her mother rocked her in as a baby. You try to find spaces you can use those things in."

Sechrist knows of what she speaks. When she married, her husband was appalled that she wanted to toss his set of glasses featuring Looney Tunes characters that he acquired in college. "He loved those glasses. That was a sentimental-value thing. I'm looking at these glasses thinking, 'These are stupid. They take up a lot of room.' But he really liked those glasses, so we ended up keeping them until my children broke them all."

Letting go of grievances is one of the big keys to making a relationship succeed. Conflict is inevitable, so if we don't learn to compromise and let go of bad feelings, says Dr. Kramer, then the relationship is doomed to fail.

Managing a Household

Dividing Labor by Two

Here's a tradition as American as beer and baseball. Once you set up house with a woman, you leave most of the household chores to her. Especially those that are tedious and need doing most often. You do this even if, like you, she works hard all week at a full-time job.

Study after study has shown that women continue to do more housework than men, even women who work outside the home. Some estimates have wives, regardless of their employment status, doing more than twice the housework of their husbands.

That's a pretty good deal if you can get away with it. But some women think that this division of household labor should go the same route as corsets and the six-day workweek.

Who Does What

Women have good reason to feel that way, especially if they're married. According to research done by sociologists from two universities, men and women who are married do the most disproportionate amount of housework, compared to unmarried, divorced, or widowed men and women. Men do increase the number of hours they devote to chores when there are children in the house. But their wives increase their hours of housework even more, further increasing their share of the drudgery.

Who does which chores is often determined by gender. Studies show that women are more likely than men to cook,

wash dishes, do laundry, and clean the house, while men tend to be responsible for things like home repairs, yard work, and car maintenance. A few tasks, such as buying groceries and paying bills, seem to be more equally divided between men and women.

Chores done mostly by women, however, tend to be those that need to be done every day, such as cooking and washing the dishes. Men, meanwhile, are apt to do mostly irregular or sporadic tasks that can be scheduled more flexibly, such as auto repair and yard work, according to a study done by two sociology professors at Bowling Green State University in Ohio. Women spend far more time on the routine chores than men do on the irregular housework.

Chore Leave

The roots of our household slothfulness run deep. Teenage girls spend about twice as much time per week as boys doing housework. And in homes where both parents work, daughters help more around the house than sons. Little wonder then that when we guys get older and set up house with women, we expect them to do most of the chores. Old habits die hard.

Yet only about 33 percent of husbands and wives think this situation is unfair to wives. The authors of one study say the reasons why women don't complain more about their share of the workload around the home include:

Ideology. Boys and girls often are brought up to believe that housework is the domain of females. As adults, we still perceive household chores as women's work.

Power. A woman who has few alternatives to the relationship she's in and who is financially dependent on a man may feel she must do the bulk of the housework.

Equity. A man who works longer hours than his partner or helps out in other areas such as child care is more likely to be forgiven for shirking his share of household chores.

It's easy, however, to understand why some women are resentful and angry over the fact that they are stuck with most of the housework—especially if they, too, work outside the home. It's not just a matter of fairness. Housework can be perceived as menial. The man who shares in these chores is demonstrating that his wife is an equal, not a servant.

Resolving Household Differences

Even if you and your partner divide household chores equally, there still may be disputes over style. She may see red when you throw colors together with whites in the washing machine. If you, on the other hand, like the house so clean that you could eat off the floor, it will bug you that your partner is content to give the floor a quick once-over with the vacuum or a mop.

"The house symbolically is your castle," says Samuel L. Pauker, M.D., assistant clinical professor of psychiatry at Cornell University Medical College at New York Hospital–Payne Whitney Clinic in New York City and co-author of *The First Year of Marriage: What to Expect, What to Accept, and What You Can Change for a Lasting Marriage.* "For one person, messiness might be freedom. For another, it might be aesthetic horror."

Most disagreements about household tasks are resolved fairly easily, Dr. Pauker says. "They call for communication and negotiation," he says. "One of the things couples usually aren't prepared for, however, is that because of

---

Mr. Clean

Even if you're not doing your share of the household chores, you probably spend more time on them than you would like. Here are a few expert tips on how to get them done faster, offered by family and consumer sciences agent Mary Longo in the Ohio State University newsletter *LifeTime* and by clinical psychologist and marriage family therapist Dr. Jonathan M. Kramer.

- Use both hands when cleaning. Finish a step with one hand while starting the next step with the other hand.
- Go ahead and splurge on spiffy cleaning tools. You'll be more likely to clean if you have them. Put supplies in a bucket to carry from room to room.
- If something isn't dirty, don't clean it. Vertical surfaces collect dirt much more slowly than horizontal surfaces.
- Keep up with cleaning all year rather than exhausting yourself right before a major holiday or family event.
- If you have children, give them responsibility for putting away their belongings. Provide a large box or basket to make it easier.
- Set a time limit for your cleaning. And when that time is up, stop. You have better things to do. Don't you?
- If you finish first, help her out with her chores, says Dr. Kramer. Be on the same team, looking out for each other's best interests.
- Take pride in your home and your work, says Dr. Kramer. Do a good job.

---

the need for negotiation, there often is a kind of transformation of love. Rather than being idealized and blissful, once you have to negotiate and argue, it changes the nature of the passionate bond."

For example, your sweetie may complain

that you don't do enough in the kitchen, then object to or criticize your attempts to help with dinner. Chances are that while she resents having to cook every night herself, she also feels that the kitchen is her turf and her area of expertise, and she's reluctant to let anybody intrude upon it.

Here are some ways Dr. Pauker says household conflicts can be resolved.

Divide and conquer. Divvy up the various household jobs according to which ones fit each of you best. If one of you has a knack for fixing things and the other enjoys yard work, there is a natural division of labor. If you stay up late at night and your mate turns in early, offer to wash the dishes so she can relax before bedtime if she agrees to prepare dinner. It's not always possible to divide chores fairly or to each partner's satisfaction, but splitting up these jobs is a good start and can reduce arguments over these matters.

Make work fun. Put on music and whistle while you work, says clinical psychologist and marriage and family therapist Dr. Jonathan M. Kramer. Bending, lifting, and cleaning are opportunities to stretch your muscles and keep limber. Take pride in doing a good job. It's your home, too.

Nix nagging. If you need to motivate a lazy partner to pull her weight around the house, don't nag and complain. Instead, make chores as easy and enjoyable as you can for both you and your partner. Do some tasks together. Put on some music that you both like and save some of the best stories from your day for now. If it's your partner who is the slacker on household chores, this approach may get her to assume more responsibilities on her own. If you constantly complain, however, she won't be eager to do so.

Curb criticism. When your partner does housework, don't act like an Olympic judge and

Keeping Score

Chances are, you ought to be helping your partner with more of the household chores because it's the right thing to do. Still not motivated? Well, consider this. You make a woman happy when you help her out around the house. A happy woman is a hornier woman.

But not all chores are created equal. A woman will place greater value on your vacuuming the house than, say, feeding the cat. To help guys receive maximum benefit from the choice of chores they do, *Men's Health* executive writer Greg Gutfeld, author of *The Scorecard*, offers this scoring system that assigns points to various tasks. Among them:

You make sure there's plenty of gas in the car . . . . . +1

You make sure there are barely enough fumes in the car to get it to the nearest gas station . . . . −1

You take out the recyclables and stack them neatly by the curb . . . . +1

You take out the recyclables at 4:30 A.M., just as the truck pulls away . . . . −1

You load the dishwasher whenever you dirty a dish . . . . +1

You leave dishes in the sink . . . . −1

start critiquing her for technical and artistic merit. At least she's doing the work. Criticism will only discourage her in the future, and she may well leave it for you to do. Try a different tack: Express your appreciation for her help.

Be flexible. If one arrangement for doing chores doesn't work, try another. Don't get bogged down with sexist stereotypes, such as thinking that since she's a woman, she ought to do the vacuuming. Be sensitive to any resentments that build up because of chores that don't get done or that take too long.

Save time for yourselves. Maybe the two of you are too meticulous. Limit the amount of time you devote to household tasks to, say, an hour per day or weekend mornings. Don't

You leave them under the bed ...... −5
You leave the toilet seat up ...... −1
You leave the toilet seat down 0
You leave the toilet seat wet ...... −3
You unclog a stopped-up toilet ...... +6
You clean up cat, dog, or human vomit ...... +7
You get rid of a dead rodent, a nest of spiders, or a nest of dead rodents ...... +8
You tackle a large household project, such as painting the den ...... +15
Or refinishing the floors ...... +16
Or rewiring the basement ...... +17
Or adding a second floor ...... +18
Or setting up a Nerf basketball hoop over the bathroom wastebasket ...... −6
And you're tickled pink about it ...... −15
You check out a suspicious noise and it's nothing 0
You check out a suspicious noise and it's something ...... +5
You pummel it with a six iron ...... +10
It's her father ...... −10

burden yourselves with too many "shoulds," such as you should always have a clean house, or you should always have the beds made. Leave time to relax and enjoy your home.

Take responsibility. It's your house, too. Look for what needs to be done and do it, says Dr. Kramer. Think of yourselves as a team and pull together in getting the household chores done.

A Man's Work...

Despite the above, there remain some domestic tasks that are universally man's work, no matter what the experts tell you about dividing work up. If you're the man of the house, sooner or later these jobs will fall to you. Do them.

Opening things. Whether it's a jar or a stuck closet latch, it's the man's job to be the opener, the provider of ingress. When it is a jar, the trick is to make it appear effortless. Don't grunt. Smack the jar on the bottom with the flat of your hand, then twist.

Pest control. From sewer rats to carpenter ants, you are expected to step in and decisively—but without too much gore—destroy or remove any bug, critter, or varmint that crosses her path. If you're required to use deadly force, do not take too much delight in the kill. No need to scream "Gotcha!" or "Look at the guts!" Just stalk it, nail it, and get it out of her way.

Inedible messes. If it's spilled milk or other foodstuffs, either one of you can clean it up. But if it's something lavishly gross—a foot-long hair ball, a decaying squirrel in the chimney, a toilet-based obstacle—it is incumbent on you to don the rubber gloves of honor and do your duty. Make a big deal of washing up after the fact so that she'll have no qualms about getting close to you and rewarding you for your service.

Checking suspicious noises. Whether it's a bump in the night, a hiss in the basement, or a knock under the hood, a man is responsible for keeping his ear to the ground of life. Your job is to listen for the signs of trouble and move quickly to cut them off.

Being mechanical. If it plugs in or has moving parts, it's your job to know how to operate it, fix it when it breaks down, or at least shut it off before it blows up. This extends not just to cars (if hers breaks down, she gets yours) but also to water valves, blown fuses, and VCR programming. If something is beyond your capacity to fix, your responsibilities include scheduling a repair and haggling with repairmen.

Making Room for Each Other

How to Avoid Couples' Claustrophobia

We consider it a classic movie fight scene—only it didn't involve fists, but rather vicious verbal sniping in the bedroom. The contenders: Jack Nicholson and Ann-Margret in *Carnal Knowledge.* "You have such contempt for me," she whimpers. "Kid, you worked hard for it. It's yours," he snarls. Sure, Jack's character, Jonathan, was a shallow, vain misogynist, but if she had just given him a little more space, he might have been a nicer misogynist.

It could be that Jonathan was experiencing what a lot of guys go through when they start living with a woman—couples' claustrophobia.

"It's an individual thing," says marriage and family counselor Riley K. Smith. "My experience is that most people need separate space as much as they need the together space."

Crowded House

Neither partner should keep his or her desire for private time bottled up, Smith advises. Assure your mate that your need for personal space is nothing personal; you would still crave occasional time alone even if Uma Thurman were sharing your place. Okay, so we've asked you to exaggerate a tad. The point is that revealing the Clint Eastwood loner side of yourself early on will pay dividends later.

"When the problem is ac-

knowledged, a certain amount of courtesy just comes out," Smith says. By getting it out in the open, your partner won't be defensive in the future if you say you're feeling a little cramped.

This is a two-way street. If it's your woman who wants a little time to herself, don't get in a huff. Unless she begins to emulate Greta Garbo and wants to be alone all the time, you have nothing to fear.

Size Matters

Even if the two of you wish you could spend 24 hours a day with each other, you may find it a little tight in your new digs. If so, there are lots of things you can do to create more space in your humble home, says Melinda Sechrist, owner of an interior design company. Here's a room-by-room blueprint.

The bedroom. Older homes, in particular, have small bedrooms and closets. If you have a spare bedroom, this can be where one of you stores clothing. "If not, you can get these great hanging racks with shelves above them. They hook in really well on the slanted ceilings that are more common in old homes," Sechrist says. Shoe racks, wall hooks, and rolling racks also conserve space. And an armoire is a fine second "closet" and a handsome addition to a room.

Plus, you can buy plastic baskets that will fit on a shelf and hold accessories. Or you can store stuff in boxes kept under the bed. Some people buy compact lacquered shelf units to replace or supplement dressers, Sechrist says.

The bathroom. If your bathroom has less space than the one in Barbie's playhouse, there is no way that you and your partner can store all your toiletries there. "You keep only the things in the bathroom that you absolutely need to have there," Sechrist says. That would include items that require water: razors, shaving cream, toothbrushes, and toothpaste, for example.

Some things normally done in the bathroom can be moved to another room, Sechrist says. "Maybe there's a place in the bedroom where she could do her makeup if you get decent light," Sechrist suggests. "You make it a good space."

Most bathrooms have room above the toilet or over the towel racks to hang shelves. And even modest bathrooms may have space for a small table or cabinet where you can stack towels. "That would leave room in the linen closet for other things," Sechrist says.

The living room. If you have a spare bedroom, it can serve as a place to put a second television, or it can be used as a sitting room. "A lot of times, though, there just isn't the space to do that," Sechrist says. "But you can have your own spot in the living room. Your chair. A spot to put your book, your glasses. It's kind of like building your own little haven within the haven."

So now we know why Archie Bunker went ballistic if anybody sat in "his" chair.

The kitchen. "If both of you have great dishes, you really don't want to throw them away. What you need to do is find space for the things you aren't using all the time," Sechrist says. Things like your partner's fine china. And, of course, your Star Trek collectors' glasses.

Some of the places you can put these items are a dining room buffet, a cupboard in the hallway, or a section of a coat closet. "I've seen people use their stereo cabinets for that sort of stuff," Sechrist says.

Getting Out

The newspaper ad for the place you and your partner moved into called it cozy. Now that you're in, you realize that was code for tiny. The logistics of creating private space for yourself are as challenging as squeezing a sumo wrestler into a Speedo. There just isn't enough room. Don't despair. You can have what you want without moving or adding on a room. Just get out of the house more.

Couples ought to have shared interests, but sometimes an individual hobby or pursuit is healthy, too. Let's assume that it's you who needs an occasional breather from your partner. If she has a night each week in which she goes out with her friends, this can be your time for solitude.

Sometimes the problem is one of psychological space, says clinical psychologist and marriage and family therapist Dr. Jonathan M. Kramer. If one or the other partner feels hurt, angry, or frustrated because some need is unmet (such as intimacy, love, or sexual variety), then any space can feel small. Some good ways of dealing with couples' claustrophobia, according to Dr. Kramer, are:

- Having your own space
- Having time out, away from each other
- Resolving interpersonal conflict

Often, too, one person (usually the guy) has a greater need for time alone than the other. In this case, he can explain that it's not about her, so she shouldn't take it personally and feel hurt, but about him and his need to be alone for a little while. Then he'll want to be with her because, as the old cliché goes, absence will make his heart grow fonder.

Having Children

Making Way for Baby

Feeling a little crowded? Weary of restaurants, movie theaters, and beaches teeming with people like human ant farms? Get used to it. By the onset of the millennium, the world's population is expected to exceed six billion people, more than double the number on Earth just 50 years earlier. Some 265 babies are born in the world every minute—7.5 of them in the United States.

And now you and your baby are contemplating making a baby.

Look, you might say. America is expected to account for a measly 274 million people as we move into the twenty-first century, a mere 4.5 percent of the world's total. Surely we won't be contributing to the world's population pressures, you argue.

But in fact, you will. Americans use 25 percent of the world's resources and produce trash and pollution way out of proportion to our numbers. The average American's energy use is equal to that of 2 Japanese, 6 Mexicans, 13 Chinese, 284 Tanzanians, or 372 Ethiopians, according to Zero Population Growth, a Washington, D.C.–based group formed in 1968 that advocates stopping global population growth. The addition of 2.5 million Americans has the same environmental impact of 80 million more Indians, the organization says.

But still you want to have a baby. You have company. A Gallup Poll found that 84 percent of childless respondents under the age of 40 said they wanted to have children someday. But before you make

that baby, here's what else you need to think about first.

A Matter of Timing

There are no hard-and-fast rules on when to have a child. Certainly there are financial implications. Not only is there the cost of an extra mouth to feed but also lost income if a parent (usually the mother) stays home with the little nipper for a few weeks or months.

If you father a child when you are young, odds are that this will be when your income is lower. You may become so engrossed in your career that you have little time to devote to a child. Some husbands and wives also need time to just be a couple before becoming a family. On the other hand, when you're young, you have the energy to truly have fun with a child.

"If you're looking for a logical time to do it, it's really different for every couple," says Jerrold Lee Shapiro, Ph.D., professor of counseling psychology at Santa Clara University in California and author of *When Men Are Pregnant.* "The notion that anybody can have it all is not realistic. So what we're down to is a series of choices."

Religion, family tradition, family pressure, finances, the age of the couple, and their romantic beliefs all influence the number of children they have. It's an issue that needs to be discussed by a couple before—not after—they get married, says Dr. Shapiro.

If you're going to have more than one child, there is the matter of how far apart to space them. Have them too close together, and you risk being perpetually pooped from dealing with diapers and feedings. And the children may be deprived of the valuable developmental experience of having the total attention of the parents, Dr. Shapiro says.

Have them too far apart, and the second child may seem like an overwhelming chore, and the age difference may prevent the siblings from becoming companions. Many experts think that 2½ to 4 years apart is optimal, says Dr. Shapiro.

Fatherhood Fears

Even the most gung ho dad-in-training is apt to be occasionally as scared as, well, a baby. This is especially true during his wife's pregnancy and after the birth of the child, says Dr. Shapiro, who has interviewed more than 2,000 guys about fatherhood. These apprehensions are normal, he says, noting some of the following fears.

• Becoming second banana to the little monkey. Before you had a baby, it was just you and your sweetie, and she made you feel like the king of the jungle. But now that a baby is on the way, you rightly wonder if you will become a little-noticed supporting player in the drama that is your wife's life.

"Most of the guys becoming fathers today have had direct experience with that in their families of origin, where they saw their fathers being replaced by themselves," Dr. Shapiro says.

• Wilting in the delivery room. Guys who plan to be present during the birth worry that they will get nauseated or faint in the delivery room. It rarely happens, but men with this concern should discuss it with their

Pay Attention

If you're going to make a baby, know that the little bundle of joy will cost you a bundle. One-fourth of those questioned in a Gallup Poll said that the financial expense was the greatest detriment to having a child. No wonder.

The U.S. Department of Agriculture (USDA) estimates that a married couple earning more than $56,700 and having their second child in 1996 would spend $350,920 on that child by the time he or she turned 17 in 2013. Married couples with an income between $33,700 and $56,700 will spend $241,440. And couples making less than $33,000 will spend $178,080.

The USDA estimated what parents would spend in seven budgetary categories, such as clothing and transportation. Housing expenses, which included mortgage interest, rent, utilities, and the like, accounted for the single biggest outlay: 33 to 37 percent of expenses, regardless of income. Food was next, accounting for 15 to 20 percent of child-rearing expenses.

And now the really bad news. Those figures don't include college costs. College tuition and fees now average $12,432 a year at private four-year colleges, and $2,860 a year at public four-year schools, according to the College Board, a national membership association of schools and colleges.

So if your wunderkind gets a degree in four years, your savings account could be lighter by anywhere from $11,000 to $50,000. Sure, there are millions of dollars available in financial aid, but nearly 60 percent of it is in the form of student loans. And if Junior goes on to graduate school—well, we don't want to make you cry.

partners, medical people, other men with the same concerns, or recent fathers. Childbirth education classes also have films that demystify childbirth.

- Pondering one's own demise. Men often become more aware of their own mortality when they become fathers. "There is no way when you're present at the beginning of life to avoid thinking about the end of it," Dr. Shapiro says. "You move back a generation psychologically. When you have a child, there's now a generation that is expected to survive you."
- Paternity paranoia. About 60 percent of the men interviewed for *When Men Are Pregnant* revealed that they had at least fleeting thoughts or doubts about whether they were really the biological fathers.

"It isn't about faithfulness; it's about how powerful and magical creating life is, and most men feel inadequate at some level to do that," says Dr. Shapiro. "It's really about thinking, 'I'm just not good enough to do anything this big.'"

Pregnancy Patterns

During the first trimester of pregnancy, men often see their partners in a new light. Men become more nurturing, doing more housework and being attentive if their partners have morning sickness, Dr. Shapiro says. He cautions that while a man should be sensitive to his partner's changing needs, he must not treat her like an invalid.

Similarly, some couples overreact and quit having sex in the usually mistaken belief that it will be harmful to the fetus. Other guys quit having sex because they now associate their wives with all mothers, including their own, leaving them repulsed at the thought of

---

Every Conceivable Option

It's one of the occasional jokes life plays on us: When you don't want to conceive a child, you and your partner have an accidental pregnancy. When you're trying to make a baby, you come up barren as the Sahara. More than five million couples are in the latter camp. Here are some other methods of having a child. Each can be costly—and is usually not covered by health insurance—and fraught with potential legal and emotional pitfalls.

In vitro fertilization. Your sperm and your wife's eggs are combined outside the body in a laboratory dish. If the sperm fertilizes an egg, the embryo is transferred to her uterus to mature. Or the sperm and eggs are mixed and injected into one or both of her fallopian tubes, where fertilization may occur. Estimated cost: $7,800 per procedure and up.

Donor insemination. At about the time your wife is ovulating, the semen from another man is injected into her cervix or inserted directly into her uterus, and subsequently, the fallopian tubes. The baby is genetically related to your wife, but not to you. Estimated cost: $300 per time and up.

Donor eggs. Eggs are obtained from the ovaries of

"incestuous" sex with their wives, Dr. Shapiro says.

During the second trimester, the reality of the pregnancy really sets in for some men as their wives' bellies grow noticeably bigger and they can feel the fetuses moving. Women often withdraw into themselves, leaving poor old Dad feeling excluded from the pregnancy experience and sometimes causing marital stress. This is a time when keeping channels of communication open is even more vital than usual, Dr. Shapiro says.

another woman and fertilized by your sperm, and the resulting embryos are placed into your wife's uterus. The baby is genetically related to you, but not your wife. Estimated cost: $8,800 and up.

Surrogacy. **Another woman carries the pregnancy for your wife. With a traditional surrogate, the woman is inseminated with your sperm. The baby is genetically related to you, but not your wife. With a gestational surrogate, your sperm and your wife's egg are fertilized through in vitro fertilization, but the embryo is nourished in the body of the surrogate. The baby is genetically related to both you and your wife, not to the surrogate. Estimated cost: $25,000 to $40,000 for a traditional surrogacy; $35,000 to $75,000 for a gestational surrogacy.**

Adoption. **It may be arranged through a public or private agency, or privately through an attorney. Check the laws in your state. Things to consider include what age child you are seeking, whether you want to adopt domestically or from another country, if you want a child of the same race or a different race, and whether you would consider a "special needs" child that has emotional or physical problems. Estimated cost: as much as $30,000.**

find themselves doing more household chores than ever as their wives become more immobile.

With a lot of women feeling so crummy and many couples fearing that sex will hurt the baby, lovemaking may now be only a memory. Some guys resort to affairs, Dr. Shapiro says. In talking to 27 men who cheated on their wives during the latter stages of pregnancy, Dr. Shapiro found that many of them did so with close friends or relatives of their wives—who, like the husbands, felt abandoned by the wives. One guy had an affair with his wife's sister; another with his wife's mother.

The wife/pregnancy/baby become the focus of attention and the man often feels ignored and left out. If so, says clinical psychologist and marriage and family therapist Dr. Jonathan M. Kramer, he should tell his wife that he needs to talk about what's going on with him—his work, concerns, friends, interests—so he won't feel left out.

Dr. Shapiro suspects that the infidelities he studied were about the marriage relationship, not sex. As with so many problems that can arise in a marriage, communication is crucial. Men who discuss with their wives their need to be included more in the pregnancy are more apt to find solutions that avert affairs.

The third trimester can be especially difficult. That radiant glow your partner had a few months ago has vanished. Now she may be as bloated as an overinflated beach ball. She may get frequent indigestion, heartburn, or other discomforts. On top of all this, she may now have doubts about her sex appeal or femininity. In a word, she's grumpy.

Guys, too, may be more tired and irritable if they are working longer hours to boost their income in preparation for the baby. They could be getting less sleep, and they may

A New Relationship

The baby has been born, and the relationship between you and your wife is forever changed. It can be both exhilarating and frightening.

Confined to the home for the most part, new mothers often feel isolated from adults. And they must be constantly attuned to the demands of their babies, to the detriment of their own needs. It's enough of a problem that as many as 8 out of 10 new moms have bouts of depression, irritability, and crying jags beginning three to four days after the baby is born.

Men may have similar, less severe feelings. They may have a new sense of responsibility and the realization that they have to provide for a family now. "Those are the things to talk over with a partner who is having equivalent fears of her own," says Dr. Shapiro. "I think a baby still affects the woman more because it's much more likely she will be the primary caregiver. But the effects on the husband are not insignificant. The pressure to provide really comes up big, psychologically, and often in reality as well."

A baby also means that your lives will lose spontaneity. You can't decide on the spur of the moment to go away for the weekend or to a movie. Some guys feel trapped, even resentful of the baby. Others, however, are so enamored of fatherhood that they are surprised how accepting they are of their new, more constricted lifestyle.

It's common for a man to feel jealous or envious of the relationship that his wife has with the new baby. A guy may resent being back at work, excluded from his new son or daughter's life. The new dad who does much of the nurturing, changing of diapers, and the like after work not only can establish a strong bond with his child but also can provide a break for his weary wife.

Post-Baby Passion

If you think that a week after your wife comes home from the hospital, the two of you will be having reckless, raunchy sex three times a week, you might be disappointed. Here are some things that can dampen your wife's ardor.

• She may be in pain for a while after the birth, especially if she had an episiotomy, a common procedure that involves making an in-

cision to widen the vaginal opening, literally making room for baby. The incision is stitched shut after the birth. She could be recovering even longer if she had a cesarean section, in which a fetus is delivered through an incision in the abdominal and uterine walls. This is major surgery on par with having an appendix or gallbladder removed, and it's done when the mother or the fetus is in jeopardy, such as when a woman has a prolonged labor or the baby is in a breech position. It takes about three times as long to recover from a cesarean as from a vaginal birth.

• She may feel anything but sexy because she hates how her body looks and feels.

• She will not have the usual amount of vaginal lubrication for a few weeks, making sex more difficult.

• She may keep distinct in her mind sensations she has when breastfeeding the baby and those she has during sex with you. In her book *The Year after Childbirth*, Sheila Kitzinger relates the story of a new mother who smacked her husband when he put his mouth to her breast. The woman said she equated her breasts with motherhood, and said what her husband did "felt like incest."

• She may be willing to resume a normal sex life, but the baby's cries or fussing keep interrupting.

Even if you consider yourself a paragon of studliness, you may also not be ready to plunge back into sex right away. Some guys now view their partners' bodies as not sexual, but maternal, and belonging to their babies. Others who have witnessed complicated births may be afraid of injuring their partners. And things you did sexually with your partner before the birth may no longer please her. This isn't as bad as it sounds. It simply means that you have to discover her body anew, like when you were first intimate. Think of yourself as Meriwether Lewis (as in Lewis and Clark) and her body as the Northwest Territory, and start exploring.

Happily, childbirth can also have a positive effect on a couple's love life. There may now be a new tenderness and a greater depth of feeling than existed before. Some men become more caring and sensitive to their wives' wishes, according to Kitzinger.

The Importance of Dad

It wasn't long ago that Ward and June Cleaver were the embodiment of the American family. June was the nurturing mother and housewife, packing lunches for Wally and the Beaver, caring for them when they were ill. Ward was the breadwinner who dispensed sage advice at the dinner table and a stern lecture if the boys got too rambunctious.

Nowadays, men are doing more hands-on child rearing. Thirty-five percent of dads in a survey commissioned by the Council on Family Health said that they missed at least one day of work in the previous year to care for their children when they were ill. Another 69 percent said that they have taken one or more of their children to the doctor's office, and 81 percent said that they are likely to administer medicines to their children.

The change is a welcome one, Dr. Shapiro says. "The influence of the father is incredibly important for the development of both boys and girls." As proof, Dr. Shapiro points to youth gangs. "There's almost a linear relationship between gang membership and no male figure in the home. The influence of the father keeps the son from seeking out alternative male role models that are dangerous."

It's not just boys who benefit from a doting dad. "Girls who grow up without fathers tend to be less ambitious and less successful, and they also tend to be involved in relationships with men who leave, just like their fathers did," Dr. Shapiro says. "Fathers are very important."

My Boy Rover

Maybe you hesitate to be a dad because you suspect that your fatherhood style will be more like that of Al Bundy than Cliff Huxtable. Consider getting a dog instead.

A pooch won't demand that you buy him Air Jordans, beg you to let him get his tongue pierced, or sass you back when you say no. Nor will a dog outgrow his clothes, smoke pot in the bedroom, or join a gang. Heck, research even shows that dogs reduce our blood pressures and stress levels. Of course, when your dog fetches a stick, it doesn't make you swell with pride quite the same way as when your child hits a home run or aces that dance recital.

All a dog asks is that you feed him, rub his belly now and then, and not make him wear stupid hats or sunglasses. Some other comparisons:

Dog: **Poops on the floor the first few weeks**
Child: **Poops in diapers for at least two years**

Dog: **Licks self in embarrassing places**
Child: **Touches self in embarrassing places**

Dog: **Whines at the vet's office**
Child: **Whines at the doctor's office**

Dog: **Chases cars**
Child: **Races cars**

Dog: **Four weeks of obedience school. Cost: $50**
Child: **Four years of college. Cost: $11,000 to $50,000—or more**

Growing Bold Together

How to Get Better with Age

> *Gettin' married's a lot like getting into a tub of hot water. After you get used to it, it ain't so hot.*
> **—Minnie Pearl**

Sometimes, after years of what others consider a successful marriage, a guy wakes up one day and realizes that the woman next to him in bed is a stranger. Maybe this epiphany comes when the last of the children has left home and there are no more ball games, dance recitals, and PTA meetings to attend. It's just him and his spouse, and it dawns on him that they've grown apart.

Sometimes, though, the guy is the one who thinks he has a successful marriage. And one day, his wife wakes up and realizes there's a stranger in her bed.

Warning Signs

Such scenarios are common, says Matti K. Gershenfeld, Ed.D., adjunct professor of psychoeducational processes at Temple University in Philadelphia, a psychologist, and president of the Couples Learning Center in Jenkintown, Pennsylvania. "They live in the same house. They see each other after work, and they get into a rut," Dr. Gershenfeld says. "Their lives can become very routine, day after day after day."

Many couples stop doing the romantic things they did when they were younger, Dr. Gershenfeld says. "The excitement of dating, per se, isn't there. When you ask someone for a date, you go out to the movies or to dinner. When it's your own wife, you don't have to do that any more, so people don't. It becomes humdrum, boring, and routine."

"Couples get so busy with the demands of everyday life that they don't make time for each other," says clinical psychologist and marriage and family therapist Dr. Jonathan M. Kramer. "There's a lot of pressure in modern life," he says. "There are dual-career households and a lot of chores. When children enter the picture, you add in the demands of caring for them. Plus, there are the high expectations that everybody has of having it all and wanting it all right now."

After children, careers, and chores, Dr. Kramer says our sense of self as a couple rates a meager fourth place. "I see a lot of couples in therapy who do nothing together as a couple once they've had children. All their time is spent on responsibilities. They don't have couple time anymore, and they get lost as a couple," he says.

If you're worried that your own marriage has become stuck in neutral—or reverse—keep your eyes peeled for these danger signs.

You no longer talk. One of Dr. Gershenfeld's pet peeves is couples sitting across from each other in a restaurant and saying nothing. "You're not bothered with cooking, you don't have to get the food on the table or clean up. But they have nothing to say to each other." At home, these couples may eat dinner while watching the television news, then go to separate rooms to do separate activities. Or when the guy comes home from work and his wife asks how his day was, he responds, "The usual." Says Dr. Gershenfeld, "That's not conversation."

You find excuses not to go out together. Some couples squabble over who should make plans for an outing. They can't agree on where to go. "I talked to one couple who said that they hadn't taken a vacation in seven years," says Dr. Gershenfeld. "They didn't want to spend the money. They didn't want to get a sitter for the kids. So every day becomes just like every other day."

You've become business partners and roommates. If emotional closeness and passion are gone, you're in danger of sinking into marital coma. Especially if your sex life is listless or gone, you need to pay attention to the danger signals and do something pronto, says Dr. Kramer.

Boredom outweighs comfort. You might have convinced yourself that your marriage isn't dull, it's simply comfortable. How can you tell the difference? "If in your heart of hearts you are satisfied with the way things are and you don't need constant surprises and drama, then you might just be comfortable, and that's okay," says Louanne Cole Weston, Ph.D., a board-certified sex therapist, a marriage, family, and child counselor, and a sex columnist for the *San Francisco Examiner*. "But if you catch yourself wondering what it would be like to be married to that woman across the room, then I think your marriage is more in the boring category."

Together Again

You needn't continue sleepwalking through a relationship that's as bland as warm

---

The Empty Nest

If your kids make Beavis and Butt-head look like Rhodes scholars, you may scoff at the notion of an empty nest syndrome. That's where one or both parents have an emotional letdown after the last of their children has left home. If it's such a big deal, you ask, why didn't Muddy Waters ever sing "The Empty Nest Blues"?

"I think it's real," says sex therapist Dr. Louanne Cole Weston. "People often preoccupy themselves with their kids when they are bored with their spouses." So who is hit hardest by an empty house? "It depends on who is using the kids more to keep themselves busy," Dr. Weston says. "Probably women, but not always."

If this sounds like a depressing prospect, there is a flip side. Once the children are out the door, it's a golden opportunity for couples to get to know one another again. It's also a chance to discover a different kind of empty nest syndrome, the one that has you both noticing how every room in the house is a bedroom...

---

milk, and you shouldn't. Here are some things you can do to put a little zip in your marriage. None requires any great sacrifices by you or your mate, just some effort and good intentions.

Say hello and goodbye. Don't enter or leave the house without seeking your partner out. And punctuate the moment with a kiss. "It says, 'You're important to me,'" says Dr. Gershenfeld. Be affectionate. Hugs, pats on the back, and hand-holding all say that you care.

Schedule time together. No matter how busy the day or how hectic the schedule, fit some time in to be together. It could simply be at dinner, as long as the television is off.

Share what happened during each of your respective days. And don't make excuses about why you can't talk. If you've had a rotten day and don't feel like reliving it, leave out the grisly details and offer an overview, Dr. Gershenfeld suggests.

And be sure to mention how it made you feel, adds Dr. Kramer—mad, sad, scared, or happy.

Schedule time apart. "It's really not good for couples to spend every night together," says Dr. Gershenfeld. They ought to have at least one night a week when they do something independently, or have their own friends individually.

Some couples do this by taking different adult education classes on the same evening. "While they go together and come back together, they're going to separate classes and interacting with different people," says Dr. Gershenfeld. Afterward, they have new topics to discuss.

Invite friends over. Contrary as it might sound, one of the best ways to get quality time with someone is to be with her in a room full of people.

"That quality of interacting with other people forces you to be social, forces you to see each other in a different perspective," Dr. Gershenfeld says. "What creates boredom is when the two of you are constantly interacting only with each other. You need bigger stimulation. You need more people."

Become more interesting. Another way to spice up your marriage is for each spouse to develop new interests, Dr. Weston suggests. "This doesn't mean that you turn your back on your partner," she says. "It means figuring out what excites you, what is

---

A Matter of Respect

If a couple who has been together for years realizes one day that they don't much care for one another anymore, perhaps the fire isn't the only thing that has died. Maybe respect is gone, too.

"They have to decide to look at what is going on between them and why they feel the way they do about the other person," says sex therapist Dr. Louanne Cole Weston. "It's a hard row to hoe. Have they grown apart because they no longer respect that person? It's a very tough thing to say, 'I don't respect you anymore.'"

There are dozens of ways one spouse loses respect for the other during a marriage, Dr. Weston says. There also are ways to regain that respect. Here are a few.

• He doesn't stand up for himself when his employer takes advantage of him. To turn that around, promote your talents at work, but don't be a shameless suck-up. Don't undervalue or overvalue your contributions. Don't spread office gossip. Do these things, and your boss probably will respect you more, and so will your wife.

---

interesting to you. Is it symphony music, touring the world, getting to be a fabulous gardener, or entering the world of politics in your community? What is it that would jazz life up for you?"

But how does this inject new life into your relationship? "When you are excited about something, you are a much more appealing and interesting person," Dr. Weston says. "If the other person has any interest left in you and they see that you have something going in your life, then they're more likely to be attracted to you. If people are constantly developing, then there is always something of interest for a partner to know."

• **One partner accepts the other's lies. After her menopause, for example, she may claim that she no longer wants sex because she can no longer conceive a child. He recognizes it for the baloney that it is and loses respect. Worse still, she knows he knows, and she faults him for accepting the lie. Talk about a vicious circle. Instead, he should get at the truth. Maybe she's withholding sex because she's angry at him. Or perhaps she's bored by the routine of their sex life. Or she could be going through some hormonal changes that have affected her enjoyment of sex—changes that could be accommodated if he showed an interest in talking about them.**

• **She fakes orgasms, and he knows she fakes them. She disrespects him for not confronting her. Rather than going along with the theatrics, he should indeed confront her to find out why she isn't having orgasms and why she feels the need to fake it. Maybe he would find out that he isn't sensitive enough to her desires in and out of bed. Maybe he would discover that he makes sex seem like a performance rather than genuine lovemaking. Maybe he would learn that she feigns sexual ecstasy because she feels pressured by him to have loud, quick orgasms. Or if she actually has a real orgasm, she may feel pressured to fake several more. Maybe he would regain her respect by doing something about this.**

Go out at least once a week. It can be dinner, a movie, skating, a concert, the planetarium, or anything—but do it without the kids.

Have fun together. "It lets you remember what the relationship was all about, why you got married to start with," Dr. Gershenfeld says.

Vacation together at least once a year. Plan an annual getaway that involves just you and your sweetie—nobody else. If one of you likes the mountains and the other the beach, compromise. Visit each in alternating years and be a good sport about it, Dr. Gershenfeld advises.

Follow the example of others. If you need helpful hints in your relationship, there's nothing wrong with looking around to see how others do it. Observe a couple whose marriage seems good and determine why it is. Emulate some of the things that seem to work for them. "Pay really close attention by talking to them," Dr. Weston says. Also, read about relationships (like you're doing now) and find out what makes them work, then do the work.

The Upside of Aging

"The thrill is gone," blues legend B. B. King wailed, and for many couples who have been together a long time, there is no denying that's true, says Dr. Weston. "Some people convince themselves this is okay and acceptable. But it doesn't have to be that way. I think it's a real matter of choice."

Indeed, for many couples, marriage only gets better as they age. That's because they have matured and have a better sense of who they are, Dr. Weston says. "They've been around the block enough to know what's there."

It's called maturity, and with it comes more tolerance and less bickering over each other's differences. "Sometimes when we're 20 or 30, we treat things that are really just preferences as though they were necessities," Dr. Weston says. "One of the things being older can bring us is a realization that many things are only preferences, not life-and-death issues. Older couples can have some of the best experiences of a lifetime." Loosen your grip on your demands, and embrace your partner instead.

Dealing with Grief

Don't Push It Away

Good grief, what's good about grief? If you're like most guys, you'd rather endure almost any other hardship than try to cope with feelings of sadness. We're not talking about the grief you feel when you're downsized from your job or the Cubs stumble through another losing season. We're talking about serious grief brought about by traumatic loss. The death of your parents. The loss of a friend or, worst of all, maybe even your partner. So what do you do? How do you cope? How does anyone?

How Men Grieve

People who study such things tell us that nowhere in the world is there a society in which men cry more than women. Some cry as much. Many others weep less. Part of the reason is physical. From adolescence on, men produce less of the hormone prolactin than women do, says Thomas R. Golden, a psychotherapist and author of *Swallowed by a Snake: The Gift of the Masculine Side of Healing.* Prolactin helps produce tears.

"The important thing is that you can't judge a man's pain by the number of tears he sheds," Golden says. "Men are often in tremendous pain, but it doesn't come out in tears."

Grief experts including Golden point out, however, that at least in North America, cultural reasons have more to do with men's comparative sto-

icism when grieving than any hormonal causes.

"We men are basically independent sorts," Golden says. "When you're in that perspective, you don't want to share your pain because sharing your pain means that you're not independent any more. Men are more comfortable sharing their solutions than their pain." Supporting that view is the fact that grief support groups are comprised mainly of women.

Expectations placed on men also have much to do with their way of handling grief, according to Alan Wolfelt, Ph.D., founder and director of the Center for Loss and Life Transition in Fort Collins, Colorado. He cites these factors in the article "Gender Roles and Grief: Why Men's Grief Is Naturally Complicated," which appeared in the journal *Thanatos.*

- Boys are usually discouraged from crying, while girls are not.
- Grief creates a turning inward and slowing down on the part of the mourner. Masculinity is equated with striving, moving, and activity. Men are taught to overcome grief, not experience it.
- Outwardly expressing grief equals weakness to many men. Being masculine is still thought to mean being composed and stoic in the face of tragedy.

The way men deal with grief can cause misunderstandings and tensions with their partners. "Often, a man will withdraw in order to heal from some sort of loss," Golden says. "Women often see the withdrawal as not dealing with it. There are all kinds of historical and spiritual stories about men healing by withdrawing. Christ would go into the desert for weeks at a time in order to heal himself. You never see in the Bible that Mary went after him and said he needed to join a support group. Men will talk about their problems after they have a handle on them. Women will talk about their problems before they have a handle on them."

While a lot of guys are reluctant to discuss their grief with others, Golden says talking about what they are going through with another guy can really help. "The support we can get from other men is great," he says. "It's very different from the hand-holding thing you might get from a group of women."

"Men do better if they have a close friend or neighbor for a confidant," agrees Anne Studner, senior program specialist for the American Association of Retired Persons' Widowed Persons Service.

The Silent Treatment

While a lot of us guys are shut-ting out the world after the death of somebody close to us, the world is shutting us out, too. Or at least, it may seem that our own family members are shutting us out. What's going on? "It's not that people don't love them and care about them. It's just that they don't know what to say because of their own pain," says Eric Cline, director of the Grief Recovery Institute in Cambridge, Ontario.

The guy who is grieving can do a lot to change this, Cline says. If on a birthday or a holiday he talks about missing the person who died, others will open up, too. "Then it makes it okay for everybody else to talk about their relationship with the person who is no longer there," Cline says. Other-wise, "people will try to carry on as if nothing has happened."

Sometimes, however, you may wish people didn't say anything

Old Yeller

Your dog has gone to that boneyard in the sky, and you feel downright embarrassed at how grief-stricken you feel. Don't be. Even tough-talking guys like actor Lee Marvin and President Harry S. Truman waxed philosophic about mutts. *Dog Music*, a book of 163 poems about dogs, including many mourning their deaths, was compiled by guys. And why not? As British poet Alexander Pope once said, "Histories are more full of examples of the fidelity of dogs than of friends." Many people feel that their dogs are their best friends—loyal, calming, and happy to see them. So it's natural to feel a powerful loss when their dog friends die.

So maybe now you don't feel silly because you're as misty-eyed over your dog's demise as you were when you watched *Old Yeller* as a kid. But what will make you feel better? Try the following suggestions from the American Humane Association and the Marin Humane Society.

- **Talk to somebody who will understand your feel-ings—somebody with a pet of his own that he loves. Tell him about your dog: the good times, the bad times, and the way it ended.**

- **Make a memorial donation in your pet's memory to a humane organization or animal care and con-trol agency. Or volunteer at such a place.**

- **Arrange pictures of your dog in a photo album or collage.**

- **If you have children, express your grief. If they are sad and their parents show no emotion, it can be confusing. If the dog is euthanized, have your vet explain to them what that means. Assure them it's not their fault that Old Red is dead.**

- **Pick the right time and place, and if you have to, do it. Cry, that is.**

because of their unintentionally insensitive remarks. People who are grieving repeatedly hear 141 different comments in the first 72 hours after a death, Cline says. "About 19 of those comments are helpful."

Some examples of what you won't want to hear—and should refrain from saying to somebody else who is mourning a loved one:

- "I know exactly how you feel." Says Cline: "That's impossible. No two relationships are the same."
- "She's in a better place." Cline again: "It doesn't deal with the problem that you miss them and you are not going to have contact with them."
- "Don't be sad." But you are sad, and this is normal.

What should be said? Perhaps, "If there's anything I can do or if you ever want to talk, I'm always here to help or listen." Or maybe nothing more than a heartfelt, "I'm sorry."

The Worst Tragedy

Perhaps no loss is as devastating as that of your child. "It's such a completely different type of grief," says Melissa Swanson, executive director of Pen-Parents, an organization based in Reno, Nevada, that puts parents of a child who has died in touch with others who have experienced the same trauma. "You expect to outlive your children."

The death of their child causes many couples to divorce, Swanson says. "If there were any problems in the marriage to begin with, these just get magnified," she says. "Men are supposed to keep that stiff upper lip. They have the added burden of feeling that they have to be the caretakers of their wives. Because they don't work through their own grief, it just festers inside. Eventually, they will resent their spouses because their spouses are taking so much from them."

Men often think that their wives are overly emotional following the death of their child, and they feel shoved aside when she gets the bulk of the support from family and friends.

This is especially true in a lost pregnancy, Swanson says.

Conversely, women are disturbed if their husbands show little emotion after the death of the child and return to work right away. Men often return to work quickly in order to give their lives a sense of normalcy and to keep busy during their grief, Swanson says.

Swanson advises men to try to do the following if a child dies.

- Communicate with your wife what you are feeling. Recount fond memories of your child.
- Find a support group.
- Keep a journal. Writing can be therapeutic. Consider keeping a second, shared journal, in which you and your wife each record your thoughts about the child's death, and respond to each other in the journal. This is helpful to parents having trouble talking to each other about the death.
- Accept the fact that your wife's grieving may differ from yours and that no one way of grieving is better than another.
- Sadness is normal. Let yourself feel your loss and let your spouse know that you feel badly, too. This can help you and your wife pull together, rather than apart.
- If it's still going badly, seek counseling.

When Your Wife Dies

Women typically outlive men, but those men who survive their wives' deaths face unique grief issues. "Men traditionally have put all their eggs in one basket," Golden says. "Their wives tend to be their entire support system. Women tend to have more elaborate systems of support. So when a wife dies, it's a big trauma."

Even more so if it's a sudden death. "Men seem to do less well if the death is sudden," Studner says. Women, however, cope better with a spouse's death that is sudden, rather than lingering.

Men also may find themselves ill-equipped to deal with certain household functions that were taken care of by their wives. They may know little or nothing about cooking, ironing, or running a washing machine.

In the awful event that your wife does die before you, Dr. Wolfelt has these tips for coping in his brochure *Helping Yourself Heal when Your Spouse Dies.*

Take the time you need. Your grief is unique and there's no need to compare your experience to others. Nor should you adopt assumptions about how long your grief should last. Take a one-day-at-a-time approach.

Don't ignore your grief. Don't push your dearly departed out of your mind because she is too painful to think about. Talk about the type of person your wife was, activities you enjoyed together, and memories that bring both laughter and tears. Avoid insensitive people who, while well-intentioned, may deny you your grief by continually making comments such as, "Stop dwelling on the past," or "Aren't you over her yet?"

Give in to your feelings. As a man, you're probably a little uncomfortable dealing with strong emotions, but expect to feel them now. And you will experience a gamut of emotions—confusion, disorganization, fear, guilt, relief, and anger to name just a few. Don't ignore them or try to fight them. In many cases, that only intensifies the feelings. Feel them and let them go. Feel them again when they return and let them go. In this way, you'll neither avoid them nor get stuck in them.

Treasure your memories. Make some effort to preserve your partner's memory. If your partner liked nature, plant a tree you know she would have liked. If she liked a certain piece of music, play it often while you are thinking about her. Make a scrapbook of photos portraying your life together.

Keep the faith. If you are religious,

When Grief Gets Worse

Sometimes grief gets so bad, you may feel like there's no end in sight. And for those whose grief descends into serious depression, it's no time to be stoic anymore; it's time to get help, says David Dunner, M.D., professor and vice chairman in the department of psychiatry and behavioral sciences at the University of Washington in Seattle. That's why it's so important to recognize the danger signs of serious depression. See your physician if you're experiencing several of the following, especially if you're experiencing them even several months after the event that has caused your grief.

- **Feeling down or low most of each day**
- **Losing interest in almost all activities**
- **Experiencing significant weight gain or loss**
- **Inability to sleep**
- **Feeling agitated**
- **Feeling fatigued**
- **Experiencing inappropriate guilt or feelings of worthlessness**
- **Inability to concentrate or make decisions**
- **Having suicidal thoughts**

embrace your spirituality in ways that seem appropriate to you. You may find that this will give you some sense of peace.

Write it out. Sometimes it's easier to put your words and feelings on paper as a way to get them out, rather than expressing them to another person. Write a "goodbye" or an "I love you" letter to your partner as a way of telling her how you really feel and of getting some sense of closure, suggests clinical psychologist and marriage and family therapist Dr. Jonathan M. Kramer.

Don't isolate yourself. Alone time is important, but it's also important to be with others, says Dr. Kramer. Spend time with friends or family, even if you need to be quiet.

Overcoming Infidelity

Cures for Cheating Hearts

Sometimes, it appears as though everybody is fooling around. Now it's true that a depressingly large number of people succumb to the urge, forever changing, if not ruining, their marriages. But contrary to popular perception, more of us remain faithful to the ones we marry than media reports would suggest.

Some 94 percent of married men and women surveyed by the authors of *Sex in America* said that they had but one sexual partner in the past year. And more than 80 percent of women and 65 to 85 percent of men report that they had no sexual partners other than their spouses at any time during their marriages. Some surveys have found higher numbers of unfaithful spouses. Whatever the number, this chapter is for those who have strayed, or are thinking of it.

Why We Cheat

There is no more surefire way to destroy your first marriage than to sleep with somebody other than your spouse, says Frank Pittman, M.D., a psychiatrist and family therapist and author of *Private Lies: Infidelity and the Betrayal of Intimacy* and *Man Enough: Fathers, Sons, and the Search for Masculinity*. "In first marriages, I just don't see many divorces unless there has been screwing around," says Dr. Pittman. As Frenchman Jean-

François Guichard once said: "Divorce is the sacrament of adultery."

A marriage in which a spouse cheats almost always is unhappy, Dr. Pittman believes. Among the reasons he says his patients have given for cheating: They thought all couples did so; they were reacting to their spouses' affairs; they were seeking more intimacy or excitement than they got from their spouses.

Adulterous behavior often runs in families from one generation to the next, says Bonnie Eaker Weil, Ph.D., a family therapist and author of the book *Adultery, the Forgivable Sin*. She estimates that 80 percent of the couples she has counseled came to her because one spouse was unfaithful, and in 9 out of 10 cases, at least one partner was the child of an adulterous parent.

An extramarital affair is a symptom of an unresolved problem passed from one generation to the next, Dr. Weil says. It can be the adultery or death of a parent, divorce, or another event that left the grown-up child feeling abandoned or betrayed.

Does Cheating Ever Help?

You're feeling neglected by that wife of yours. She takes for granted how hard you work, and she seems indifferent to sex. Maybe, you tell yourself, I'll dally with Sally or play with Kay. If she finds out, she'll appreciate me again. Heck, an affair will improve my marriage, won't it?

That's just blind rationalization, says Dr. Pittman, who has been counseling couples since that reputed philanderer John F. Kennedy was president. He recalls few cases in which both partners said an affair was more helpful than harmful to their marriage. More often, it's a catastrophe.

An affair can have the positive effect of letting a

spouse know the marriage is in trouble, Dr. Weil allows, but he adds that the deep pain and intimacy problems it causes will never go away.

With AIDS and other sexually transmitted diseases lurking under the sheets, fewer infidelities nowadays are one-night stands than in the past, says Dr. Pittman. In a way, that's even worse news on the adultery front, because current affairs tend to be more intimate—and hence more destructive.

While most of us think of infidelity as sexual intercourse with somebody, this isn't always the case, especially with the proliferation of phone sex and cybersex. But like traditional sex, they, too, require secrecy and subterfuge. Still, these diversions can't be a big deal, can they? "Anything you have to lie about is harmful to your marriage," Dr. Pittman warns.

When You Cheat

Studies show that married men cheat more often than married women do. They do so earlier in the marriage, and with more sexual partners. Still wonder why women bad-mouth us? Men are more apt to engage in extramarital sex with little or no emotional involvement, while women are more likely to have an extramarital emotional involvement without sexual intercourse.

In a study reported in the Journal of Sex Research, Shirley P. Glass, Ph.D., and Thomas L. Wright, Ph.D., tried to gauge the difference in men's and women's attitudes about adultery by giving them a questionnaire listing 17 justifications for an affair, such as for fun, sexual excitement, a romantic experience, and to advance one's career.

Naughty in North Dakota

Is any place in America more bland than North Dakota? The people are 95 percent white; the state beverage is milk; the state dance the square dance. One of its best-known natives is Lawrence Welk. Yet these stoic Dakotans can become as inflamed with extramarital lust as the randiest among us.

"There's a lot more going on than you would think," says Russell Hons, a private investigator in Grand Forks, North Dakota. "We've had cases in real small towns that have involved groups of women sharing themselves with groups of men."

When somebody hires him to learn if a spouse is cheating, the client is already suspicious, says Hons. Unfaithful wives tend to be more elaborate in their scheme to avoid detection than husbands, Hons says. He recalls one who would drive a variety of different routes to a McDonald's parking lot, where she would meet her lover. The two would then leave in one car for their trysts. "I think the women, in general, are probably a little more clever, a little more sneaky," Hons says.

But more careless, too. "Women keep souvenirs," Hons says. Photographs, love letters, and cards. "We've had people come to us with suspicions, and we'll tell them to check around the house" for these items.

Hons is not one of those private eyes who will enlist a sexy woman to try to seduce a guy he has been hired to check out. In the business, it's called integrity testing. Others call it entrapment.

"I don't think it's an ethical way of going about it," Hons says. "My theory is if a man is going to have an adulterous affair, there's no need to set it up. He will do it on his own, and we can catch him at it."

Twenty percent of the men said that they would not feel justified in having an affair for any of the 17 reasons listed. The other 80 percent, however, were more approving than women of extramarital sex when the justification was curiosity, novelty, or sexual excitement.

Regardless of why you are in an affair, if you want to salvage your relationship, there is one thing you must do, says Dr. Pittman. Confess. Not to your priest. To your partner.

But, you plead, it was a one-time fling. It meant nothing to me. Telling my wife will only hurt her and make life hellish for me.

Dr. Pittman makes no exceptions. "The lying is what damages the relationship," he says. "Yes, the incident was meaningless. Your mate would understand this." (We hear you bellowing, "Not mine!")

"I fully recognize that most people aren't going to take this advice," says Dr. Pittman. "But if people develop secrets in their marriage, the marriage loses its capacity for intimacy. The important thing is to reveal everything and take total responsibility for your actions."

Everything? "If you're holding anything back, the secret takes on more significance than it deserves," says Dr. Pittman. "You should be a gentleman first, but you have to be honest. The truth will hurt, but the lie will hurt worse."

And if your biggest fear in admitting an indiscretion is that your wife will dump you, consider this: Among a sampling of 50 adulterous couples whom Dr. Pittman counseled but who divorced anyway, 37 of the break-ups were initiated by the spouse who was unfaithful, and only 13 by the partner who was wronged.

If you do admit to an affair, Dr. Weil has this advice.

Don't gloat. If you're repentant and genuinely want to repair the damage, don't crow about your affair or admit to it out of anger. You'll only enrage or alienate your spouse, even if you feel it was she who drove you to have an affair. If you're going to own up to it, do so when you're feeling clear-minded and level-headed.

Reassure her. If you've just confessed to an affair, one of your partner's first reactions is going to be that you strayed because you don't love her anymore. In all likelihood, that's probably not the case. If you still love your wife, reassure her of that fact. It may sound hollow to her, and she may scoff, but it needs to be said. By you. And sincerely. And more than once.

Answer questions. Not surprisingly, she may demand information about your lover and start asking questions. Be willing to answer those questions, but not too explicitly (no need to rub her nose in it). Answering such questions may seem counterproductive. But remember that not answering them may cause her to dwell on them and imagine the worst.

Let her vent. She has good reason to be furious with you, so if she blows her stack, stand there and take it like a man. And expect her to stay mad for a long time.

Naturally, when you admit to an affair, you ought to apologize and ask for forgiveness. But don't expect the relationship to revert quickly to whatever it was before the affair. How long it takes before, or if, your wife forgives you depends on things such as how good the relationship was earlier and how forthcoming you are, Dr. Pittman says.

"Recognize that you'll be on a short leash for a while. It's a year of mourning for the lost relationship. You have to go through a new courtship."

When She Cheats

"When a woman is having an affair, she's looking to get out most of the time," says Dr. Weil. "Men are not as forgiving as women. A woman knows that she's taking more of a risk if she's going to have an affair. A lot of women who have affairs did not marry for love. They married for prestige or the biological clock was ticking or they married for money. They are looking for that romantic feeling."

If you're a typical guy, once you learn of her affair, you will be angry and hurt. Here are some suggestions from Dr. Weil on what to do next.

Put down that phone. Naturally, after learning of an affair, your first reactions are going to be clouded by anger and rage. While it's okay to feel anger, it's not such a good idea to act out of anger. Don't do anything you'll regret later, like physically hurting her or, say, reaching for the phone to call a divorce lawyer. Give your anger a chance to recede, and plan the next step when your cooler head prevails.

Do insist that the affair end. If you are going to have any kind of a future together, it's vital that she end the affair. Tell her that in no uncertain terms. While relationships are things that thrive on compromise, this is one situation where there's no room for debate. Let her know: It has to stop.

Take your share of responsibility. Don't let her put all the blame on you. Ultimately, the decision to be unfaithful was hers, not yours. But there may be some validity to her blame, says Dr. Kramer. If most women have affairs for emotional intimacy, it means that her man is not close enough, not making her feel loved or special. The silver lining in this case is the realization of how to make her happy and avoid future affairs: Be more emotionally intimate with her.

Reach out to others. At a time like this, you're going to be feeling some pain. To make it worse, the person you normally turn to when you're feeling bad is the very one who's causing those feelings. So to whom do you turn? Parents, siblings, or friends. Don't be ashamed to talk to them about this. They're there to help you, not judge you. They can help get you through this. Don't shut them out. Let them in. If you're like most men, though, you'll probably want to keep it to yourself and avoid embarrassment and further pain. But, says Dr.

Danger Signs

Here are 10 signs that you have a wayward woman, according to family therapist Dr. Bonnie Eaker Weil.

1. She spends a lot more time away from home on business trips or nights out with friends.
2. She devotes excessive time to doing nice things for you, as if to make up for guilt.
3. Her hair or clothing smells of men's cologne— and it's not your brand.
4. She's been piling up a lot of mileage on her car.
5. She suddenly mentions a colleague or neighbor a lot in conversation, or conversely, has abruptly ceased talking about a man whose name used to come up often.
6. She suddenly loves working out at a gym or sticking to a diet.
7. You now make love noticeably less—or more— than usual.
8. She no longer calls you endearing pet names.
9. Her credit card statements show unusual charges for purchases that never appear around the house, or she is secretive about her credit card bills.
10. She provokes more fights or is more hostile when you argue.

Kramer, it can help if you talk to even one person you trust.

Ask hard questions. Once you've recovered from the initial sting of her infidelity, you have to deal with the next step—whether you want to try to repair your marriage or not. That's up to the two of you, of course. But you need to answer some hard questions first. Do you still love each other? Did you do things in the marriage that helped drive her to somebody else? Are you willing to trust her again? Are you a forgiving person, or are you the sort who holds a grudge? How you answer these questions will be your best indicator of how to proceed.

Enjoying Your Golden Years

Life after Retirement

Retirement. Ernest Hemingway called it the ugliest word in the language. But then how would he know? Papa didn't live long enough to find out if retirement is so bad—he shot himself shortly before his 62nd birthday. Like a lot of men, he might have envisioned his life in retirement as suddenly being rudderless, of no longer having any purpose.

He was wrong.

"I'm always amused when I see people link retirement with premature death," says Mark D. Hayward, Ph.D., professor of sociology and gerontology and director of the Center on Aging and Health in Rural America at the Population Research Institute at Pennsylvania State University in University Park. People should want to retire, he says. It's a positive thing.

Take This Job...

The ranks of retirees are bulging, and the graying of America will only accelerate. Consider:

- Since 1900, the year after Hemingway was born, the percentage of Americans age 65 and older has more than tripled, from 4.1 percent of the population to 12.8 percent in 1995. In raw numbers, that's nearly an 11-fold increase, from 3.1 million to 33.5 million.
- People are living longer. Between 1900 and 1960, life expectancy at age 65 increased by only 2.4

years, but it has gone up by 3 years since 1960.
- The most rapid increase in older Americans is expected between the years 2010 and 2030, when baby boomers begin turning 65.
- By 2030, there will be about 70 million older Americans, making up 20 percent of the population, compared to 13 percent in 2000.

Most of them will be retired and glad of it, says Dr. Hayward. "The vast majority of Americans hate their jobs," he says. "They had to work to make a living. As they get older, retirement is a much more attractive option than their current work situation. Otherwise, they wouldn't retire."

Assuming a New Identity

Conventional wisdom is that men derive much of their identity and self-worth from their work. Without it, they are lost, which makes them understandably reluctant to retire.

That wisdom really only applies in certain situations. "The people who are least likely to retire are those with a lot of autonomy and creativity in their jobs," Dr. Hayward says. "It's true that they derive a lot of their identities via their work environments and tasks. But at some point, it's still more positive for them to move into retirement."

There is evidence to support Dr. Hayward's view. In one study, researchers followed more than 800 older workers in North Carolina to gauge the psychological impact of retirement. They found that those who retired were less depressed than when they were still working.

"Men tend to work in jobs that are bureaucratic and controlled. A lot of men, especially blue-collar workers, don't have a lot of autonomy," Dr. Hayward points out. Thus, retirement can be a boon for them since it offers a kind of freedom that they haven't known before. When men in these types of jobs do retire, Dr. Hayward says that they tend to seek out opportunities that allow them to take risks, do new things, and do the things that they never had the chance to do before.

Spending Time, Saving Money

However you spend your time after you retire, one of the best ways to help ensure that you enjoy that time—and make a smooth transition to life as a retired guy—is to plan for it financially.

Otherwise, a financial shortfall can cause all sorts of strain, especially on your marriage, says Temple University's Dr. Matti K. Gershenfeld. If you save enough that you and your wife can have the place in Florida, or fly to Europe at will, you're probably not going to have much of a problem. But if finances are limited and you find that your pension income or Social Security benefits don't allow you to live the life you were hoping for—or even what you were used to before retirement—it can make for a hard adjustment, one that could spill over into resentment and petty squabbles.

We're not saying that you can't enjoy retired life on a budget, though. "Many people get along on a shoestring quite nicely," Dr. Hayward says. "There is still a lot of freedom to do what you want, and people adapt to different levels of income. People don't suddenly become poor, generally, after retirement."

But for your own peace of mind, make sure that you've planned ahead so that you won't spend all of that free time worrying

> # Discount Days
>
> **Here's something to look forward to: Being a senior citizen means getting lots of great stuff at junior-size prices. We're not talking about Medicaid but, rather, the fun stuff you can do with your wife or your retired buddies. Things like these.**
>
> - **The Empire State Building's 86th floor observatory is half price.**
> - **Many restaurants have "early bird" dinners in the late afternoon—their regular fare at reduced prices.**
> - **Some golf courses offer discounts.**
> - **Many airlines and car rental companies give reduced prices.**
> - **Hotels and motels often provide discounts, ranging from 10 to 50 percent.**
> - **For a nominal fee, the National Park Service sells a lifetime pass that gets you into any national park free.**
> - **The Rock and Roll Hall of Fame and Museum in Cleveland lets aging rockers in for the same lower price as kids. Maybe you and Keith Richards can go together some day—and take your grandchildren.**

about money. As a general guideline, you need to be saving or investing between 10 and 20 percent of your gross income for about 25 years—that's if you want to retire at 100 percent of your income. And every time you get a raise, put half of that increase into some kind of investment plan.

Pest Control

Once you retire, odds are that the problems you'll have won't be coming from your wallet, but your wife. Not to put too fine a point on it, but retired guys have been known to make pests of themselves around the house, mightily testing the patience of their wives. "Women say that their husbands retire and they have nothing to do," Dr. Gershenfeld says. "Men have been used to going to work and having a structured day. Now that they don't, it's very strange to them." So they drive their wives crazy.

What often happens is that retired men, who likely have done far fewer household chores than their mates, now see themselves as experts on such matters. "Now they're telling their wives how to vacuum, how to dust," Dr. Gershenfeld says. It's a big enough pain that she offered a course teaching women how to counsel husbands to help them cope with retirement. Luckily—for your wife—there are myriad other ways you can occupy yourself.

Keeping Busy

American clergyman Harry Emerson Fosdick had this advice many years ago: "Don't simply retire from something; have something to retire to." That wisdom is still valid today. After you retire, there are plenty of things to do that you once had no time for. Spending more quality time with your partner is one of them. Here are just a few examples of the things you can enjoy together. And if she's looking for an excuse to get you out of her hair, we've provided some suggestions that might just save your relationship.

University courses. Universities often let older citizens sit in on courses for free. "So if you always thought you could be the writer of the great American novel, or you always wanted to know how to really invest or take a course in American literature, you could do that," says Dr. Gershenfeld. Or you can sign up for a course that you and your wife can take together, like cooking, dancing, or even massage.

Elderhostel programs. Elderhostel is a nonprofit organization that provides

educational programs usually of a week or longer at colleges and universities, museums, theaters, and national parks. That's great for the two of you. If you want to do something on your own, Elderhostel also offers "adventure learning classes" that include learning to drive a dogsled, studying yoga or tai chi, dancing in all forms, and horseback riding. "It appeals to a population that's brainy, that likes to study," says Dr. Gershenfeld. "It's also a place you can comfortably go if you are a widow or widower. It's outstanding." For a free catalog from Elderhostel, write to Elderhostel, 75 Federal Street, Boston, MA 02110.

Part-time work. Some retirees, especially blue-collar guys, hire themselves out doing odd jobs or freelance and consulting work, Dr. Hayward says. "They desire the extra activity, and they're looking for a way to somehow combine work and leisure." A few years ago, Dr. Hayward helped conduct a study that concluded that one out of three retirees returns to work within one year. If work gives you some measure of purpose and satisfaction, go for it. Look at it this way—you'll have a little more mad money to spend on that woman of yours.

Networking. There is at least one valuable thing in retirement you will have more time for that costs you nothing—friends. "People's social networks actually expand after retirement; they don't contract," Dr. Hayward says. "People tend to reach out to each other even more than they did when they were working."

Volunteering. There is a huge variety of organizations that needs and welcomes volunteers. You can inquire through civic and religious groups. Or write to the American Association of Retired Persons, 601 East Street NW, Washington, DC 20049, to be placed in their volunteer talent bank, a nationwide pool that matches your skills to available jobs in your area. This, too, is something that couples can do together.

Part Five

Real-Life Scenarios

Quest for the Best
They're making their mark in the world—and making their relationships work, too. Here, these successful men share the wisdom that has helped them excel at life—and love.

You Can Do It!
They're guys like you, with real lives and real relationships. They've also tackled real problems and learned from them. Now, so can you.

Quest for the Best

They're making their mark in the world—and making their relationships work, too. Here, these successful men share the wisdom that has helped them excel at life—and love.

Michael Zane, Founder and Chairman, Kryptonite Corporation

Locked in Love

It takes 15- to 20-hour days, seven days a week, week after week, year after year, to become a successful entrepreneur. That doesn't leave much time, or energy, for a serious relationship. Or any relationship.

That's what it was like for Michael Zane, founder and now chairman of the board of Kryptonite Corporation in Canton, Massachusetts, makers of those nearly ubiquitous—and nearly indestructible—bicycle and motorcycle locks.

"I was always doing trade shows, working late," says Zane, a bearded and balding six-footer who is as kinetic a person as you'll ever meet. "I'd meet a woman at a convention or on a plane or a train and start to get into a relationship, but I just didn't have the time to invest in getting to know someone well." A series of short-term relationships—"20, 30, I can't even count," he admits—left Zane doubtful that the timing would ever be right for a long-term involvement, much less marriage.

Not surprisingly, he met Elizabeth Fritz in the course of another busy workday: on a visit to the Emmaus, Pennsylvania, headquarters of *Bicycling* magazine, where she worked. She was his match—a tall, energetic, adventurous, ath-

letic, striking, and strong woman who was on the move from the moment she woke up. But the two did not immediately get romantically involved. "The first personal comment I ever made to her was to tell her how beautiful her teeth were," he recalls. "I said it in front of six guys and walked away feeling like a real ass."

Within a year, they were dating regularly, or as often as they could considering his schedule and the 300 miles between their homes. When he suggested they live together, she upped the ante, saying that if they did that, they ought to consider getting married. "I thought about it 10 seconds and said, 'Let's do it,'" Zane remembers.

Routines and Rituals

Zane was 43 when he married Liz, as she is known. She was 39. It was the first marriage for both, and they are committed to making it their only marriage. But for two people who have spent most of their adulthood in the singular tense, the adjustment from "me" to "we" doesn't always come naturally, as they discovered.

"How hard is it to change my ways?" Zane asks rhetorically. He offers his own answer: "It's definitely an ongoing learning experience."

Says wife Liz, "When you're single for so long, you develop a routine, even for the simple things, like how you get up in the morning. You're focused on yourself, your life, your needs. And there's no one else you have to consider. Compromise goes totally against the grain of how you've managed to survive alone. But in order for it to work, there has to be a willingness to bend on both your parts."

As an example of how they've adjusted to each other's idiosyncrasies, they both cite the morning coffee ritual. It's a minor thing in life but, they both assert, one of those little details that can say so much more. When she was single, Liz loved to get up in the morning, grind fresh beans, brew the java, and mix in hot milk. Zane, for his part, was an early riser—as in 4:00 or 5:00 A.M.—who also loved his cup of joe but not with the heated milk. The new morning ritual they worked out: He would make the coffee with the milk warmed to the way she liked it, and he would wake her each morning and serve it to her.

"It's a wonderful luxury," she says. "And this may sound ridiculous, but it took some time to get used to it. But now I think it's the best time of our day. We see each other's smiling faces first thing in the morning, and it fills me with happiness that he's stopping what he's doing to perform this little act of love. It means the world to me."

Love Takes Time

Making time for each other, they found, was the hardest task of all. They each had their own lives; they each had been conditioned in all those years of singlehood to pursue their interests with passion—alone. One time in the middle of a busy day in which Liz realized Zane was being pulled in too many directions to pay attention to her, in frustration she blurted out, "All I want is a little bit of your time, but I want it all." It became their motto, a reminder. "It means that when we're together, even if for just a couple of minutes, we are completely focused on each other," explains Liz.

Zane wrote the line down and kept it in view on a notepad pinned to the dashboard of his Volkswagen van.

Another way the couple makes sure they spend time together is by taking what they call joyrides. They get in the car and just go. The destination is unimportant. It could be to the hardware store. It could be to get some ice cream. "Where we go is not the point," Zane says. "It's just an excellent time to touch base, to laugh, to talk without interruptions of phones, faxes, or someone ringing our doorbell."

Zane incorporated Kryptonite in February 1973 with personal savings of $1,500. Now it's estimated that annual sales are in excess of $15 million. "But money was never the driving force," he says. More important to the art history major who graduated from Franklin and Marshall College in Lancaster, Pennsylvania, was seeing his designs for the Kryptonite K-4 Lock placed in the permanent collection of New York's Museum of Modern Art in 1983. In 1988, the lock received Japan's Good Design Prize and Germany's Museum of Utilitarian Art Award.

All of this has made Zane a wealthy man. He modestly admits that his worth is probably several million dollars. He oversees the company's product development efforts from his home on Martha's Vineyard, the tony island playground off the coast of Cape Cod, Massachusetts. Though he would be the last to think of it, we couldn't help but speculate that being a "man of means" would have made him a great catch for some gold digger. Did he fear that with Liz?

"Not for a second," he responds quickly. How did he know? "You just do," he replies. "It's instinctive. The fact is neither of us are in it for the money. We both love to work. We love to work together. We love to work separately."

When they're not working, they're playing—biking, swimming, making love. ("The sex has never ever been this wonderful—ever, ever," Zane effuses.)

"I think it's been so great because basically she has taken me as I am," he concludes. "And she has honored my attempts to meet her halfway, to compromise, to make room for her in my life."

Al Joyner, Olympic Champion

Gold-Medal Lover

If there were an Olympic gold medal for romancing, Al Joyner would surely win it. He could put it next to his other gold medal for winning the triple jump at the 1984 Olympic Games in Los Angeles. But after speaking with him, you get the distinct impression he would value that gold for good loving more than the one he earned for his athletic accomplishments.

He trained for many years to win the heart of a fellow athlete named Florence Griffith, who in 1988 in Seoul, Korea, became the first American woman to win four medals (three golds and a silver) in a single Olympics.

He still remembers the day he first set eyes on her—June 11, 1980. She was walking with several other women athletes at the University of Oregon during the U.S. Olympic Trials. "I said right then that that was the woman I wanted to marry," he recalls. Her reaction was not exactly the same. "She said she didn't pay much attention to me." Later that year he found out she was enrolled at the University of California at Los Angeles (UCLA), where his sister Jackie, a track star in her own right, was also a student. He asked his sister to introduce them. The message came back that Florence wasn't interested in meeting him. "Jackie was no help whatsoever," he adds.

Jumping Over Love's Hurdles

A lesser man would have given up. Not Joyner. "I told everybody she was going to be my wife. She just didn't know it yet," he says. He returned to UCLA several years later to train for the 1984 Olympics, but only

one thing was on his mind then: winning a gold medal. Mission accomplished, he saw Florence briefly and asked her to show him around Los Angeles the next time he came out. She said sure. He returned to Arkansas State University to coach and train. "I told people at State that I was going back to California to train for the 1988 Games and the only reason I wouldn't come back would be if I had married Florence," he says. "They said, 'Yeah, well, you'll be back.'"

On his return to Los Angeles in 1986 to begin training, he caught up with Florence not long after his arrival. The first sign that she was interested was when she said, "I thought you were going to call me." Still, since high school, Joyner had grown used to ending up as women's friends. "Women would say, 'He's a great guy but just a friend type.' It never went further than that." He figured this was another one of those situations, but this time he made a conscious decision to maintain the friendship. "I decided, either way, I wanted to be her friend, so why not just enjoy it?" This didn't stop him from sending her flowers every Tuesday or inviting her to dances or giving her a friendship ring. He clinched it with this very suave but sincere line: "I know you think I'm giving you this to impress you, but this is just the way I am. I'm a caring person, and no matter what happens, I really cherish your friendship."

In truth, he was head over heels in love, but he played it cool. When he thought he was going overboard, he stopped sending the flowers, stopped the calls. It didn't take long for Florence to start asking after him. "After that, I never looked back again," he says. The dating, the dancing, and the Tuesday flowers commenced again in earnest.

The day he proposed in 1987 could have been scripted by a love-struck Hallmark card writer. "I had this thing about the number seven," he says. "I knew she was the seventh child, so I decided to propose on the seventh month, July, on the 17th, at seven o'clock. If she was going to say no, it would have to be on all my lucky numbers." He rented a limo and drove her around until he finally got up the nerve to throw a pillow on the floor, get on one knee, and say, "You're the most straightforward woman I know. Will you marry me?" She proceeded to cry for 45 minutes. But because she promised her niece and nephew she'd say yes in front of them, she waited to respond until the youngsters were around to witness the moment. The answer, by the way, was yes.

The wedding was planned for October 1988, after the Olympics, but a Southern California earthquake shook the couple up and they decided to get married immediately in Las Vegas. That was 1987—seven years after Joyner first laid eyes on Florence.

A Man among Powerful Women

Eventually, Joyner took over coaching his wife. Now he is president of FAMJOY Enterprises, a sports and celebrity management and marketing company based in Mission Viejo, California. His main client is Florence, who has acted in films and on television, has a clothing line, and gives motivational speeches. Joyner explains his own motivation for promoting her activities: "Someone said in 1988 that Florence would be a flash in the pan, that after the Olympics nobody would remember her. I never forgot that quote, and I was going to make him eat those words."

Joyner, now in his late thirties, is often asked how he, an Olympic champion in his own right, handles being known as the brother of Jackie Joyner-Kersee and the husband of Florence Griffith-Joyner rather than being known for his own accomplishments. "First of all, it doesn't bother me because I grew up surrounded by powerful and successful women, plus I've always been one of their greatest fans," he says proudly. "Not to mention that I was the

first in the family to win a gold. I know my own worth, and if you're true to yourself, you will shine no matter who you're with."

And frankly, adds Joyner, he gets the impression that the guys who taunt him for being the man behind the women "in fact would die to be in my shoes."

Nonetheless, he has to admit it isn't always easy holding his own against a wife billed as "the world's fastest woman," who also happens to be a flamboyant dresser and extremely beautiful. He also admits to a dynamic tension between them, but he sees it as healthy. It makes sense that when two competitive people live together, there is the potential for Olympic-size contests over everything from washing the dishes to child rearing.

"It's true," Joyner says. "When we do become competitive, we just go for it and see who's right. And we always add, 'May the best person win.' Afterward, we make sure the loser doesn't hold a grudge because the winner won fair and square. But we have this running joke: If she cleans up the house, I say that I could have done better."

When push comes to shove, the Joyners tackle arguments the same way. They're competitive but fair.

"If I was wrong, I say I'm sorry. You never want to go to bed upset with each other. What if you die in your sleep?" he says. Their other tactics: They keep joy and laughter in their lives; stay focused on raising their daughter, Mary; worship together; and try to be real with one another. "I'm the same person in front of my wife that I am in front of other people," he says.

They also support each other in their ambitions. After Joyner helped Florence complete her cosmetology degree, she planned to back him as he trained one more time to make the Olympic team. "I still have the drive, and it's still fun," he says. "I want to know what my place in history will be. If it's as Flo-Jo's husband and Jackie's brother, that's fine. But it would be nice to make a little history on my own."

Noah Adams, Author and Host of National Public Radio's *All Things Considered*

A Gift for Giving

One of the most esoteric skills any man can master in the game of relationships is the high art of gift giving. Any man who has proffered a dud to the woman in his life can bear witness to the heartache it can cause—cause him, that is. If she loves the gift, you are made in the shade with your fair maid. If she looks at it, her eyes glaze over, she smiles that stiff smile she uses when she greets your mother, and then she mumbles, "Oh, a gift certificate to Al's Amazing Car Wash and Dry Cleaners. Just what I always wanted..."—well, let's just say, dear brethren, you may need a lesson from Noah Adams. A piano lesson.

Adams is best known as host of National Public Radio's (NPR's) program *All Things Considered*, but he's also the author of a book entitled *Piano Lessons: Music, Love, and True Adventures*. It's about his decision, which he made at the age of 51, to learn to play the piano. The 12 chapters chart each month in the first year of this sometimes-trying endeavor. Near the end of the year, to stay motivated, he decides to master (or at least stumble through) a difficult piece—German composer Robert Schumann's "Träumerei"—as a surprise Christmas present for his wife, Neenah.

So on the day before Christmas 1994, he dons a full tuxedo and strolls into a room where she's wrapping presents. He's carrying a candle, a brass candlestick, and matches. "What?" she asks, grinning.

He then sits her in a chair to the right of the piano bench, turns off the radio, lights the candle, and proceeds to blow her away with what has to be the most thoughtful gift any man has ever given to any woman. He describes the moment in *Piano Lessons*: "The candle flame dances with light...the world becomes small. And I play." Halfway into the three-minute piece, he writes, "the music begins to sound hushed, eloquent; even the wrong notes seem to have a special quality. I can barely see Neenah, off to my right; I would dare not turn to look." By the final chord, Neenah is crying. And, much to his surprise, so is he.

Third Time's a Charm

Adams gave his wife another gift as well. After all, the $10,000 piano had been a personal indulgence for himself. For her, he bought an elegant wooden sailing dinghy. It, too, was a surprise. When Neenah comes along to talks he gives at bookstores now, women approach her. "They know it's idealistic and that books, while honest, never tell the entire truth, but they still say, 'I wish I were married to a man like that, somebody who was thoughtful enough to find the perfect present, someone who would think about it, actually get it done, and not be clumsy about it,'" he says. "I tell you, most gifts fail, but that present worked. The moment worked, everything worked."

Divorce is a great teacher. It took Adams two previous marriages to learn these lessons. He and Neenah met on the job. She was a producer at NPR. They had worked together on projects, even traveling to places like Japan, Yugoslavia, and France together to produce shows during the troubles there. But they didn't get romantically involved for quite a while and didn't get married until much later because of NPR's policy forbidding marriage between employees who are working together.

He believes the workplace "creative friction" is what brings many men and women together. But it's a double-edged sword. "Sometimes it's more difficult," he now reflects. "After a bad day, I'd come home and still be fighting internal battles about mistakes I made in that day's show. Then she'd mention something she didn't like." While he's on a leave of absence working on another book, the tables are turned. "I'm home cooking and shopping, and when she comes home, I want to jump right into what she's doing at work, even though I promised I wouldn't."

Ultimately, their relationship, working and otherwise, works because of one word: honesty. He elaborates: "We have respect for each other's abilities and each other's opinions. Sometimes she'll have an idea that I may not agree with, and 24 hours later she'll agree with me. I tend to write with too much sweetness and romanticism, and she reigns me in."

We Can Work It Out

Aside from the art of gift giving, Adams has also learned the art of fighting. "We tended to let things build up, then typically some issue which was not really the issue would be the touch-off point," he explains. "While I'm never going to be one who talks a great deal about feelings and what's going on, I'm very cautious about not letting things build up. Instead, I'll very calmly ask about what's going on or explain that I'm having some difficulties."

Another thing he has learned about keeping a marriage vibrant is to "try hard to make something special happen from time to time, whether in a day or a week or a month or a summer."

Also, he suggests that men especially should try to "go as far outside of their personalities as possible, to stretch their definitions of

themselves." For example, if you're not the romantic candlelit dinner type, try organizing a romantic candlelit dinner one evening anyway. Or take her to a blues club and actually make an attempt to dance. Or learn to play the piano and play her a piece as a present.

"You have to make the effort to push at the envelope of what you are," Adams says. "It's not going to kill you. You don't want to be the same old guy you've always been, because life moves on."

Being mutually supportive in all this also helps. Allow and encourage each other to change and grow, he says. And, at the same time, tolerate each other's differences and limitations as well. He offers a simple example. He likes to mountain bike. She goes along for the ride, but he can tell she's less than wholeheartedly enthusiastic. "She can't see why you're riding a machine on a trail where you could be walking," he says. "It just doesn't make sense to her. I suspect there will come a time when she'll just not want to ride with me." Meanwhile, her favorite activity—sailing—is not high on his list. But this, he has learned, is part of the compromise of marriage. "We can live with that," he says. "She can sail by herself, and I can ride my bike by myself."

One of the reasons that Adams thinks *Piano Lessons* struck a chord with both men and women (it made the *New York Times* bestseller list) is that "I write about her in a loving and honest way," he notes. "And we don't get to read much about good relationships in nonfiction today."

As for Neenah's reaction to the book, "she says she loves it and is very proud of it." But Adams is quick to note that despite the hundreds of letters he has gotten from adults sharing their sob stories about trying to learn the piano late in life, the intention of the book was "not a sales pitch for taking piano lessons in adult life. It's about doing anything to bring new meaning and depth to your relationship with your wife." And it's about doing anything to bring new meaning and depth to your own life.

Sam Keen, Ph.D., Best-Selling Author

Fire in the Heart

He freely admits to the mistakes he made in his first marriage. But he has taken the lessons he learned and applied them to his second and, he pointedly notes, last marriage.

"More than half of what I know about being a good man I've learned from both of my marriages," says Sam Keen, who holds a Ph.D. in the philosophy of religion. That realization alone would set him apart from a lot of other men who remarry only to fall into the same old patterns that destroyed their first go-round. It's almost more impressive than the fact that he has written 14 books, among them the *New York Times* bestseller *Fire in the Belly: On Being a Man*, and devoted himself to the examined life as a self-declared "freelance intellectual gypsy."

For many years, he was a consulting editor to *Psychology Today* magazine. The PBS documentary based on his book *Faces of the Enemy* was nominated for an Emmy Award. Further, one of his first books, *Apology for Wonder*, was named by *Time* and *Newsweek* as one of the 10 best books published in 1969.

"Like most men, I unconsciously took my success from how I appeared in the eyes of women," he says. "Their applause and their approval was crucial to my sense of manhood."

He is reclining in his writer's cottage about 75 steps from his house on 70 acres of rolling hills in Sonoma County, California, about 40 miles north of San Francisco. Across from his desk is a quote from his favorite movie, *Zorba the Greek*. It reads, "I am my own man—I mean free."

In his second marriage,

which began in 1976, he learned that a man shouldn't take his identity from a woman. "I didn't make my wife into a surrogate mother or my audience," he says. "I realized I had to find my manhood on my own."

The Art of Loving

The subject of love is very much on Keen's mind this summer morning. His book *To Love and Be Loved* has just been published. Asked why he wrote it, he says, "There are a lot of books out there about how to get love, but very few about how to give it." He cites psychoanalyst Erich Fromm's 1956 classic *The Art of Loving* as one of the few that tried to offer a practical guide to one of the world's oldest art forms.

He says that too often we fall in love and get married expecting an idyllic happily-ever-after script. "We think about conflict as the antithesis of love, but that's not my experience," he says. "The conflicts of marriage are the forge of the spirit. All love requires the ability to be with somebody but also to stand against her— to be able to say no as well as yes. We say, 'For better or worse, for richer or poorer.' But we mean, 'So long as you stay above the poverty line, so long as you don't gain 30 pounds...'

"Marriage is also for the worse, and it's going to get worse," he says. "Sometimes I think marriage is designed so that you fall out of love into reality. That worse part of you and her is going to come out. And you're going to have to deal with it. That's when love gets interesting, when it moves beyond illusion to reality. Can you love a person who doesn't dust the house or who leaves dishes in the sink? Now you have to face the fact that you're married to a failure, and so is your wife. And you have to go on loving each other in spite of your and her so-called failures. Unconditional love doesn't come at the beginning of a marriage. It comes at the end—at the point that you're feeling like either committing murder or suicide. When you stop performing for each other, when you can relax and be yourself, when you can let her be who she is and let yourself be who you are, then you've achieved unconditional love."

The Road Less Traveled

Keen's own education has been out of the ordinary, to say the least. It started traditionally. He was raised in the South by loving parents in the Presbyterian fundamentalist tradition. After earning a masters degree from Harvard Divinity School and a doctorate from Princeton, he went on to become a tenured professor. Married with children, living on a tranquil tree-lined street, things then began to unravel. His naturally inquisitive mind began to question every paradigm by which he had lived his life. It was the 1960s. He separated from his wife of 17 years, took a sabbatical in California, and decided to quit his very secure job and become a freelance writer, lecturer, and workshop leader. Since then, there has been no looking back.

Throughout it all, he has always been physically active. "The life of the mind was not enough," he says. At Harvard, he took up wrestling. He also became an avid skin diver. He started jogging long before it was fashionable. "I remember running along the Charles River in the 1950s, and people would stop me and ask if I was in trouble or needed a ride," he recalls. And then there were horses. He loved riding so much that eventually he moved with his second wife to Washington and lived on a horse ranch. He and his wife still own several horses and ride frequently.

"I've always had strange passions," says Keen, now in his mid-sixties. "But, come to think of it, all passion is strange." His latest strange passion is the flying trapeze. You read that right: flying trapeze. It's been one of his boyhood dreams to fly through the air with the greatest of ease. When he was 62, he happened to see a feature on a TV news program about the San Francisco School of Circus Arts, where it was being taught. He was hooked after his first class. So much so that within a year, he had a trapeze rig built on his Sonoma ranch, within view of his writer's cottage.

For Keen, it's more than a physical exercise or the playing out of some childish dream. It's an exercise in life, love, and relationship. "It's about the Zen of flying, of being airborne," he says. "And I use that as a metaphor of the spirit, of transcendence and freedom and trust. I enjoy trapeze because it puts me out on the edge, literally and figuratively. It's about overcoming fear, going beyond personal limits, testing yourself, and trusting yourself." He could be speaking about the fears and challenges of loving as well.

"They're both complex skills that require practicing and mastering a number of moves," he says. "They are both practices about trusting other people as well as yourself. They're both about finding the balance between knowing when to hold on and when to let go. They both involve timing and spontaneity."

Now Keen hosts classes twice a week at his home trapeze, run by the San Francisco school. A center for at-risk adolescents and female victims of drug and physical abuse in San Rafael, California, leads workshops there, helping people build self-confidence and camaraderie.

Keen had just received a sizable advance to write a book about trapeze, to be published by Broadway Books. "It's not my plan to become the guru of enlightenment through trapeze," he says. But just as it wasn't his plan for *Fire in the Belly* to put him at the forefront of the men's movement, you can't help but expect his new interest to motivate a lot of people to reach beyond their personal limits to love and live as fully as they can.

You Can Do It! They're guys like you, with real lives and real relationships. They've also tackled real problems and learned from them. Now, so can you.

Marriage Metamorphosis

Eric Shambaugh,
Blue Bell, Pennsylvania

Date of birth: March 17, 1970

Profession: Restaurant manager

Marital status: Married June 18, 1994

Four years ago, I was a single, 20-something bartender partying my way through life. Marriage was not for me. I wore my hair long, slicked back. If I wasn't smoking a cigarette, I was actively looking for one. I was a bit overweight (okay, 80 pounds overweight), and I never worked out—exercise might have interrupted my sleep schedule. Marriage was far from my mind. I knew that it would wreak havoc on my lifestyle.

Then I met Cindy. We worked together, and we were instantly attracted to each other. Slim and beautiful, Cindy had a dramatically different lifestyle than I. She exercised, for one thing. And she ate vegetables.

Admiring Cindy, I realized that I was careening down a really bad trail. I had to face facts—I was out of shape. You've heard of endomorph and ectomorph body types? Mine was a new category—the big slob body type. Cindy got me into a regular exercise regimen, and I began losing weight. We moved in together, and I started eating better. She made some subtle hints, and we both quit smoking. Since I obviously couldn't live without her (my old lifestyle had me headed for a heart attack), I married Cindy in 1994.

For Better, Not Worse

People say things change when you get married. They're right, and the thing that changed was me. Cindy started me on a regular exercise regimen. She exercised, and I wanted to spend time with her, so it wasn't too hard a sell. We tried out a few sports together, such as tennis, walking, and running. Then finally we hit upon one I loved—mountain biking. In the beginning, I loved the fact that deep in the woods, I could hop off my bike, push it up the big hills, and nobody could see me. But I improved and discovered that mountain biking is scary, exciting, painful, and beautiful. It's just you, your bike (your wife if you want), and your woods. I deal with people at work every day, and to go to a place where there's nobody except me and my wife is magical.

Plus, I got bitten by the exercise bug. I love the sense of accomplishment after slugging up a big hill. I crave the stress and aggression-release of charging down a rocky trail. Also, there's the technical aspect of biking—the parts, the gear, the never-ending excuse to buy new things. Biking is my hobby, not just a sport.

The more I enjoyed biking, the more I rode, and the more I rode, the more weight I lost. In just one year, I lost 80 pounds. Of course, the weight didn't just melt off. First I stopped drinking, which saved me lots of calories. Then I traded in my eating habits for my wife's. She showed me that just because it's green doesn't mean it tastes bad. She eats a lot of vegetables and fruits, whereas I ate lots of fast food. Cindy changed that. And so the weight came off.

Marriage literally was the best thing that ever happened to me.

The transition from living-together life to

married life was an easy one. I didn't have high expectations about married life. I hadn't expected to ever get married. I did have great role models, though. My parents have been married for 40 years. They have a very supportive relationship. Sure, they faced tough times, but I don't remember ever thinking that they wouldn't be together. My parents gave me the keys to a happy marriage.

Everything I Learned...

What I learned from them was that first, you have to make time for each other. That's a challenge for Cindy and me since we work opposite shifts. She leaves for work as I'm coming home and vice versa. We leave a lot of notes for each other. We only see each other one day a week, and that's when we try to fit in everything—family, friends, and our own personal time. Often it's the most exhausting day of the week, but it's also the most joy-filled, even when we're doing chores. In the afternoon, when I'm off work, I do all the errands, plus day-to-day maintenance around the house— dishes, laundry, making the bed. But on our day off, we do major cleaning projects together. (I have to admit, though, when it comes to scrubbing the bathroom, I find something else to do.)

Luckily, Cindy and I like to do the same things in our spare time. Our marriage wouldn't work if that didn't happen. We'd spend time together wishing we were doing something else. But we have many interests in common, especially bicycling. We love to go on long, challenging rides together. We participate in charity rides in support of cancer research or multiple sclerosis, and we race mountain bikes in the summer. It's amazing how a relationship can cause you to tailor your interests. But that's important in a marriage, to evolve together.

Growing together as a couple is especially important so you can weather the storms that inevitably brew. Cindy and I agree on the major issues, such as how to spend money, where we want to go with our lives,

and how we want our family to be. So when we do argue, it's about small, inconsiderate things that one of us did, usually me. For example, my work schedule is so erratic and I get home so late that I don't usually call to tell Cindy when I'll be home. She'd be sleeping anyway. So that habit runs over into personal time also, and if I'm going to be two hours late from a bike ride, I forget to call, too. I'll come home, she'll be upset, I'll get defensive, eventually I'll realize I'm wrong, and I'll apologize. So then I'll call the next time, and probably the time after that, but then I'll forget again. Scheduling is not one of my strengths. This is something we work on.

Something to Talk About

Being able to work through problems is obviously one of the reasons why communication is so important in a marriage. And that's probably why it's so hard. Often I'll say something that sounds clear to me, but Cindy hears something completely different. Different people take different slants on the same series of words. And it's not just talking that's hard; sometimes listening is harder. Sometimes when Cindy is talking, I think I know what she's about to say, so I finish her sentences. Half the time I'm wrong, which is bad, but when I'm right, it's even worse. Because then she knows that I just didn't have the patience to let her make her statement. It's as though hearing her say it isn't interesting enough.

Along with communication, I think support is important in a marriage. It's comforting to know that no matter what I do, Cindy will support me. Also, in a good relationship you have to love one another, but you also have to like each other and enjoy each other's company. Most of all, I think you have to be able to laugh together. If I can make Cindy laugh, I feel that I've accomplished a goal. Because above all else, I want her to be happy. It makes sense to me that if each person in a marriage lives to make the other person happy, they'll both be happy. And I am.

Love in the First Degree

Anthony Kivela, Houston, Texas

Date of birth: October 11, 1955

Profession: Police Lieutenant, Gang and Tactical Unit Commander, Houston Police Department

Marital status: Married June 9, 1973

I know police officers have a notoriously high divorce rate, but I think a satisfying, healthy relationship is possible, even for us, if you are really willing to make the woman in your life your number one priority.

Diane and I were high school sweethearts, and we grew up just a few blocks away from each other. We were married for almost four years before I became a police officer, so dealing with the related stress from my job was a brand-new experience for both of us.

Emotions Under Arrest

Because of the nature of our work, police officers have to be experts at masking emotions and feelings. We see some pretty gruesome things on the job, and many officers then go home, open up a beer, and keep these experiences bottled up inside. Maybe I'm the exception, but as a young officer, I was eager to go home at the end of the night and tell my wife about the car chases or raids I'd been on during my shift. I developed this habit early on, not even realizing that it was bringing Diane and me closer together and helping me cope with stress from the job.

Of course, Diane is concerned for my safety on the job, but I don't believe it has caused her too much stress. In part, this is because she says I'm a good officer and she has

complete confidence in my ability to protect myself. But I largely attribute it to the countless years of open discussion we've had about my work. She's fully aware of the painstaking planning that goes into a five-minute raid—it's like a carefully thought-out game of chess. She knows that I wear my bulletproof vest religiously when I'm working the streets and that I'm constantly looking for new ways to improve safety on the force. I've always tried to defuse tense situations on the job by taking the extra time on a scene to talk things through, and I've never had to fire my weapon. We've all heard of police officers who lose their cool in high-pressure situations, and unfortunately, those are the type of officers who have loved ones at home constantly worrying about their safety. I've always worked at making sure that I do everything within my power to come home safely, and Diane knows this.

The Laws of Love

Unfortunately, a major pitfall for many men in my line of work is the tendency not to trust. When every encounter you have during the day is with crooked people, it's easy to become wary of everybody. Diane and I now trust each other completely, but it wasn't always that way. She has trusted me since the beginning, but my trust had to develop over time. Part of building this trust was never doing anything that would breach it. We've never been unfaithful to one another—that's just not a possibility. Of course, we encounter problems in our relationship, but we've developed our own method of working through them.

Perhaps it was partly my fear of failure, but I knew from the day I married Diane that we had something special, and I was absolutely determined to make it work.

After more than 24 years of marriage, I've learned that communication is a key ingredient to a successful relationship. However, I've also learned that when you discuss your problems is just as key. Diane doesn't want to hear about my problems as soon as I walk in the door at the end of the day. We've learned to allow each other time to unwind before unleashing the day's frustrations upon each other. Secondly, we never go to bed angry. It's an unwritten rule for us. And, no matter how angry I am, I will never sleep on the living room couch or take off in the car. I admit to an occasional pout, but after a couple of hours I'm able to put the problem in its proper perspective. I'll then lean over and hug her, and she'll immediately hug me back. And before you know it, I'm wondering why I didn't do this hours before. We end up talking about the problem, sometimes into the wee hours of the morning.

Divorce is just not an option for us. I don't threaten her with it in the heat of an argument, nor do I joke about it. We constantly tell each other that we're going to be married for the rest of our lives. I think that if you say this often enough during the good times, it really reinforces your determination to work through anything.

Making It Happen

These days I think that a lot of people just pay lip service to making a relationship work, and they aren't really prepared to put forth the extra effort needed to make it a reality. A successful relationship is not going to just happen on its own. You have to make it happen. There are so many little things that Diane and I do to show how much we appreciate each other.

We leave each other love notes, take community classes together (a recent offering was massage for couples), and keep one night a week open as "date night"—an evening out for just the two of us. Date night became a tradition back when our two children were still at home and we needed the time to ourselves. But

it's still going strong even after our kids have grown up and moved away.

I also make the time to include Diane in my plans whenever it's feasible. For example, I attend and often conduct periodic community meetings. I've asked Diane to attend these meetings with me, and actually some of the other officers have followed my lead. I'm sure the meetings aren't extremely interesting to her, but just asking her to come along sends the message that she's important to me. We don't always get to sit next to one another or even talk during the meeting, but just knowing that she's there, seeing her reactions, and being in her presence is what it's all about.

Another tip: Diane and I touch each other constantly. Now, of course, by touching, I don't mean anything overtly sexual. I hug her or lightly touch her arm. This nonverbal communication keeps us connected, and it's a great way to show affection. Along these lines, I also learned long ago that you don't come home late at night and jump into bed expecting sex. The process of making love really begins hours before the actual act. It can begin by noticing and thanking your wife for doing something that she routinely does, or complimenting her just because you mean it. Or it can begin just by being with her, by doing something else that you like doing together— and it doesn't have to have anything to do with sex.

It may sound like a cliché, but I tell Diane several times a day that I love her, and I say it with sincerity. We also exercise and really take care of ourselves physically. This not only helps us to stay fit and attractive to each other but it's also a great stress reliever.

There's a small pillow on our bed that I gave to Diane that says, "Happiness is being married to your best friend," and I think that sums up our relationship. Rough times are inevitable, but if you have an honest, trusting relationship and are willing to really work at it, your spouse can be your best friend and so much more.

A Mixed Match

Ray Wolff,
Emmaus, Pennsylvania

Date of birth: August 12, 1945

Profession: Owner of a human resources management consulting firm

Marital status: Divorced; Remarried: 10 years

Many people say that it's tougher to keep interracial marriages together than same-race ones. But from my own experience, I would say that it has been easier. The fact that I'm White and my wife, Lorna, is Black has only given us more to share with each other.

I think interracial marriages become more challenging when there is a lot of family involved. Lorna is the only child of very professional parents. Her father was a doctor and her mother is a nurse who had become accustomed to traversing in White society long before I came along.

Negotiating my family was more difficult. My mother made it clear upon first meeting Lorna that she didn't like her. Lorna, to her credit, was straightforward enough to respond with, "You don't know me. How can you not like me? Maybe it's just the color of my skin that you don't like." That was just the tactic to take because from that moment on, my mother was all warm and fuzzy toward Lorna. My mother actually became instrumental in winning over my sisters. Within a year of introducing Lorna to my family, all of their race issues were resolved.

An Office Romance

Lorna and I met when she was hired by the company I worked for in central New Jersey. Physical appearance is what logically first attracts one person to another. And I was attracted to Lorna's appearance, but more than that, it was her kindness and her sensitivity. She is such a caring person about so many things.

That trait is so much a part of her that it's evident upon first meeting her.

In the course of dating someone, you inevitably ask yourself (or at least I did), "Would I want this person to be the mother of my children?" It was Lorna's kindness and gentleness that made the answer to this question "yes."

Although I had never dated interracially before, Lorna had. She went to the University of Delaware, where she had dated interracially occasionally. So early on in the relationship, she tried to warn me about some of the possible racial backlash that we as a couple, and I as a White man, might encounter from family, friends, and even salespeople in stores. I couldn't comprehend this at first, but then some of what she forecasted happened.

There weren't any overt measures such as people burning crosses on the lawn. The slurs were much more subtle, but just as noticeable. For instance, when we would go to a restaurant where I had eaten many times on business, we wouldn't get my normal, fairly decent seat. Instead, we would get seated next to the bathrooms. Lorna handles these incidents more calmly than I usually do. I tend to address them head-on. I guess these types of problems could drive a wedge between a couple, but facing them has helped me understand life better from her perspective. And that ability to see the other person's point of view helps in all kinds of situations, not just those related to race.

Brady Bunch of the 1990s

Before getting married, Lorna and I talked about the problems we thought we'd encounter as a married couple. The race difference was definitely one of them, but it turned out not to be as big a problem as some other things.

I had been married to another woman for 15 years before getting together with Lorna. From that marriage, I had two boys of whom I have custody. Lorna, who was 28 when we got married, wasn't prepared to become the stepmother to a 4-year-old and a 7-year-old. There was a tremendous amount of adjustment that took place. The divorce and my new marriage were hard on the kids. And when they wanted to act out, Lorna and I became the drum that they beat on. Things didn't start getting better until the oldest was about 13. It was around then that he started to develop real interests of his own, such as karate, that he could devote his attention to. Also, as both boys matured, they realized that Lorna has been better to them than their own mother has. At one point when Lorna and I were moving from New Jersey to Pennsylvania, we let the kids decide if they wanted to live with their mother or come with us, which would mean that they would see less of her. They chose us.

My ex-wife and I have had problems regarding my custody of the children, but they never revolved around Lorna. She's always had a great deal of respect for Lorna. She knew Lorna before we ever started dating, and she liked her. In fact, when I told her I was starting to date Lorna, she said, "I don't think so. Lorna has too much class for you."

Lorna and I have a seven-year-old daughter, Stephanie, together. The difference in our races affects Stephanie far more than it ever did us. And she feels the impact more strongly the older she gets. When we lived in a more diverse community, she invited 25 kids to her birthday party, and only 5 couldn't come because of illness or vacation reasons. Since we've moved to a more homogeneously White community, only 3 of the 25 children she invited to her party this past year came. Some of the kids told her that their parents didn't like her mother. Unfortunately, kids don't stay color-blind forever.

Twenty-five years ago, I would have been extremely intolerant of this situation, calling up these parents and telling them off. I guess age has mellowed me because, now that I'm in my fifties, I just looked on this as an opportunity to teach Stephanie some values that

she'll need to learn anyway. Lorna and I both figure that if we raise Stephanie the right way, she'll be strong enough to handle anything that comes along. It will be a challenge to do that. But it's a challenge that Lorna and I face together.

Using People Skills

Given our training—we're both human-resources professionals—we are both pretty adept at resolving issues. Unfortunately, the problem-solving skills we use in our jobs don't work at home. I've been through the same types of training courses as Lorna, so I recognize the psychological tactics. Of course, I'm not a co-worker at her place of business; I'm her husband. So if she starts using these tactics on me, I resent it. At the same time, I think we still handle our problems pretty well.

We have a few unspoken rules when it comes to arguing. First, we don't engage in name-calling. Calling the other person a pigheaded ignoramus might feel good at the time, but it doesn't solve the problem. If we need a cooling-off period to prevent ourselves from exchanging insults, we take it. Lorna is usually able to talk things through right away, but I sometimes need half a day before I'm ready.

We try to stay focused on the issue at hand. If one of us brings up a different issue, we set it aside for later. I've also realized that sometimes you have to say you're sorry, even if you still think you were right.

Lorna and I have such a solid marriage because we share so much. We have a common view of the world and similar values and interests. It seems that too many interracial marriages are born from a desire to be rebellious, rather than a desire to be with the other person. Lorna and I are together because we choose to be. Our marriage, like others, has had its problems. But we talk through them, and in the end, those difficulties make our marriage even stronger.

In Love through It All

Ed Bruin,
San Francisco, California

Date of birth: July 6, 1931

Profession: Retired engineering manager for Westinghouse

Marital status: Married February 20, 1960

Do you know how it feels when your heart skips a beat? Well, that's what happened when I fell in love with Paula, my wife of 38 years. We met at the University of Illinois, where we both went to school back in the late 1950s. We dated about a year and were married a few months after I graduated. She had nearly completed her junior year of college but postponed finishing school so that we could get married. She went back to earn her degree several years later, which was something I didn't want her to do. I wanted her to be a stay-at-home wife.

Paula and I had both come from families with seven children. I liked having a big family and wanted lots of kids. She wanted children, too, but not as many—and not as soon. When we first got married, Paula was more interested in starting a career than starting a family, but she soon had a change of heart and decided we would start a family anyway. Our first child, Kathy, was born after we were married about two years. Paula and I were fascinated with Kathy—from her first words to her first steps, we were just in awe of the neat little person we had created. Sharing the joy and excitement of watching our child grow really gave a deeper meaning to our marriage.

It was only about a year later when we had our second child, and the third came soon after that. In fact, in a period of four years, Paula had given birth to three children. And our fourth child came just a few years later. As much as we loved our children, having so many so close together was really tough on Paula, and I knew it. I think she didn't feel good about herself having this brood of children. She wanted to be something more than just a mother.

We also moved a lot, especially in the early years of our marriage. Each of our four children was born in a different place—Kathy in Jackson, Mississippi; Eddie in Ottawa, Ontario; Carrie in Severna Park, Maryland; and Meg in Walnut Creek, California. Since we've been married, we've moved a total of eight times. Many of those moves were tough on Paula. They made it difficult for her to establish her career as a journalist, and she was often leaving friends to go to a place where she didn't know anyone. The moves weren't so bad for me because in most cases, I either knew people who were at the new work site or I was moving with a group of co-workers to the new location.

Weathering the Rough Spots

After all four kids had started school, Paula decided to go back to school herself. This was something that I resisted. I was brought up in a generation where the husband worked and his wife stayed home, particularly the wife of a successful man. I grew up in this blue-collar mentality that said you worked for money. You didn't work for fun or professionalism. You worked because you had to support your family.

My father, who was an alcoholic, was not a good provider, and when you have seven little mouths to feed, not bringing home enough bacon can really put a strain on your family—not to mention your marriage. As I watched my parents struggle to make ends meet, I became determined that, unlike my father, I would be a good provider for my wife and children. That's part of the reason why I disapproved of Paula working outside the home. Since we didn't need a second income, I felt that with her working, it somehow meant I wasn't doing my job as provider.

Paula knew that I didn't want her to go back to school. The combination of my lack of support and her determination to do what I clearly disapproved of really created a lot of conflict. So after 15 years of marriage, Paula suggested that we split up for a while. With all of the hostility between us, I thought it was probably a good idea.

The separation lasted about two months. I rented an apartment where I stayed during the week while Paula was at home with the kids. Then on the weekends, she would stay with a friend so I could spend time with the children. When we got back together two months later, things were better, but not everything was resolved. I had accepted the fact that Paula was going to pursue a career whether I liked it or not, but I still didn't support her decision and she knew it. She had also adopted a lot of the feminist ideas and attitudes of the times, which really made me feel threatened. I thought the whole feminist movement was overblown, which was another thing that made Paula angry. All of these unresolved issues really put a strain on our relationship. We managed to stay together for about a year, but then we split up for a second time.

A Separate Peace

This separation lasted about three months. Like the first separation, I rented an apartment and Paula stayed at home with the children. This time the kids came to visit me a lot. They had a ball swimming in the pool at the apartment complex. Sometimes Paula would make excuses to come and see me. One night we ended up going to dinner together, and we really had a wonderful time. It brought back memories of all the good times we had shared in the past. We went on a few other dates while we were separated, and we didn't see other people. We didn't really have an appetite for

fighting, either. We've never been yellers. But one of the problems with not fighting is that sometimes you don't communicate enough. When there are bad feelings between you, you end up not discussing them to avoid the conflict. That's what happened to us. We still loved each other, but we needed some time apart to work out our differences.

I really thought we were going to work it out, but there was no guarantee. We did go to some counseling sessions. I think counseling can be helpful, but in our case, we really worked things out on our own. It took me a while, but I finally came to understand that Paula couldn't sit at home and be fulfilled. She wanted to achieve professional success, and she needed the self-esteem that comes along with it—something she didn't get from being a mother. After two years of her telling me what she wanted out of life, I came to realize why having a career was so important to her, and for the first time, I truly supported her decision to go back to school. It wasn't that I had given in to her and what she wanted to do. It was that I came to understand her needs better.

Now it's been more than 20 years since those separations. At this point in our marriage, I'm retired and Paula is still working. Sometimes that's hard for me. I don't see her all day, and then she comes home from work and needs some time alone to relax and unwind. But even so, we still spend more time together now than when the kids were all at home. And when we do spend time together, we always have fun, whether we go for a drive down the California coast or spend a lazy Saturday in bed. We're still very much in love after 38 years. In fact, I hope our kids' relationships are as good as ours has been. I hope they've learned how to deal with conflicts from the way we did it right as well as from the way we did it wrong. But most of all, I hope we've taught them to be optimistic about things. It makes your life more cheerful. That's true in every aspect of your life, and it's certainly true in your marriage, too.

Credits

"Confirm Your Compatibility" on page 35 is adapted from the PREPARE/ENRICH couple compatibility questionnaire. Copyright © 1995 by Life Innovations, Inc. Reprinted by permission.

"Speaking and Listening" on page 52 is adapted from *Fighting for Your Marriage: Positive Steps for Preventing Divorce and Preserving a Lasting Love* by Howard Markman, Scott Stanley, and Susan L. Blumberg. Copyright © 1994 by Jossey-Bass Inc., Publishers. Reprinted by permission.

"Sentence Starters" on page 58 is reprinted by permission of PAIRS International, Inc. Copyright by PAIRS International, Inc.

Index